NEWEST BORN OF NATIONS

A Nation Divided: Studies in the Civil War Era

ORVILLE VERNON BURTON AND ELIZABETH R. VARON, *Editors*

NEWEST BORN OF NATIONS

European Nationalist Movements
and the Making of the Confederacy

ANN L. TUCKER

UNIVERSITY OF VIRGINIA PRESS

Charlottesville and London

University of Virginia Press
© 2020 by the Rector and Visitors of the University of Virginia
All rights reserved
Printed in the United States of America on acid-free paper

First published 2020

1 3 5 7 9 8 6 4 2

Library of Congress Cataloging-in-Publication Data

Names: Tucker, Ann L., author.
Title: Newest born of nations : European nationalist movements and
the making of the Confederacy / Ann L. Tucker.
Other titles: Nation divided.
Description: Charlottesville : University of Virginia Press, 2020. | Series: A nation
divided : studies in the Civil War era | Includes bibliographical references and index.
Identifiers: LCCN 2019057959 (print) | LCCN 2019057960 (ebook) |
ISBN 9780813944289 (cloth) | ISBN 9780813944296 (ebook)
Subjects: LCSH: Nationalism—Confederate States of America—History. |
Nationalism—Europe—History—19th century. | United States—History—
Civil War, 1861–1865—Causes. | Confederate States of America—History. |
Southern States—History—1775–1865.
Classification: LCC E459 .T88 2020 (print) | LCC E459 (ebook) |
DDC 973.7/13—dc23
LC record available at https://lccn.loc.gov/2019057959
LC ebook record available at https://lccn.loc.gov/2019057960

For my family

CONTENTS

ACKNOWLEDGMENTS

This work has moved with me through many chapters of my life, from graduate student to assistant professor, through multiple new jobs, and across the Southeast in a series of interstate moves. At each of these stages, I was fortunate to receive support and assistance without which this book would not be possible. I want to thank everyone who helped me with and through this project.

This book would not be what it is without the guidance of Don Doyle, who patiently helped me take a few unformed ideas and turn them into something meaningful, who provided countless suggestions for fruitful avenues of inquiry, who helped me clarify the parameters of the project and the ideas within, and who helped me parlay this work into a career.

This work also benefited from the mentorship of many other scholars who have been generous with their time and assistance. My professors at the University of Alabama and the University of South Carolina helped me develop the knowledge and skills of a historian. In particular, my committee members Thomas Brown, Lacy Ford, and Paul Quigley helped refine my ideas and set me on the path to this finished book. My fellow graduate students also provided helpful advice and insight as I was shaping this project.

As this project developed from idea to research to manuscript, many friends and colleagues have read portions of this work and shared their thoughts and suggestions. In particular, colleagues and graduate students at the University of Mississippi read and provided critical feedback on the newer portions of this work. My department and administration at the University of North Georgia, led by Jeff Pardue, have also been immensely supportive of this project, providing the support I needed to finish it. Additionally, friends and colleagues Kari Frederickson, Vernon Burton, Amy Fluker, Charles Eagles, Michael Woods, David Prior, Thomas Scarritt, Beatrice Burton, and Kathryn Tucker have provided significant support for this work or my career.

The earliest ideas for this project originated when I studied abroad in Venice, Italy, while an undergraduate at Wake Forest; I immediately fell in love with Italy and knew I wanted to study connections between Italy and the South. Such an opportunity would not have been possible without the help of Thomas Phillips and Randal Hall, then scholarship directors at Wake Forest, who mentored me through my undergraduate career and early historical research.

The University of Virginia Press, especially Dick Holway, have been endlessly patient as this project has spanned perhaps more stages and years of my life than we had initially anticipated. Knowing that my editors wanted a good book rather than a fast book enabled me to write a better book. I also appreciate the assistance of everyone at the press who worked with me on this project and helped turn the manuscript into the final product. The readers selected by the press provided insightful and useful feedback in their reports that helped me strengthen this work. I also want to thank Beatrice Burton and Margaret Hogan for their invaluable help and work with indexing and copyediting.

Beyond my professional life, friends at every step along the way have also supported me and helped make this work possible.

Most of all, however, none of this would be possible without my family. My love of history comes from my family, from my grandparents to my parents to my siblings. My family showed me how fascinating history can be, happily discuss and debate history with me, and have always supported and continue to support me and my interests. My sister Elizabeth, joined by my brother-in-law, Andrew, have helped me keep perspective on this work and life. My sister Kathryn has lived every step of this project, and of my larger career, with me. She has been an invaluable resource, both in providing the critical insight and knowledge of another historian and in being there with me through my journey. My parents, Mike and Diane Tucker, have supported me in countless ways, both small and enormous, through this project, through my career, and through my life; I could not have completed this work without them. Every scholar needs someone to help them relax and recharge, think through tricky ideas, support them through the inevitable hard places, and celebrate their successes, and my family has done this and so much more for me.

NEWEST BORN OF NATIONS

Introduction

In the spring of 1861, as questions of nationhood consumed the United States, southern and northern minds alike turned to an unexpected figure. Giuseppe Garibaldi, a prominent Italian nationalist who had led a military expedition to help achieve Italian unification in 1860 and who had previously earned fame in the 1840s fighting for the cause of national independence in South America and Italy, presented the world with an example of a seemingly ideal nationalist. To Americans, struggling to answer many of the same questions of governance, rights, and self-determination that had fueled nationalist movements through-out the Atlantic world in the nineteenth century, Garibaldi presented possible answers. White southerners who sought to legitimize the new nation they were creating hoped that self-comparisons with Garibaldi and his nationalism strengthened their case for independent nationhood.[1] In contrast, for leaders within the U.S. government seeking to preserve the same union that southern secessionists threatened to destroy, Garibaldi's acclaim proved so compelling that they invited him to come fight for the U.S. Army.[2] As these beliefs in Americans' ideological connections to Garibaldi reveal, both sides in the American Civil War conceived of their national mission as part of the broader international debate over proper expressions of nationhood.

Indeed, as demonstrated by Garibaldi and his international career and appeal, the first half of the nineteenth century appeared full of new possibilities and questions for supporters of aspiring nations around the globe, not just for white southern nationalists. Led by the Enlightenment-inspired American and French Revolutions, and driven by attempts to decolonize the Americas and to dismantle the European system of power established by the Congress of Vienna, an age of revolution saw potential nationalities throughout Europe and the Americas rising up and attempting to form independent nations out of multi-national empires. A desire for national self-determination and self-government tied these revolutions together, and participants and observers alike recognized these ties. The goal of national liberty, however, did not resolve the troubling questions of how best to enact a program of self-government or how to build an independent nation, much less of who should be able to participate in these processes. Nor did even the loftiest of goals guarantee success, with more European nationalist movements failing than succeeding in the first half of the nineteenth century.[3] Nonetheless, the promise of national independence proved so enticing that in February 1861, white southern nationalists in seven southern states, later joined by four more, met to declare themselves the Confederate States of America, a new nation, soon, they planned, to be welcomed as an equal in the international community of nations. For the elite white southern men who created the Confederacy, an international vision of the aspiring southern nation as one of many new nations seeking membership in the family of nations was central to their national self-conception.

Although primarily inspired by the desire to protect slavery and white supremacy, the men who created the southern nation were also influenced by a longstanding southern tradition of understanding issues of nationhood through an international lens. Throughout the antebellum era, Confederates' predecessors had analyzed the values and expressions of nationalism as new and aspiring nations throughout the nineteenth-century Atlantic world sought to throw off the bonds of empire and establish independent self-governing nations. Critically, antebellum southerners connected these nationalist movements abroad to their own American nationhood, evaluating European nationalist movements, particularly the revolutions of 1848, on the basis of these American values, albeit an interpretation of American values that increasingly echoed elite white southerners' particular concerns. This process ultimately aided white southerners in clarifying their definition of these national values and therefore in developing a southern interpretation of nationhood, even as they remained loyal Americans.

As sectional tension in the United States mounted in the late antebellum period, white southerners applied this vision of nationhood to their conflict with the North over the territorial expansion of slavery, dramatizing their fears of the growing threat to slavery by comparing themselves to defeated and oppressed nations in Europe. Self-comparisons with failed nations in Europe particularly aided white southerners in translating their concerns about slavery into the international language of nationhood. These comparisons, utilized both in the debate over slavery in the territories gained in the Mexican-American War and in the debate over filibustering as a potential method for expanding slavery and the power of slavery interests, began preparing white southerners to see the South as a unit capable of being discussed within the larger Atlantic discourse on nationalism and as a unit supposedly facing serious threats to its self-government, comparable to those faced by European nationalists. This developing international perspective was bolstered by the presence of European revolutionaries within the United States and, critically, by the differing northern and southern reactions to these revolutionaries, which taught white southerners to begin conceiving of the South as holding different national values and a different national identity than the North. Through their antebellum international analysis, white antebellum southerners created an international perspective on nationalism that they used to understand issues of nationhood and to shape their sense of possibilities for their own national future.

When the debate over southern nationhood turned to secession, this understanding of issues of nationhood as comprehensible through international analysis was readily available for both supporters and critics of secession to deploy at will. White southerners did just that, developing three competing international perspectives on southern nationalism, each of which white southerners used to define, defend, and legitimize their vision of the proper form of nationhood for the South. Secessionists utilized this international perspective to explain and defend their actions and legitimize the new nation they created. Among secessionists, a more liberal perspective claimed that the aspiring southern nation was legitimate because it followed in the footsteps of new and aspiring nations in Europe in seeking national self-determination in the face of oppression. This perspective allowed white southerners to continue discussing their concerns about the preservation of slavery through the guise of legitimate concerns about rights. An alternative conservative secessionist perspective claimed legitimacy for the Confederacy through the conservative, slaveholding Confederacy's supposed purification of what it argued was the excess liberalism of nationalism as expressed in Europe, particularly by focusing on the key role of racial hierarchy in creating a stable nation and society. Not to be left out of the internationalization of their nationhood, Unionist southerners likewise developed an international perspective to argue that the best national future for the South was continued unity with the United States, which, they claimed, already represented the best international model of the desired national values, and which would also ward off the harms of disunion as revealed by failed attempts at nation-building abroad. On all sides of the debate over secession, white southerners used an international perspective to make their case for their visions of nationhood.

The creation of the Confederacy and outbreak of war, combined with wartime realities, challenged each of these groups' international perspectives.

Secessionists, now Confederates, were forced to grapple with why, despite supposedly emulating or improving on the model of nationalism found abroad, the Confederacy gained no official international support. The proposed alliance between Garibaldi and the United States likewise threatened Confederates' symbolic claim to equivalency with Garibaldi's own Italy. Further, impending military defeat created additional challenges for southern nationalists' claims to be the most perfect, successful nation. These challenges required Confederates to reassess and reject or manipulate their claims to legitimacy based on an international perspective. Southern Unionists, meanwhile, depleted in number and strength by the rise of the Confederacy, shifted from trying to block secession to seeking to find a way to help reunite the American nation. Despite these challenges, however, each group of white southerners remained committed to their international perspective throughout the war, continuing to use it to advance their visions of the South's nationhood.

Throughout the antebellum and Civil War periods, elite white southerners used an international perspective to understand, imagine, and defend their visions of nationhood. Their international perspectives functioned as a mechanism for translating their concerns about their own government and society—usually related to slavery and race—into the more internationally resonant language of rights, values, and nationhood. As such, white southerners' international perspectives on their nationality constituted a well-known, easily understood, and readily accessed means of discussing issues of nationhood for the mid-nineteenth-century southern elite. The complex, changing, and conflicting ways in which southerners utilized international perspectives reveals that the making of southern nationhood was a long, dynamic, and contested process. Throughout the antebellum and Civil War eras, white southerners' international perspectives on their own nationhood were central to their discourse on and actions regarding nationalism, and played a critical role in shaping white southerners' nationalism by helping them define their relationship to American nationalism as well as by helping them imagine and create southern nationalism.

Elite white southerners who utilized an international perspective to understand issues of nationhood in the antebellum and Civil War eras had ample subject material to draw on as they looked across the Atlantic Ocean. The mid-nineteenth century was a period of revolution throughout Europe, as first in 1830 and again in 1848 aspiring nations rose up to challenge the monarchs and empires that claimed power over them. Although the majority of these revolutions failed, the Italian Risorgimento, which succeeded in uniting most of modern Italy in 1860, right on the eve of the American Civil War, meant that southerners had at least one successful model of nation-building to add to their collection of unsuccessful examples.[4]

Historians have begun the work of analyzing the American Civil War in the context of this larger age of nationalism. Most notably, Don H. Doyle, Paul Quigley, and Andre M. Fleche have all identified transnational connections within the American Civil War and southern nationalism. Doyle's work reveals that northerners, southerners, and Europeans alike understood the American Civil War as relevant to the national questions of the time. Quigley identifies nationalism in Europe, particularly romantic nationalism, as one of the leading influences on the development of southern nationalism, and Fleche argues that the legacy of the revolutions of 1848 shaped both northern and southern beliefs and actions during the Civil War.[5] This book advances the work of these scholars in several ways.

By analyzing the development and usage of white southerners' international perspective during the antebellum era, this work explains how and why white southerners during the Civil War drew the international comparisons that other scholars have identified. In particular, examining the deep antebellum roots of elite southerners' interest in European nationalist movements and demonstrating white southerners' use of international analysis to understand the developing sectional crisis of the 1850s, including events such as the conflict over slavery in the western territories and the filibustering movement, reveal how this antebellum analysis of events in Europe shaped southerners' national self-perception and identity before and as southern nationalism developed. My analysis of the secession crisis and wartime era builds on this antebellum understanding to explain how an international perspective actively aided white southerners in imagining a distinct southern nationalism and constructing their competing visions of the ideal forms of nationhood for the South. In doing so, this work reveals the process through which white southerners developed, expanded, manipulated, and utilized these international comparisons to shape their own nationhood. This work also examines the evolution of these perspectives as wartime realities threatened white southerners' claims, emphasizing the lasting commitment white southerners had to their international perspectives and complicating our understanding of how developing events intervened to shape southerners' vision of the South within the international community.

Further, this work identifies three competing international perspectives that liberal secessionists, conservative secessionists, and Unionists used to advocate for their specific visions of the South's national future during secession and the

Civil War, demonstrating that white southerners' international contextualization of their nationalism during the Civil War was more complicated and diverse and less homogenous than we have understood it to be. In particular, incorporating southern Unionists into the internationalization of the Civil War expands our understanding of the widespread appeal of international ideas on nationalism, as well as their flexible nature. Indeed, the widespread nature of this discourse across the full spectrum of white southern political thought indicates that international analysis was not just a minority opinion but central to white southern thought on nationalism. My analysis of white southerners' international perspectives thus reveals the making of southern nationalism to be a long, fraught, complicated, and dynamic process.

Moving beyond southern thought, this book also seeks to contextualize white southerners' developing international perspectives within the larger transatlantic debate over nationalism. In particular, by incorporating analysis of the extent to which secessionists' and Unionists' international perspectives resonated with or were adopted by northerners and Europeans, this work contextualizes southern thought and provides insight into how viable white southerners' claims were within the mid-nineteenth-century Atlantic world. The analysis of white southerners' manipulation of the ideals of nationalism as understood abroad highlights the malleable and adaptable nature of nationalism in the age of revolutions.

This work utilizes sources from southern print discourse to engage in this analysis of the international dimensions of the Civil War. Print discourse, including newspapers, magazines, pamphlets, and printed speeches, represents the bulk of the ideas and information that would have been available to the elite white southern men who ultimately decided the national fate of the South. Just as importantly, it is in print discourse that we can see how these men publicly used international ideas and information to actively shape their fellow southerners' thoughts about nationhood. Because this is an analysis of the creation of ideas of nationalism, print discourse provides the best source base for understanding what elite white southerners wanted their fellow countrymen to know about their nationhood, and thus for accessing white southerners' attempts to shape and reshape their nationalism.[6]

Southern print culture in the mid-nineteenth century undeniably lagged behind that of the North but nonetheless was growing in both quantity and influence.[7] Importantly, European affairs featured prominently the developing southern journalism industry; a typical southern newspaper from this era printed articles on European affairs at least weekly, if not daily in the case of more internationally focused papers. The number of European-focused stories could range from one a day to as many as six or seven in one day, at which point foreign news dominated the typical four-page length of antebellum newspapers. Although many southern journals made ample use of reprinted articles from northern periodicals, southern journalists and editors also added their own voices to the conversation on Europe. While I have used articles reprinted from northern periodicals and wire services as indicators of what information was available to southern audiences, my analysis primarily focuses on sources that reflect, to the best of my knowledge, the perspectives of writers who were producing work specifically for southern audiences, and I indicate if I am quoting or discussing a source that I know to have originated outside the South.

The nineteenth-century journalistic tradition of unsigned or pseudonymous articles makes assigning authorship difficult when using periodicals, meaning that for many sources, the newspaper or magazine that printed an article is the only information available about who might have penned the piece. I have identified authors and editors where possible or likely, but much of my analysis of which southerners utilized an international perspective is by necessity analysis of which journals printed such perspectives (and therefore of which editors ran these journals), rather than which individuals endorsed them.

In my decade of working with these sources and this subject, the most important finding regarding the identity of white southerners who endorsed an international perspective is that almost all subsets of educated white southern men did indeed utilize an international perspective. I have found an international perspective in newspapers (of both partisan affiliations, as well as those unaffiliated with either political party), magazines, speeches (political and otherwise), and government documents including diplomatic instructions and congressional debates. Among these sources I have also found an international perspective in the voices of less influential southern men who wrote letters to the editors, gave toasts at both political and social gatherings, and attended and voted at political meetings. Although the larger, urban newspapers such as the *New Orleans Picayune, Charleston Mercury,* and *Richmond Daily Dispatch* made most frequent use of international comparisons, newspapers both big and small, rural and urban, also published pieces that internationalized southerners' nationhood. At times, the Natchez *Mississippi Free Trader,* for example, also prominently and frequently utilized international context in its discussions of nationhood. As the prominence of newspapers from both Richmond and Natchez reveals, newspapers' embrace of an international perspective likewise spanned both Upper and Deep South.

The widespread nature of these comparisons indicates that an international perspective did not break down neatly along partisan lines, despite the critical influence of the second party system on antebellum politics. Both Whigs and Democrats actively used international perspectives to advance their visions of the ideal nationhood for the South. Although both parties embraced international analysis, however, a slightly higher percentage of international comparisons were made by Democrats, which, during secession and the Civil War, held true for both the liberal and conservative secessionist perspectives. The Democratic emphasis on defending slavery possibly primed southern Democratic politicians to focus on either the ways in which threats to slavery potentially re-created European-style tyranny or, conversely, the ways in which the preservation of slavery protected (white) freedom and rights, including the ability to direct a government in accordance with their own slaveholding interests.[8]

While partisans of both parties used international perspectives to advance their positions, cultural analysts not primarily known for their political affiliations also utilized international comparisons. In particular, southern magazines focused on issues including culture and economics, such as *DeBow's Review*, frequently advanced a vision of the South as part of an international community debating issues of nationhood. Additionally, while fire-eaters, or radical secessionists, were among early and enthusiastic advocates of an international perspective, southern Unionists likewise turned to a larger international context to make their case for continued national unity during secession and the Civil War. International perspectives, then, existed among elite white southerners in all regions of the antebellum and Civil War South, in all types of social and political commentary, and across the political spectrum. International analysis was not a fringe idea in the antebellum and Civil War–era South. On the contrary, the widespread nature of this analysis demonstrates the centrality of an international perspective to white southern thought.

As elite white southerners developed and advanced international perspectives on nationalism, they made free use of the ideas and information available to them about nations and nationalism. Such ideas were plentiful, as the nineteenth-century Atlantic world was a place rife not just with revolution but with related debates over the proper forms of government, nationhood, and nationalism. "Nationalism" generally refers to the modern idea that a certain group of people should be able to govern itself within a sovereign state.[9] In the middle of the nineteenth century, ideas of nationalism were transitioning away from the Enlightenment-inspired liberal, or civic, nationalism, which defined nations on the basis of shared ideas such as natural rights and self-government, and toward romantic, or cultural, nationalism, which defined nations on the basis of cultural traits such as history and ethnicity.[10] Elite southerners in the middle of the nineteenth century were inspired by both strains of thought, with new ideas of romanticism resonating in southern views of nationhood.[11] Because the revolutions they watched and analyzed abroad were still largely, if imperfectly, attempting to adhere to ideas of liberal nationalism such as republicanism or national self-determination, however, and because of the United States' own history with liberal nationalism, these elite white southerners still sought the values of a more liberal nationalism, particularly as they developed an international perspective on nationalism.

In addition to utilizing different versions of nationalism, nineteenth-century southerners could also draw directly from the political ideologies of both liberalism and conservatism. In the nineteenth-century Atlantic world, Enlightenment-inspired liberals battled tradition-based conservatives to determine the best form of governance. Liberalism developed out of Enlightenment-based views of government that hold that the people have rights, including the right to determine their own government, and that the people should therefore be able to consent to and participate in their government. On the more liberal end of this spectrum, republicans advocated for government in which the people were sovereign and therefore directed the government themselves. Other nineteenth-century nationalists accepted more limitations on the self-government of the people, seeking constitutional monarchies instead of absolutist empires. Nonetheless, liberals shared a belief in the rights of the people and the duty of the government to protect those rights. In the nineteenth century, however, the definition of "the people" was less certain; while more radical liberals were moving to at least oppose enslavement, a restriction of "the people" to white men was still generally acceptable throughout the Atlantic world, with significant implications for ideas of self-government and nationhood.

Conservatism, on the other hand, sought to maintain tradition and avoid change, particularly as it related to hierarchy and power within society. For conservatives, a hierarchical political and social system, such as aristocracy and/or monarchy, provided needed structure for society. While European conservatism did center on monarchy, in the United States, conservatism instead often focused on social order, local control, and other ways of ordering power in a traditional manner. Conservatives feared that without the protections of a clear division of power and tradition, self-government would descend into chaos, violence, or anarchy, thereby destroying society.[12]

The southern intellectual class drew from both of these traditions as it developed its political beliefs and, ultimately, international perspective. The southern elite, much like the intellectual classes in the rest of the United States, felt a strong connection to and affinity for the heritage of the American Revolution. Accordingly, the liberal traditions of republicanism, liberty, and self-government were critically important to antebellum southerners as they evaluated their government and their place within it. A conservative respect for tradition and social order, however, increasingly combined with a robust defense of slavery that enshrined a racial hierarchy and challenged liberal ideas of freedom and equality, constituted an additional influence on southern politics, helping pave the way for the white southern defense of states' rights and limited commitment to full democracy. For antebellum southerners, these liberal and conservative strains of thought coexisted in their political worldview.

White southerners' embrace of both liberal and conservative perspectives shaped southern politics in the nineteenth century. Southern political thinkers blended these traditions by merging elements of both and indeed saw them as intertwined. For antebellum southern elites, for example, slavery was not a regressive, repressive institution incompatible with modern society. Instead, for many white southern thinkers, slavery was a necessary element of a modern, liberal, republican society; slavery, they argued, protected society against the harms of excess democracy by supposedly preventing the degradation of lower-class whites, thereby warding off labor radicalism and providing necessary stability for a republic. Such a formulation obviously relied on limiting the "people" who could to participate in self-government to white men only (a not-uncommon definition in the nineteenth century). For many elite white southerners, this redefined vision of a liberal government, tempered by the stabilizing influences of conservatism, was the best expression of the modern form of republican governance.[13]

Thus, as elite southerners analyzed their government and their national values through an international lens, they did so using both their liberal and conservative values. Southern thinkers and writers who prioritized the southern liberal tradition, including values such as liberty and republicanism, saw much to admire in the attempts to create liberal governments abroad. For their counterparts who prioritized the conservative southern respect for tradition and social order, and focused their analysis on the potential harms of social and even racial equality, however, failed nationalist movements abroad were examples of liberalism run amuck. Due to these competing political influences, secessionists ultimately developed two competing perspectives on the place of the South relative to the international community, with the liberal perspective claiming that the South emulated nationalist movements abroad while the conservative perspective asserted that the South purified these same nationalist movements.

Even in the emergence of competing international perspectives, however, much overlap occurred between the liberal and conservative visions of the international influences on the South. Many of the same newspapers and journals endorsed both perspectives at various times, revealing that these perspectives could peacefully coexist. In a demonstration of this ideological blending, even the liberal perspective depended on the limited southern vision of self-government that excluded full participation in democracy on the basis of race and gender. And even the conservative perspective generally sought to correct, rather than reject, the liberal model of governance based on the rights and sovereignty of the people. While I have identified the liberal and conservative perspectives as competing on the position of the South relative to European nationalist movements, these perspectives were nonetheless overlapping in goals, vocabulary, historical and political influences, and even values. These shared political beliefs explain the lack of clear-cut difference between the southerners endorsing the two perspectives. Southerners embracing the liberal versus conservative international perspectives were not fundamentally different from each other in background, political orientation, or visions of the southern nation. As such, these two international perspectives reveal variations within the mainstream of southern political thought, demonstrating the diverse ways that white southerners applied their shared assumptions about goals for nationhood.

The ubiquity of the international perspective on nationhood throughout the South, utilized by both conservatives and liberals, secessionists and Unionists, as well as in all areas of print and public discourse, is significant in and of itself. An international perspective was not exotic to mid-nineteenth-century white southerners; instead, it was part of their general worldview and part of how they understood their national values and nationhood. Internationalized ideas of nationhood were freely available for white southerners to make use of as they would—and use them they did. Because the international context of issues of nationhood in the middle of the nineteenth century was so well understood, as were the ways in which that context could be applied to the South, an unreflective appeal to an international perspective was an easy way for white southerners to dramatize the stakes in sectional tension, define the action of secession, or defend a vision of the nation.

Accordingly, an international perspective developed as a form of almost instrumentalist nationalism. Although nineteenth-century white southerners deeply engaged with political ideologies, these southerners often inserted their international comparisons into their larger discourse with relatively little ideological precision or analysis of how these comparisons fit with broader ideas and political models. Indeed, elite white southerners had no problem manipulating political ideas in order to achieve their end, a reality demonstrated not only through their international perspectives but also through many of their larger claims, such as the defense of slavery as a positive good. An international perspective was not a logical, well-developed political policy. Instead, it was a readily available metaphor for speaking to an audience of fellow white southerners, one that allowed its adopter to translate the concerns of slaveholders into the language of international nationalism. An international perspective on nationhood was a set of ideas that antebellum and Civil War–era white southerners developed and utilized despite the required ideological manipulation, because it served their larger purpose of advancing their interests.

The widespread and malleable nature of the international perspectives allowed white southerners to utilize these ideas in combination with their more well-developed political concepts. The international perspective interacted with larger claims about states' rights, white supremacy and democracy, and self-government. For example, southerners' international perspectives overlapped with broader sources of southern nationalism and southern nationalist justifications for secession.[14] Claiming that northern antislavery interests constituted European-style tyranny embellished the larger argument that secession was legal because the North had violated the constitutional compact and southern rights, while the position that slavery purified nationalism of the excesses found in the North and Europe fit closely with the larger strategy of claiming Confederate nationalism as the purest iteration of national ideals.[15] The ability to attach an international perspective to any of these larger ideas, and to trust that the audience would understand what was meant, made this international perspective a valuable element of southern discourse and increased its influence over the development of southern nationalism.

Elite antebellum southerners were not unique in crafting a vision of liberal nationalism that was altered in accordance with local concerns and realities. Most of the revolutions of Europe likewise blended elements of liberalism and conservatism, some by design and some by pragmatism. The Italian Risorgimento, for example, grew in part out of a movement for not only Italian independence but also a republican government, as expressed most famously in the vision of leading republican and nationalist Giuseppe Mazzini. After fighting for decades for republican independence, however, the creation of the modern

Italian nation ultimately happened under a monarch, Victor Emmanuel II, king of Piedmont-Sardinia.[16] Thus, although white southerners responded to the concerns of their own particular, self-interested blend of liberalism and conservatism, they were not alone in lacking ideological purity for their movement. Nor were white southerners unique among Americans in assessing the European revolutions through a lens of their own values. Indeed, many Americans throughout the nation shared southerners' desire for the establishment of independent nations in Europe, as well as a concern that the revolutionaries failed to live up to the model of the United States.[17]

Therefore, what made the southern vision of nationhood significant was not that it alone blended the many visions of governance and nationhood resonating throughout the nineteenth-century Atlantic world, or that it uniquely connected domestic ideas to foreign events, but that it did so in accordance with the particular values, politics, and concerns of elite white southerners, in a way that served the interests of the southern elite. Because southern reaction to the European revolutions affirmed elite southerners' visions of nationhood and taught southerners to apply this vision to international affairs, southern analysis of these European nationalist movements played a critical role in preparing southerners to conceive of a southern nationalism and to defend or reject the idea of an independent southern nation.

To nineteenth-century residents of the Atlantic world, issues of nationhood and governance mattered deeply, as nationalists, monarchists, revolutionaries, and conservatives debated what a nation and a government should be. Elite white southerners envisioned themselves as part of this international conversation. From the antebellum period, in which these southerners used their analysis of nationalisms abroad to refine their sense of their own national values and possibilities; to secession, in which southern nationalists and Unionists alike positioned themselves as following or rejecting European nationalists in a quest to secure the best national future for the South; to the Civil War, when battlefield realities forced southerners to expand and alter their international perspectives to continue defending their visions of southern nationhood, white southerners understood their own nationhood through an international perspective. An international perspective on nationhood thus played a central role in the development of southern nationalism, and southern visions of nationhood, in the antebellum and Civil War eras.

PART I

Age of Revolutions, 1820–1850

Residents of the nineteenth-century Atlantic world could easily see themselves as living in an age of revolutions. Inspired in part by the American Revolution of 1776 and French Revolution of 1789, Latin American nations broke free of the Spanish Empire in the early nineteenth century and aspiring nationalities in Europe sought independent nationhood in two waves of nationalist movements, first in 1830 and again in 1848. Americans eagerly watched these events abroad. In particular, antebellum-era Americans sought evidence that the inspiration and model provided by their own revolution was leading to the triumph of republicanism and self-government, not just at home but also abroad. Elite white southerners, like their counterparts in the North, found events in Europe of interest and import. Although still loyal to the United States, southerners in 1830 and especially 1848 sought evidence not just of American values but also of the particular version of American values that resonated among white southerners, who combined respect for the liberalism of the American Revolution with a conservative, slavery-based desire to limit expressions of equality and freedom. Southern analysis of European revolutions thus helped white southerners refine their beliefs about proper and appropriate expressions of nationhood. Critically, this analysis also taught southern commentators to link revolutions and nations across international boundaries. By helping white southerners clarify and internationalize their vision of nationhood, southern analysis of the European revolutions in the first half of the nineteenth century led elite southerners to develop an international perspective on nationhood that they could use to evaluate issues of nationalism at home and abroad.

1

The Revolution of '76 Extending Itself across the Seas

SOUTHERN ANALYSIS OF EUROPEAN REVOLUTIONS

In September 1849, journalist George W. Kendall, former soldier and adventurer, former war correspondent during the Mexican-American War, and current European correspondent for the *New Orleans Picayune,* took it on himself to explain to his readership why his enthusiasm for the European revolutions of 1848 was so tempered with skepticism. Using the short-lived but failed Roman Republic of 1848 as an example, Kendall described his analytical process, writing, "had [the Romans] succeeded in driving off the French, and in freeing themselves forever from popish rule and priestly bondage, I should have rejoiced as loudly as the loudest and thrown my cap as high as the highest. But they did not; and the final result of their struggle shows that something was wanting." Critically, Kendall blamed this poor result on a failure of both the people and the leaders in Rome, who he argued were ill-prepared for republican governance. The only figure to escape Kendall's critique was leading nationalist and Italian military leader Giuseppe Garibaldi; according to Kendall, the sole chance that the Roman revolution had for success would have been if "all, leaders and citizens, [had] come out and battled with as much zeal as Garibaldi and his foreign legion."[1]

In this short statement, Kendall touched on many of the central themes of white southern intellectuals' analysis of the revolutions of 1848. Kendall was skeptical and made no attempt to hide his criticism, particularly of what he saw as the poorly suited nature of Europeans for liberal governance. His concerns, however, focused on the means rather than the ends of the revolutions. Kendall supported the ideas behind and goals in front of the European nationalist movements; as such, he wanted to support the revolutions and wanted them to succeed in establishing independent republics. When the revolutions failed, however, they seemingly confirmed Kendall's fears that the nationalists and their movements were simply not equal to their ideals.

By evoking Italian general Giuseppe Garibaldi, Kendall tapped into additional trends in southern analysis of nationalist movements in Europe. Kendall evaluated each revolution, and revolutionary, on its own merits; when revolutionaries such as Garibaldi seemed capable of achieving their goals, Kendall cheered, even as he criticized the other leaders who supposedly failed to live up to Garibaldi's standards. In celebrating Garibaldi while explaining his own general skepticism of revolutionaries, Kendall echoed the worldwide—and southern—support that Garibaldi enjoyed as a supposed exemplar of the best of the nationalist movements.[2] Additionally, as Kendall elevated Garibaldi as the best model of an appropriate nationalist, even while criticizing Garibaldi's fellow nationalists, Kendall combined a desire for national self-determination with a wariness of the dangers of excess democracy—specifically, the danger of giving power to people who failed to achieve Garibaldi's virtuous standards. In this analysis of Garibaldi and the Roman Republic, Kendall advocated for a vision of nations and possibilities for nationhood that reflected his own concerns and values, a vision that he shared with many of his fellow elite white southerners.

Kendall was just one of many elite southerners analyzing the meaning and significance of nationalist movements in Europe. Although an ocean away, educated southerners had the opportunity to learn of European events through frequent publication of European news in southern periodicals. Southern men from the intellectual and political classes devoted much attention in the first half of the nineteenth century to studying and assessing the course and meaning of European nationalist movements. Beginning with the Greek independence movement in the 1820s and continuing through the revolutions of 1848 that spread across Europe, southerners followed the attempts of Greeks, Italians, French, Hungarians, Poles, Irish, and other nationalities to overthrow monarchies or gain independence from multinational empires and to create responsive governments in their place.

Elite white southerners' analysis of these European nationalist movements was complex and shaped by white southerners' particular political visions and concerns. White southerners, including Kendall, drew on their conservatism to evince wariness of the liberalism of the attempts to establish independent republics throughout Europe. In particular, as these southerners discussed European nationalist movements, they emphasized the importance of social order and hierarchy and the necessity of limiting freedom and democracy, reflecting their defense of their own slaveholding power structure.[3] Their concern with unchecked liberalism abroad, however, was tempered by an ongoing respect for the enduring liberal values of the American Revolution, and therefore for the values of the American nation of which southerners were a part. Republicanism, self-government, and national self-determination were particularly central for white southerners' analysis of nationalism and of the values of a good nation. White southerners' discourse on especially the revolutions of 1848 thus drew from both their conservative concerns about excess democracy and their liberal respect for republicanism, creating a nuanced discourse on the meaning of nationalist movements abroad. As white southerners weighed and balanced their conflicted responses to the events in Europe, they clarified their own vision of what a nation should be, as well as of proper expressions of nationhood.

Ultimately, such analysis created a southern international perspective on nationhood that constituted a critical tool for white southerners' evaluation of nationalisms. Although they were not alone in viewing issues of nationalism through an international context, white southerners' international perspective, like the perspectives of their counterparts throughout the Atlantic world, incorporated their own particular political and national concerns, connecting them to a broader transnational debate about the meaning of nationhood and allowing them to see issues of nationalism as connected across national borders.[4] White southerners utilized their international perspective to clarify, understand, and advance their ideas about nationalism; with it, they could evaluate foreign nations through their own domestic concerns, assess their own nation's adherence to international ideals, and develop a deeper understanding of national values and the meaning, forms, and expression of nationhood. This international perspective would thus shape southern thought, beliefs, and action in the antebellum era, in turn preparing future southerners to consider the South as a potential nation, worthy of discussion within the broader international debate over national values and independence.

Issues of nationhood attracted white southerners' attention from the very beginning of the antebellum period. As cotton boomed in the South and industry in the North, the second party system developed, and northerners and southerners prepared to move to more extreme positions on abolition versus the defense of slavery, Europe entered a new stage of its age of revolutions, beginning with the Greek independence movement of the 1820s, then expanding with nationalist movements occurring throughout the continent in 1830. Contrary to the more skeptical response of their later counterparts in 1848, white southerners' reports on these early nationalist movements in Europe flowed with enthusiasm, indicating deep-seated sympathy for movements they saw as seeking to establish the values they held as Americans. White southerners' thoughts on these events set an initial positive tone in their analysis of nationalism abroad.[5] Since southerners had yet to develop a distinct southern nationalism, their reactions to the early European revolutions derived from their self-image as loyal Americans. Accordingly, white southerners' response to the revolutions of the 1820s and 1830s echoed rather than challenged the broader American response. By responding to the first wave of nationalism through Europe on the basis of their American nationalism, however, white southerners nonetheless reinforced their commitment to what they saw as the values of their own nation while enhancing their sense that nations abroad could emulate the American nation, thereby internationalizing their concept of nationhood.

Commencing this international analysis, as Greece fought for independence from the Ottoman Empire, American minds turned to the glories of the Greece of antiquity, lauding Greece's historic role in establishing the governmental practices of self-representation and democracy that nineteenth-century Americans so revered.[6] Elite white southerners joined their fellow Americans in celebrating Greece and the cause of Greek independence, with southern-produced analysis of Greece heaping praise on Greek nationalists. For example, the *Natchez Gazette* analyzed foreign reports to inform its readership that "the glorious cause of National Independence, will prevail in Greece, and that she will soon take her station in the rank of nations."[7] White southerners' actions echoed the positive tone; Charlestonians, for example, were the first Americans to respond to the Greek call for aid.[8] Virginia legislators and citizens of Richmond, following the example of northern pro-Greek organizations, met in 1824 to pass resolutions expressing sympathy and calling for support for the Greek cause, and the Louisiana legislature passed an official resolution in support of Greece, as reported in Milledgeville, Georgia's *Southern Recorder.*[9]

While Greece, revered as the birthplace of democracy, won significant sympathy from antebellum Americans, it was far from the only nascent nationalist movement that southerners supported in the 1820s and 1830s. As nationalist movements increased in the wake of the conservative Congress of Vienna of 1814–15, which restored post-Napoleonic Europe to the control of emperors and monarchs, southerners turned a sympathetic eye toward Ireland's desire for independence from Great Britain, the various Italian states' struggles for freedom from foreign empires and monarchs perceived to be despotic, France's creation of a constitutional monarchy in 1830, Poland's fight for freedom from Russia and Prussia, and Belgium's bid for independence from the United Kingdom of the Netherlands.[10] As with Greece, white southerners publicly displayed their support in a variety of ways. Hibernian societies and other organizations formed for the support of Ireland in southern cities and towns ranging from Savannah and Charleston to Annfield, North Carolina, often using St. Patrick's Day to celebrate the cause of Irish independence.[11] Support for Neapolitan independence exploded in the early 1820s as Naples sought freedom from Austria, with Leesburg, Virginia's *Genius of Liberty* characterizing the revolution as "among the singular and wonderful events of the day," although such optimism was crushed when Naples failed in its mission.[12] France's struggles to create a more responsive government won widespread praise from southerners, complete with parades, musical performances (including at least one instance of "La Marseillaise"), and even an official letter of congratulations from the state legislature of Louisiana that declared the support of the people of Louisiana for the people of France.[13] Poland's revolution, inspired by France's, also warranted southerners' sympathy, as southerners "look[ed] with feelings of enthusiasm" to "this gallant, chivalrous and noble country" fighting "in defense of their rights and liberties," according to Samuel Snowden's *Alexandria Phenix Gazette*.[14] Meanwhile, the settling of Belgium's independence was nothing less than a "promise for civilization" in the words of the Charleston *City Gazette*.[15] All of these revolutions were a common subject of toasts at southern gatherings, showing resonance beyond just the leadership class.[16] Often, southerners connected the European nationalist movements in their toasts, as did South Carolinian Patrick Cantwell, who celebrated "the Parisian heroes of July, 1830—a bright example for the Irish agitators, to teach them how Despotism may be overthrown, and Liberty won."[17] Such support for and celebrations of revolutions and nationalists in Greece, Italy, France, and other areas of Europe reveal white southerners' generally positive views of early nationalist movements.

Southern, and American, support for these nationalist movements was not incidental. Demonstrating their commitment to the liberal ideals of the American Revolution, southern commentators praised these movements because they believed that these aspiring nations in Europe fought for the same political values of liberty, self-government, and republicanism cherished in the United States.[18] Celebrating this republicanism abroad, Virginia congressman, writer, and professor George Tucker argued in his "Discourse on the Progress of Philosophy" that the fight for the rights of the people against monarchy, as in Belgium and Greece, was the key to the progress of mankind. To Tucker, the end of divine right of kings was the "extension of the empire of reason," and after this reason was implemented through revolutions, government "is now judged according as it tends to promote the welfare of the community," rather than that of the aristocracy. Such an assertion of reason over privilege deserved celebration in Tucker's estimation.[19] Similarly, a committee of citizens of South Carolina resolved of Greece that "the mere contemplation of a people rising to assert its rights . . . excites the sensibilities of every friend to liberal principles."[20]

If reason and the rights of self-government warranted enthusiasm from southerners for advancing the proper American vision of governance, tyrannical or despotic governments violated that same vision, earning criticism and censure from white southerners, who were largely convinced that aspiring nations such as Italy, Greece, Poland, and Belgium were indeed the victims of tyrants and despots. For example, the revolution in Naples promised to end "arbitrary and despotic government," according to the Leesburg, Virginia, *Genius of Liberty*.[21] Likewise, the *Louisiana Courier* exclaimed that the "heroic Greeks" made "such sacrifices to fling off the yoke of their tyrants."[22] In doing so, they sought "emancipation" from "despotic thralldom" in the words of the *Alexandria Herald*.[23] Similarly, the revolution of 1830 saw Louisianans congratulating "illustrious France" for rising and "trampling under foot a hoary headed tyranny," as reported in the *New Orleans Bee*.[24] Such reports often relied on emotion as they responded to southern writers' perceptions of which nations seemed to be best modeling the values that antebellum Americans tended to support, allowing these ideas to become widespread throughout southern print discourse.

Although shared ideals were important in informing white southerners' positive views of these revolutions abroad, southerners' sense of connection to these revolutions went beyond just mutual values. In particular, southerners, as with other Americans, celebrated their own American Revolution as a direct model and inspiration for inculcating these values and overthrowing tyranny in other nations. Isaac Croom in New Bern, North Carolina, declared in a Fourth of July speech, for example, that the United States stood as "a splendid example that a republican government is best calculated to promote the dignity and happiness of man."[25] Similarly, a committee of South Carolinians solicited aid for the Greeks on the basis that the United States had "fought and conquered in the cause for which Greece is now contending," declaring, "we therefore can triumph in [Greece's] victories and commiserate her reverses."[26] Ireland, according to a Judge Guyol of Terrebonne Parish, Louisiana, was "fettered and bending under the heavy iron rod of England," and was thus in the same "predicament" as the American colonies before their revolution.[27]

While white southerners, like their fellow Americans, celebrated American-style values and the inspiration of the American Revolution abroad, they nonetheless retained their sense that the United States constituted the most perfect representation of these values. Due in large part to the widespread failure of

European nationalist movements, southern and northern onlookers alike eventually concluded that, despite the admirable example of the United States, aspiring nations abroad had failed to achieve the standards of the American nation. For example, in a speech celebrating the Fourth of July 1823, Philip Richard Fendall claimed that the United States "surpassed Europe, and marched to the enjoyment of equal rights" without the "painful delays" and "vicissitudes" that plagued other aspiring republics.[28] Similarly, William A. McRea, despite praising Greece and other nationalist movements, informed his Alexandria, Virginia, audience in 1824 that the United States was "the only free and happy government in the world," as "we are blessed with institutions purely republican; and live under the genial ray of a constitution, which declares, in the spirit of freedom, all men to be equal."[29] Such comparisons strengthened Americans' vision of what made their nation different and therefore what defined their nation.

Southern analysis of early nationalist movements in Europe thus not only engendered southern support for these movements but also caused southerners to reflect more deeply on the values of their own American nation. Comparing and contrasting movements abroad with the United States refined white southerners' sense of which values led them to support nationalist activity in Europe, as well as which values underpinned their own American nationality, in particular reinforcing white southerners' commitment to the liberal ideals of the American Revolution. This deeper knowledge and understanding of nationalism was available for later white southerners to draw on as they responded to future revolutions as well as when they undertook their own. While white southerners in this early antebellum period still conceived of themselves as Americans, the sense of international connectedness that southerners strengthened in the 1820s and 1830s played a critical role in later antebellum southerners' ability to conceive of the South as an independent nation. After secession, this international vision of nationhood would also enable Confederates to justify their nation on the basis of its supposed place in the international family of nations. Without an earlier understanding of nationalisms as connected, and without the practice of using foreign nationalisms to understand one's own nation, the international contextualization of the Confederacy would have been meaningless.

Although nationalist activity in Europe began to diminish after the wave of revolutions inspired by France's July Revolution of 1830, antebellum southern attention to events abroad did not end, and European nationalist movements were only temporarily inactive. In the spring of 1848, revolutions once again broke out across Europe as French, Hungarians, Germans, Italians, and others sought to overthrow monarchies and empires and replace them with more liberal, republican governments. Discontent began growing across the continent once again as Enlightenment ideas of self-government conflicted with the post–Congress of Vienna Europe that saw control of the continent returned to a handful of monarchs, and that the earlier revolutions had failed to alter. The spread of liberalism and the idea of republicanism drove a desire for greater political representation and inspired people to fight for equality and freedom. The rise of nationalism, which elevated the idea of the nation and sought the establishment of independent nation-states in place of large, multinational empires, further inspired the midcentury revolutions. Meanwhile, increasingly difficult economic situations primed workers and peasants for revolution. When these philosophical ideas met with real-world issues such as economic crises or revolutions in neighboring countries, peasants and elites alike began to fight for new forms of government.

The first widely publicized revolution occurred in France in February 1848, when revolutionaries pushed for and gained the establishment of a republic, forcing Louis-Philippe to abdicate. After the declaration of the Republic of France, revolution swept the continent. Revolts and mass demonstrations in the Italian peninsula and German states forced monarchs, dukes, and other rulers to grant constitutions. Austrian chancellor Klemens von Metternich fled the empire as a result of mass insurrections in March 1848, and Hungarians attempted to set up an independent government. Peasants, workers, and women all joined the cry for reform and fought for equality, engaging in uprisings and demonstrations throughout Europe. The thread tying together these revolutions was a common desire for more liberal representative governments, preferably republics or at least constitutional monarchies, that gave more power to the people.

Despite the widespread nature of these movements, they were ultimately unsuccessful. The French Republic was dissolved after Louis-Napoleon staged a coup in late 1851. The Italian Kingdom of Sardinia, which had united Italian nationalists to fight against Austria, failed to win its war against the Austrian Empire, and the short-lived Roman Republic fell to the combined forces of Pope Pius IX and Louis-Napoleon's French Army. The Hungarian independence movement lost to combined Austrian and Russian forces in the summer of 1849 after almost a year of fighting. Although the revolutions gave early indications of success, by 1850 most of them had been defeated and monarchies restored. The possibility of revolutionary change in Europe had been postponed.[30] The defeat of the movements could not erase the impact that they had on the international conversation about nations and nationalism, however. The revolutions of 1848 significantly influenced the thoughts and beliefs not only of the revolutionaries who participated in them but also of citizens around the world, including in the southern United States, where white southerners would soon enact their own experiment in nationalism.

Americans were among the many people throughout the world who followed the revolutions of 1848 closely. Because of their faith in the importance of the United States as a model nation, Americans from all regions eagerly watched to see if their model of nationhood would be implemented overseas.[31] Although American civil war was far from inevitable, the United States in 1848 was increasingly dealing with sectional conflict due to the divisive issue of slavery. While still retaining their American loyalties and identities, Americans, including elite southerners, were very aware of the issues threatening their own nation at the very same time they watched Europeans attempt to create new governments and nations in 1848.

The lessons that white southerners learned about the meaning of nationhood through their discussion of the events of 1848 reinforced their American nationalism, even as they also enabled white southerners to define this American nationalism according to their own concerns, some of which were indeed national but others more sectional. In particular, southerners responding to the revolutions of 1848 blended the liberalism of their American national heritage with the conservatism of their slaveholding society, developing an international perspective on nationhood that fit with the specific concerns of white southerners. White southerners initially looked for evidence of their liberal value of republicanism in the nationalist movements in Europe; in the wake of the failure of these movements, however, white southerners drew on their conservatism to criticize excess democracy and extremism for leading the revolutions astray. Southern reactions to the revolutions of 1848 thus helped southerners clarify their vision of the best form of national values and nationalism. While in 1848, most white southerners still believed the American nation largely conformed to this vision, later white southerners would be able to use this new southern perspective on nationhood to argue that the American nation violated the southern interpretation of national values. In both teaching white southerners to see issues of nationhood as part of an international conversation and in helping them clarify their vision of ideal and acceptable expressions of nationhood, southern analysis of 1848 helped white southerners develop an international perspective that they could use to evaluate issues of nationalism both abroad and at home.

The majority of southerners commenting on the revolutions of 1848, like their earlier counterparts, found much to praise in the events abroad, or at least much to hope for in terms of the establishment of republican governments in Europe. This response echoed broader American patterns, including a search for American inspiration in the revolutions abroad.[32] Indeed, in a reflection of their American nationalism, southern commentators from across the political spectrum, including Democrats, Whigs, and independents, praised European nationalist movements in 1848 for emulating the American Revolution, as the independent *New Orleans Picayune* did by claiming that the revolutions abroad were "the revolution of '76 extending itself across the seas."[33] The documents of the American Revolution, not just the revolution itself, provided material for this comparison, as Georgians read in the Whig newspaper the *Augusta Chronicle and Sentinel* that the founding documents of the new governments in Germany, France, and Italy were based on the Constitution of the United States.[34]

Further, as with the revolutions of the 1820s and 1830s, Americans, southerners included, supported the revolutions of 1848 because they believed these revolutions fought for the same values that the American Revolution had established in their own nation. In this, white southerners still praised attempts to enshrine at least some form of more liberal values abroad. Echoing earlier southerners' focus on self-government, for example, southerners continued to support expressions of national self-determination in the revolutions of 1848. Hungarians were one aspiring nationality to earn accolades for seeking national self-determination, with a writer in the *Southern Literary Messenger* praising them for "contending manfully for representation" and "a substantial share in the government."[35] Similarly, South Carolina doctor J. F. G. Mittag, who had toured Europe in the early 1840s, wrote to the *Charleston Courier* to praise European nationalists who "seem determined, at the peril of every thing, to resume the power" that monarchs had taken from them.[36] Such concerns with the power of monarchy also reveal continued criticism of tyranny and despotism, which southerners continued to characterize as the forces oppressing aspiring European nations.[37]

Republicanism, or government conducted by the people for the protection of the rights of the people, constituted the most significant national value that elite southerners, in keeping with their American nationalism, sought in the nationalist movements in Europe. Southerners were not just interested in republicanism on an abstract level, however. As they debated the revolutions of 1848, southerners ultimately used their evaluation of whether or not a revolution fit their standards of republicanism to determine their level of support for that revolution, demonstrating the continued resonance of liberal values in the South. Indeed, the type and strength of republican virtue shown by a nation or movement dictated its place in southern ranking of movements. Republicanism thus became the primary value that emerged from southern analysis of 1848 as a clear standard for evaluating nations and nationalisms.

Southern preoccupation with republicanism is apparent throughout reports on 1848, from the praise for self-government and rights to the criticism of tyranny and monarchy. For example, Hungary earned praise for fighting for republican self-government in the face of oppression. As a writer for the Tallahassee *Floridian and Journal* declared, "If there be any point to which the eye is directed with more interest than to any other, that point is Hungary," as what was once "lightly spoken of as a rebellion . . . has now assumed the more respectable name . . . REVOLUTION," since "arms taken up first to resist oppression . . . are now retained to establish Independence." By approvingly including excerpts from the Hungarian Declaration of Independence that cited the desire for a government based on "inalienable natural rights," the editor connected his praise for Hungary to the republican ideas of self-government by a people exercising their natural rights.[38]

In contrast, lack of republican virtue was sufficient to earn a revolution condemnation. Italy, which united under a monarch rather than a representative, elected government, constituted one target of criticism of insufficient republicanism. Southern reporters tolerated Sardinian king Charles Albert's leadership of the Italian independence movement as a necessary evil until he failed to secure a united, independent Italy, at which point they accused him, and the Italian Risorgimento in general, of being insufficiently republican from the beginning. For example, the Democratic *Macon Telegraph*'s correspondent "Excelsior" criticized Charles Albert before adding, "No one sympathizes with him. All liberalists on the contrary are thankful that the cause of progress in Italy is rid of connection with any crowned head ruling, by the Grace of God, rather than by the free election of the people of his country."[39] With republican revolutions earning praise and monarchical regimes earning condemnation, republicanism was the clearest value by which foreign events could be evaluated. As they used republicanism as a standard for judging the revolutions, white southerners in 1848 began engaging more deeply with the issues behind the revolutions than had their earlier counterparts, allowing them to differentiate their responses to the various movements.

Republicanism was not the only value that white southerners used to assess foreign revolutions, however. In particular, although a majority of southern analyses of the revolutions of 1848 drew on a liberal American heritage to evince support for nationalist movements abroad, as they debated the events abroad, white southerners also drew from the conservatism of their slavery-based social system. The incorporation of the conservative southern desire for social order and fear of unchecked democracy into the discourse on foreign revolutions limited more conservative southerners' support for the revolutions of 1848.[40] Southern analysis of the revolutions of 1848 thus blended liberal and conservative traditions.

These values and concerns, both liberal and conservative, transcended geographic and partisan divides, meaning that southern discourse did not break down neatly along such lines. Instead, individuals debated the meaning of these movements, adopting positions that evolved over time, combined contradictory ideas, and continued in many cases to skim the surface of the issues despite the deepening of the overall debate. Significantly, as they debated the meaning and expression of nationalism abroad, conservative southerners' wariness of excess liberalism in foreign revolutions, while not unique to the South, began preparing them to develop a vision of nationalism that as yet remained loyal to the American nation but also adhered to white southerners' particular values and concerns, helping them refine their vision of what a nation, and what their American nation, should be.

If republicanism was the primary positive value that southerners sought in the revolutions abroad, fear of unchecked democracy and liberty constituted the key southern concern. Guided by their conservative desires for social order and limited democracy (of particular interest to slaveholders committed to a racial hierarchy), some southerners found much to critique in the revolutions of 1848, despite the initial republican intent of many of the movements. This white southern fear of unchecked liberalism frequently found its expression in the belief that Europeans were unequal to the task of self-government, and that giving rights and power to these ill-equipped Europeans would create chaos and anarchy. For example, no less a figure than John C. Calhoun argued that revolutionary action in Europe would lead to anarchy, due to his opinion that Europeans were ill-prepared to sustain a republic. He admitted, however, that if he were wrong and the revolutions succeeded, then the positive values of freedom, liberty, and republicanism would replace oppressive monarchy throughout Europe.[41]

George W. Kendall was one of the leading southern skeptics of Europeans' fitness for republicanism. Kendall, who had cofounded the *New Orleans Picayune,* served as its foreign correspondent from his home in Paris between 1849 and the mid-1850s. Kendall's dispatches from Europe were particularly vocal in revealing his wariness about Europeans' ability to properly direct their nationalist movements. In fact, Kendall's lack of faith in foreign revolutionaries helped to shape his generally skeptical tone toward the revolutions of 1848. As early as May 1848, for example, Kendall pondered what appeared to be a coming wave of revolution, asking, "Once commenced, where is it to end? Not until rivers of blood have flown; and it is almost hoping too much to believe that the result will be favorable to the masses in all the nations of Europe; for the most sanguine and ultra republicans cannot but feel and know that the majorities are but ill calculated, as at present educated, to live under and enjoy the blessings of free representative government."[42] Similarly, in November, Kendall dismissed the possibility of further popular revolution in Italy by suggesting that the people were disinclined to revolt, declaring that the Italian people, "without leaders and without spirit, appear well enough contented if they can for the present be allowed to eat their maccaroni in quiet."[43] Kendall's skepticism was well-recognized enough that, even as Kendall's editors defended his stance on revolutions against criticism from competing newspapers, they admitted that Kendall perhaps went a bit far, explaining that while his "only anxiety is to see a Republican Government," for Kendall, that same proposition required eliminating "political agitation." Since he tended to see such agitation in the events he analyzed, his attitude toward the revolutions became one of "distrust," leading him to become "less charitable than he should be toward the tribe of dreamers who would have their Utopias recognized by fundamental law."[44]

Elite southerners were so concerned with the fitness of Europeans for republicanism largely because they, like Kendall, feared that people unprepared for democratic rule would fall prey to the dangers of excess democracy due to their inexperience and poor virtue. For white southerners who were wary of extremism in the revolutions of 1848, mobs were the result of democracy run amuck, as people unsuited for governance and determined to destroy the social order gained power. Kendall, for example, in describing his fears of mobs, lamented not just "bloodshed" but also "anarchical influences." Because of what he viewed as a French tendency toward mobs, he characterized the French as irrational and overly excitable, thereby exhibiting a nature ill-suited to self-government.[45] Similarly, a correspondent with the initials P. C. G. described a mob scene in Paris for the Democratic *Richmond Examiner* that was characterized by "bloody" and "savage" fighting by people acting like "blood-hounds," again suggesting the mob's lack of suitability for serious political action.[46] To elite white southerners, revolutions that granted too much power to people incapable of self-government ultimately led to mob rule; thus, these revolutions were too violent, radical, and dangerous, and had no place in the proper process of nation-building.

While the extremism of mobs represented one consequence of unvirtuous people and unchecked liberalism, extremism of ideology constituted an even graver threat in the minds of many white southerners. Ideological extremists violated white southerners' vision of an appropriate form of governance and nationhood by threatening not only the execution of nationalism but also the intent behind it. In particular, white southerners, drawing on their conservative desire for hierarchy as well as their defense of slavery, were concerned with ideologies that sought a more egalitarian social order. Accordingly, "red republicanism," a more liberal form of republicanism that pursued, among other goals, redistribution of property, stood for white southerners as a clear example of the European revolutions' embrace of dangerously liberal ideology. Elite southerners were too invested in the slave system and in a hierarchical power structure that benefited white slaveholders to favor any ideas that promoted equality by granting more power to those at the bottom of the social hierarchy. White southerners levied harsh criticism against French red republicans in particular for supposedly driving moderates away from a more temperate republicanism. Kendall, for example, repeatedly blamed red republicans and their allies for creating the chaos that harmed the republican potential of revolutions. Indeed, to Kendall, the French Revolution of 1848 was characterized by such conflict among the various factions that inevitably the revolution would grant "one of the monarchical factions the upper hand" or allow "Red Republicanism and Socialism" to "triumph over all," including over the more moderate, reasonable "men of character" who were in short supply, and shorter influence, in Kendall's vision of France.[47]

If a more liberal form of republicanism went too far for white southerners, even more radical ideas such as socialism and anarchy earned greater criticism for the threat they posed to white southerners' own vision of society, based as it was in racial inequality. In another report, Kendall told of meeting a "hearty, decided republican" shopkeeper who lamented, "we can do nothing" against the power of the mob, even though "we know that there can be no endurance in the wild theories of the ultras." Kendall noted a "species of despondency" in this man's concerns, one that raised the issue of how much "true republicans" elsewhere need guidance.[48] Critically, both Kendall and his despondent shopkeeper distinguished between "true republicans" and the "ultras" who made success impossible for the former. Similarly, William W. Mann, Paris correspondent for the *Southern Literary Messenger,* joined several ideologies together in describing what he called the "socialist, terrorist, red Republican Party" to his readership. In Mann's estimation, although each of these radical parties individually was a small minority, combined with what he described as three monarchist parties, they together "constitute the majority of France," a situation that made republicanism impossible for France, as none "of these parties would frankly and sincerely submit to the will of France expressed at the ballot-box."[49] Conservative fears of the fullest implications of equality led white southerners to view red republicans and more extreme revolutionaries with great wariness. Such fear of extremism in the revolutions abroad clarified white southerners' belief that radicalism violated both the revolutions' goal of republicanism and the proper method of seeking republican nationhood.

While extremism—either of action, as in the case of mobs, or of ideology, as in the case of red republicanism—threatened the republican goals of the revolutions, the southern elite believed that conservative values would protect against the harmful forms of revolution. In particular, social order and limited liberty emerged as key checks on the excesses of liberalism as attempted abroad. To white southerners, invested as they were in slavery, a hierarchical social order constituted a necessary and beneficial check against the feared extremisms, enabling republicanism to exist without violating traditional societal norms. Additionally, with a hierarchical social order, liberty could be reserved for only white men. Indeed, many white southerners believed that social order was among the American founding values that the United States modeled for nations abroad. The *Charleston Courier* declared in a celebration of the Fourth of July, for example, that "our government, founded on principles of rational liberty, and social order . . . commands peace at home and respect abroad."[50] Similarly, "quality of order," which derived from "conservative tendencies," was the *New Orleans Picayune*'s standard of good governments.[51] Kendall was a common advocate of social order, fearing as he did that European revolutions would harm society in their failure.[52] His editors, even while gently chiding him for his pessimism with regards to the revolutions in Europe, supported his positive view of social order and limited liberty, praising his belief in the "philanthropic and beneficent influences which rational liberty exerts in restraining evil passions [and] inculcating a love of order."[53] While white southerners did not reach consensus on whether the harms of the revolutions outweighed their promise, they shared common assessments of both the desirable republican goals of the revolutions and the potential drawbacks of more extreme and liberal revolutions' execution of those goals.

Critically, even in this criticism of mobs and radical ideologies, southern commentators maintained their belief that republicanism itself was a worthy goal, if only it were to be executed properly. White southerners' concerns with the revolutions of 1848 were less that they sought independent republican nations and more that they failed to live up to the glorious model of the United States, and therefore failed to establish new nations in accordance with the southern elites' expectations and values. As white southerners debated the merits, values, and events of foreign nationalist movements, they largely agreed that republicanism, self-determination, and social order were the key values that nations should seek, and that extremism of both ideology and action should be avoided. These values, then, set the standard by which white southerners could assess nations in the middle of the nineteenth century, creating a southern international perspective on issues of nationhood. Through this international perspective, which blended liberal values such as republicanism with conservative values such as social order, white southerners clarified their vision of what a nation, and a nationalist movement, should and should not be.

In 1848, this southern international perspective did not necessarily differ drastically from that of other Americans'; on the contrary, southerners were themselves still loyal Americans, and Americans throughout the rest of the nation shared many of these same reactions, including the desire to see American values enacted abroad, as well as a fear that the people of Europe were incapable of exercising self-government.[54] Southern discourse on the revolutions of 1848 was nonetheless critical to the later development of southern nationalism, allowing white southerners to participate in the larger national and international debate over the meaning of nationalism. This participation not only enabled white southerners to interject their own voices and concerns into the international dialogue but taught them that they were able to do so, and therefore able to place themselves into the international debate over nationhood.

As they expanded on and clarified their vision of a good nation that held republicanism as good and extremism as bad, white southerners displayed remarkable nuance in the ways they viewed nationalist movements abroad. In particular, while southern analysis of revolutions abroad led to fairly widespread agreement about the desired values a nation should exhibit, southern commentators never fully agreed on whether the dangers of extremism outweighed the potential for good in the revolutions in Europe. The debate over this question, and the subsequent mixing of praise and criticism in southern analysis of the revolutions of 1848, produced complex and varied southern interpretations of foreign nationalist movements.

In one example of this nuance, as southerners debated the revolutions abroad, southern judgment varied from revolution to revolution. The Hungarian Revolution, for one, earned praise for its rational liberty and order, as well as for lacking the red republicans and socialists that had plagued France's revolutionary efforts and earned France criticism. As the *Augusta Chronicle and Sentinel* assessed bluntly, "We have higher hopes of the establishment of a republican government in Hungary than in France," largely due to Hungary's avoidance of French "red republicanism" and reliance instead on "rational liberty under stable law and order."[55] Kendall, the eternal skeptic, likewise distinguished between the many nationalist efforts in the Italian peninsula, criticizing what he saw as the ineffectual Italian monarch Charles Albert, the squabbling Italian people, and the tyrannical king of Naples, even while praising the short-lived Venetian republic for holding to the positive standards of the revolutions.[56]

Southerners exhibited this nuance not only in their assessment of the contrasts among revolutions but also in their analysis of various elements within the same revolution, further complicating their final determinations about the positive or negative meaning of the revolutions. Southern writers frequently pointed to what they saw as differences among the various revolutionaries who made up each nationalist movement, distinguishing between red republicans, who were supposedly corrupting the revolutions, and the more moderate republicans who upheld the positive values of the revolutions. For example, the *Charleston Courier* informed readers that in France, "there is a burst of indignation in all the organs of the moderate parties, of every shade, against the atrocious conduct of red republicanism."[57] This report was also published in the *New Orleans Picayune,* indicating it found favor with multiple southern editors.[58] Extremism, particularly of red republicans, earned condemnation from southerners, but southerners nonetheless continued to support the extremists' more moderate counterparts, allowing them to support certain aspects of the revolutions, even while rejecting those they found threatening.

Elite white southerners also used their beliefs about what a nation should be to alter their support for nations and revolutions over time, adding additional nuance to their discourse. France provides the best example of this process by which southerners continually revised their opinions of a nation based on changing circumstances and the shifting values represented by a nationalist movement. The French Revolution of 1848 initially enjoyed support and praise from southerners, with the *New Orleans Picayune,* for example, enthusing that unlike in the first French Revolution, in which "the French people had little knowledge of the principles of liberty" and therefore "commit[ed] excesses," the revolution of 1848 promised "liberty itself!" as "within the space of a single life the world has been tutored in the science of self-government."[59] As the French movement became increasingly radicalized and as Louis-Napoleon consolidated his power, however, southerners began criticizing the French Revolution of 1848, although their criticism still focused on the harms that excess did to republicanism.[60] After the French Army invaded and defeated the Roman Republic, southern commentators recognized what they saw as the defeat of republicanism in France and began to describe France as a despot equal to much-reviled Austria. The *New Orleans Picayune,* for example, in 1849 called France's efforts to restore the pope to temporal control in place of republican Rome a "sad blow" that would "enthrone a worn-out principle" of autocratic rather than republican rule; later, in 1851, the paper declared France's actions in Italy to be in defense of despotism.[61] Despite their criticism of the failed French attempt at republicanism, as well as France's emerging role as a despot in its own right, however, southerners nonetheless continued to support the principle of republican nationhood, as well as other revolutions in Europe, in particular those that they saw France as oppressing.[62] Such a shift of sympathy demonstrates elite southerners' commitment to the values of republicanism and self-determination, as well as their consistent rejection of what they saw as extremism and tyranny, highlighting an enduring reliance on certain principles to guide analysis of revolutions abroad and emphasizing southerners' nuanced approach to assessing the presence of these values in movements abroad.

While southerners' continued loyalty to the United States and commitment to American nationalism meant that southern commentators' responses to 1848 were not entirely unique and specific to the South, they nonetheless shaped white southerners' views of nationalism by providing them with a clear guide to evaluating expressions of nationhood and nation-building. Southerners' analysis of 1848 depended on careful selection of which values of liberal nationalism southerners believed were important for a nation and which aspects of liberal nationalism conservative proslavery southerners rejected as harmful to social order and therefore the nation. As elite white southerners established these criteria for nations and nationalist movements, they ultimately crafted an international perspective on issues of nationhood that adhered to their vision of American nationalism but was also in accordance with southern politics, values, and concerns, and that could be used to assess nationalism at home and abroad.

The writers of the *New Orleans Picayune* offered some of the clearest depictions of the values that were central to the international perspective which emerged out of the discussions of the revolutions of 1848. In 1848, one writer for the *Picayune* defined his ideal nationalism by combining liberalism and conservatism to celebrate "the law-abiding nature of true liberty, its quality of order, its conservative tendencies, its peaceful attributes."[63] Similarly, the *Picayune* editors praised the analysis of their foreign correspondent Kendall, which was characterized by his expression of "a profound conviction of the conservative tendencies of true liberty . . . and devotion to the fundamental principles of republican freedom."[64] To the *Picayune,* the revolutions of 1848 taught that "true liberty" could only be found in combination with "conservative tendencies."

Kendall explained his own international perspective in response to criticism that his skepticism of the revolutions threatened his commitment to republicanism. Kendall refuted this charge, declaring, "If in my desire to tell the truth, I happen to throw a doubt on the ultimate success of this or that revolution, giving it as my opinion that it has been started by men incapable of carrying it out, the mildest sentence passed upon me is that I . . . have joined the miscellaneous party who are in their hearts praying for the downfall of republicanism." Explaining why such a sentence was unfair, Kendall declared "the tactics of the [extremists] . . . I cannot but think subversive of true liberty, and thinking so I must say so." After calling out "reckless demagogues" who celebrate "outlawry," and "discontented Socialists" who force the support of the populace through "muskets and menaces" as examples of the harms of such failed republicanism that he had witnessed firsthand, Kendall turned to the Roman Republic as an example of his thought on European revolutions. Contextualizing his skepticism toward the failed Roman Republic, Kendall wrote that "had I been convinced that a rigid system of economy would be at once established; that measures would be taken having in view the ultimate education of the masses; that . . . the habeas corpus and trial by jury guaranteed, and the free toleration of religion extended . . .—and I am simple enough to believe that all this must be done before any government can go on and prosper in these latter days—then I might have had more confidence in the success of the great Republican and Unitarian movements of Rome."[65] To Kendall, the problem with the Roman Republic was not its attempt to establish a republican government in place of a monarchy; on the contrary, the problem with the Roman Republic, and the European revolutions in general, was that they failed to do so. Excess liberalism was problematic mainly in its betrayal of republicanism, especially because it supposedly doomed republican movements to failure. For Kendall, for his editors, and for many southern intellectuals, their analysis of European nationalist movements created an international perspective that utilized southern values to confirm that the proper form of governance retained much of the liberal ideals of liberty and republicanism but tempered these ideas with the conservatism of a clear social order.

Critically, while white southerners viewed the revolutions of 1848 with nuance that allowed them to create a southern international perspective on nationhood, their analysis of the revolutions of 1848 also encouraged these southerners to see nationalism as an international movement. Frequently, southern accounts spoke of the revolutionary fervor that grasped all of Europe, grouping the revolutions together. The Whig newspaper the *Texian Advocate,* for example, declared the news of ongoing revolutions in Europe to be "most important," and asked, "Will Europe again relapse into a system of despotic governments, or will the people of

France, Germany, Austria, Hungary, Italy, &c., show to the world that they are capable of self-government?"[66] Southern writers did not just group the revolutions, however; they also believed that the revolutions actively inspired more revolutions. Early on, the French Revolution of 1848 received support for the positive influence it would have in leading other nations to follow in revolution; in one such display of support, the *Augusta Chronicle and Sentinel* praised the overthrow of the French king, stating, "The reigning dynasties of Europe must learn to respect the rights and interests of the people, or their long-suffering *subjects* will rise in their might and successfully claim to be *sovereigns*." Singling out a particular region that would be thus challenged, the author declared, "recent events in France will have a powerful influence on the progress of revolutions in Italy."[67] This idea that one revolution would inspire another ran throughout southern discussions of the revolutions. With their belief that the American Revolution was the ultimate inspiration for these events in Europe, southern commentators further learned to put themselves into the international conversation that was developing about issues of nationalism.[68] Connecting the revolutions, to each other and to their personal American nationalism, led these southerners to see issues of nationhood and nationalism as part of an international conversation, enhancing their developing international perspective.

Just as importantly, elite white southerners believed these international connections could be used to increase support and chances of success for nationalist movements. Southerners commonly expressed their belief that all republicans should support other republics and republicans, linking the movements not just through common ideals but also through mutual support and sympathy. Residents of Clarksville, Texas, for example, met and resolved that "as Republicans, we fraternize warmly, in the great demonstrations for popular Government, which have lately been made in France and Italy."[69] Such solicitations taught southerners that claiming common national values was an effective strategy nationalist movements could utilize to gain support, or at least to gain a sense of legitimacy. This was a critical step in the development of later southern nationalists' strategy of winning legitimacy for the Confederacy through comparisons with foreign nationalisms. With their analysis of the revolutions of 1848, elite white southerners firmly internationalized their vision of nationhood.

As elite white southerners used their international perspective to assess the revolutions of 1848, they found an example of their ideal vision of nationalism in leading Italian nationalist Giuseppe Garibaldi. He was internationally renowned even before 1848 for joining and leading independence movements in Brazil and Uruguay, and his popularity exploded when he became associated with Italian nationalism through his defense of the Roman Republic in 1848. Despite the failures of 1848 and his subsequent exile, Garibaldi continued hoping for a united and independent Italy, gaining further fame in 1860 by leading an army of one thousand "red shirt" volunteers, named after Garibaldi's signature uniform, to conquer Sicily for the new Italian nation being assembled under Sardinian monarch Victor Emmanuel II. Because of these actions, Garibaldi was internationally recognized as a hero of nationalism and as a representative of the best virtues of nationalism. Even during his own lifetime, the developing cult of Garibaldi celebrated his bravery, strength, and devotion to nationalism.[70]

Antebellum southerners joined the rest of the world in celebrating Garibaldi as an exemplar of the best of nationalism. To southern audiences in the wake of 1848, he embodied the very traits and values that they had identified as positively associated with nationalism, both for Americans and for foreign nationalities. As they reported on Garibaldi, his life, his family, his actions, and his health, displaying deep southern interest in the Italian general, southern journalists also praised Garibaldi's patriotism and heroics, which tied him to the cause of nationalism.[71] For example, an article republished in multiple southern newspapers referred to Garibaldi as "this distinguished votery of freedom" and "brave warrior" after an exiled Garibaldi sought temporary refuge abroad.[72] In an emotional tribute, an author for the *Southern Literary Messenger* wrote in 1850 that although Garibaldi had been defeated, he had nonetheless ensured a position "in the arms of the historic muse, to be by her crowned with the freshest of laurels." Looking ahead, the author added that "when . . . the great social feast of free nations shall arrive," Garibaldi, along with Hungarian patriot Lajos Kossuth, would be praised as abundantly as were the ancient Roman gods.[73] To antebellum southern commentators, Garibaldi's commitment to nationalism deserved adulation and praise, despite his military failure.

Garibaldi emerged as such a lauded figure despite the failures that had earned criticism of other nationalists, in part because, unlike radicals and extremists, he fit with the southern vision of the proper form of nationhood. Garibaldi fought for national freedom, seeking to achieve the liberal goals of self-determination and republicanism that southerners, as with all Americans, inherited from the American Revolution. Critically, however, as a military general who was known for leading armies rather than for democratizing national politics or encouraging an activist populace, Garibaldi fought for these liberal goals while seemingly avoiding the threats of extremism such as mob action and radicalism. While Garibaldi fought for an independent Italy, in other words, he did not fight for an overthrow of the social order. Because he properly adhered to both the liberal and conservative values of white southerners, then, if southerners needed a concrete example of the values of nationalism they had learned to celebrate through their analysis of the revolutions of 1848, they needed to look no further than Giuseppe Garibaldi.

Beginning with the Greek independence movement in the early 1820s and continuing through the revolutions of 1848, elite white southerners found much to praise in nationalist movements abroad, particularly in these movements' expressions of southerners' own cherished political values, including the liberal value of republicanism. Conservative southerners, however, also had cause to fear the implications of the liberal ideals of liberty, freedom, and equality. The contradiction between conservatism and liberal nationalism led white southerners to use their analysis of nationalist movements in Europe to clarify their beliefs about what a nation and nationalist movement should represent. Southern commentators learned to continue to laud the values of republicanism and self-determination in the face of tyranny, even as they rejected extremism and the fullest implications of foreign revolutions. Although they still adhered to American nationalism, the process of evaluating which aspects of the movements deserved support and which did not guided white southerners in developing an international perspective on nationalism that reconciled southern respect for some liberal values with a conservative desire for social order. This international vision of nationhood, combined with elite southerners' new belief in the connectedness of nationalist movements, provided white southerners with a means of evaluating issues of nationhood both abroad and at home, and of doing so according to American nationhood, but a vision of American nationhood tempered by white southern values. This perspective would ultimately allow later southern nationalists to claim connections between their own anti-liberal aspiring nation and more liberal nations in Europe as a way of defining the Confederacy, according to the southern rather than international definition of nationalism.

PART II

Antebellum Sectionalism, 1850–1860

Sectional tension increasingly claimed Americans' attention in the 1850s. The decade opened with a fierce debate over the extension of slavery into the territories that the United States had gained from the recent war with Mexico. Prompted by their desire to continue the territorial expansion of slavery, fire-eating southern radicals, particularly from South Carolina, began calling for southern unity and secession from the United States, and delegates from slaveholding states met twice in Nashville in the summer and fall of 1850 to discuss the protection of what they saw as southern rights. In September, Congress passed the Compromise of 1850, which did temporarily calm the tensions, albeit without fully satisfying either section or solving the underlying sectional issues. However, the spread of abolitionism in the North and increasingly radical defenses of slavery in the South, including calls for the creation of a southern empire of slavery through annexation of territory in the Caribbean and Central and South Americas, kept conflict simmering throughout the decade. Amid this growing sectional division, Americans from both sections began to question their national mission and values, as well as their section's place within the nation.

As white southerners navigated this sectional tension, elite commentators turned to the international perspective on nationhood that they had developed through their analysis of nationalist movements in Europe, using this international perspective to help them make sense out of the problems threatening their own nation. The recently concluded, and failed, revolutions of 1848 were still fresh in educated southerners' minds in the 1850s. Even while remaining overwhelmingly committed to the American nation, the southern elite found it useful to compare conflict at home to the conflicts that they had followed in Europe.

Elite white southerners expanded on their previous strategy of analyzing events abroad through a domestic lens to now begin analyzing their own nation through an international lens. Through the crisis of 1850 and the popularization of territorial annexation and filibustering expeditions, white southerners applied the knowledge of nationalism they had developed through analysis of the revolutions of 1848 to help them understand the boundaries of their own nation. Similarly, the arrival of exiled foreign revolutionaries in the United States including the South provided southerners with an opportunity to directly compare their views on these nationalists to those of northerners, with the result that many white southerners increasingly identified distinct differences between southern and northern analyses of issues of nationalism. In particular, proslavery southerners' fears of intervention in slavery led them to reject Hungarian Lajos Kossuth's requests for intervention in Hungary, even as Irish nationalist John Mitchel's proslavery ideas corroborated white southerners' claims that their vision of a proslavery liberal nationalism could be a legitimate interpretation of the international ideas of nationalism. Such support for their international comparisons enabled white southerners to later compare themselves with acclaimed Italian nationalist Giuseppe Garibaldi, enhancing their sense that southerners best represented the international values of nationalism and therefore could potentially form their own nation.

Through the crises of territorial slavery, the filibuster expeditions, and the arrival of European revolutionaries, white southerners used their international perspective to make sense out of their own nationhood. This international contextualization of their own values, as well as of the challenges and issues facing their own nation, helped white southerners to continue refining their beliefs about their own nationhood. Just as critically, these southerners' use of an international perspective to analyze the sectional issues of the 1850s ultimately encouraged and enabled them to conceive of the South as distinct from the North on issues of nationhood, paving the way for the idea of an independent southern nation.

2

Let the South Take Warning

SLAVERY AND EXPANSION
IN AN INTERNATIONAL CONTEXT

The opening of a new decade of the 1850s witnessed Americans clashing over the expansion of slavery into the Mexican Cession. Concerned by the precedent that would be established by allowing northern antislavery interests to block slavery in the new territories, elite white southerners actively debated the best course of action for preserving and expanding the institution of slavery, and therefore southern power, within the United States and its government. To some, the situation of the South, fearful of having its interests blocked by a growing antislavery contingent in the North, echoed the sad state of the failed nations they had recently followed in Europe. Virginia state legislator and future Confederate congressman James Lyons drew on the southern international perspective as he debated whether Virginia should send delegates to the proposed southern unity meeting in Nashville. As Lyons interpreted the situation, "gentlemen North and South say, that it is treason in Southern men to assemble together to consider their wrongs. If this be true, we have . . . the most despotic government on earth—worse than Russia or Austria's system towards Hungary." This comparison of treason and despotism was a bold statement, especially since an American audience who had just sympathized when Hungary failed to gain its independence would have immediately recognized the oppression inherent in Hungary's political situation. To supply proof, then, that the South risked finding itself in the same position, Lyons added even more dramatically that "slaveholders are now cursed, because our Northern brethren poison the air we breathe, the water we drink, and peril the lives of our wives and children."[1] Bolstered by such dire predictions of European-style oppression of the South at the hands of the North, Lyons himself would go on to represent Virginia at the Nashville Convention.

Lyons's embellished claims reflect little of actual reality but reveal much about the mindset of southern slaveholders at the dawn of a new decade in

1850. Territorial expansion of slavery was one of the critical issues by which late antebellum white southerners judged their oppression or liberty. From the Northwest Ordinance through the Missouri Compromise, Americans had long debated whether the institution of slavery should be expanded or should be contained where it already existed. Despite a series of compromises that had each promised to resolve the issue, the expansion of slavery once again came to the forefront of national attention in the late 1840s and 1850s, driving increasing sectionalism. By 1850, a growing free-soil and abolitionist movement in the North sought to block slavery in the new western territories, particularly the new territories gained from Mexico, enraging many white southerners who were increasingly committed to a defense of slavery as a positive good. Although the Compromise of 1850 determined the future of slavery in the Mexican Cession, even providing for the potential expansion of slavery, it did not entirely resolve the issue, not only as the proposed admission of Kansas and Nebraska refueled the domestic debate but also as the rise of filibustering expeditions throughout the decade encouraged white southerners to dream of an expanded southern empire of slavery and to seek the creation of such an empire through private military expeditions that would conquer and pave the way for the annexation of territories in the Caribbean and in South and Central America.[2] With the issues of slavery and territory so intertwined with white southerners' vision of what their nation should be, debates over slavery ultimately became for many white southerners debates over their national future.

Slavery was so critical to elite southerners' visions of their nation in large part because their concerns about slavery and territorial expansion were intrinsically linked to their ideas of governance, especially their cherished right of self-government. As Lyons's statement revealed, the Hungarian-style oppression the South feared was the "wrong" not just of limiting slavery but also of limiting white southerners' ability to advance their own interests within the national government. The slaveholding elite prioritized slavery as the critical southern institution, and thus interpreted the protection and expansion of slavery as a crucial function of their government. Believing slavery needed a geographic buffer against the abolitionists, slaveholders argued that any attempts to limit the expansion of slavery would ultimately give abolitionists the political upper hand, infringing on the ability of the South to advance and protect its interests within national politics. Carrying this logic forward, the southern elite feared that northern attempts to limit slavery would strip white southerners of their right to self-government, initiating what they anticipated would be impending southern oppression at northern hands. These concerns about oppression were greatly exaggerated and premised, for the most part, on anticipated rather than actual developments; nonetheless, such fears ran rampant throughout the late antebellum South.[3]

Faced with a seemingly dire scenario, elite southerners including Lyons used the international vision of nationalism and nationhood that they had developed through their earlier analysis of the European revolutions of 1848 to process their own national issues. In particular, southerners' international perspective proved useful in helping white southerners translate their concerns about the preservation and expansion of slavery into the language of more broadly accepted international principles and values. Accordingly, during the crisis of 1850, southerners crafted self-comparisons with defeated nationalities in Europe to help them express their anxieties about limitations of the territorial expansion of slavery. In these comparisons, antislavery forces in the North equaled, or if left unchecked would equal, the supposedly despotic tyrants who had crushed the European revolutions. Through these comparisons, the southern fight to preserve and extend slavery into the western territories thus became nothing less than the fight for self-government.

As white southerners extended their territorial aspirations with filibustering expeditions, they again drew international comparisons, processing these private attempts to conquer foreign territories through the lens of European nationalist movements in order to clarify their vision of proper expressions of nationhood, including the proper federal treatment of the South. To many late antebellum southerners, the ability to spread slavery through filibustering constituted another necessary function of their self-governance, as well as a possible method of nation-building, or at least empire-building. Any federal attempts to block filibustering would constitute more oppression of the South. With these comparisons, elite southerners applied their international knowledge to their own nationhood, furthering the development of their beliefs about the South's national values and its place within the nation, and ultimately beginning to conceive of the possibility of a distinct southern nation.

The crisis of 1850 proved to be a turning point in elite southerners' usage of an international perspective to understand their own nationhood. As the nation debated the future of slavery in the Mexican Cession before the passage of the Compromise of 1850, southerners turned to international comparisons with the same European revolutions of 1848 that they had just eagerly watched and passionately debated. Southerners, like other Americans, largely lamented the failure of the revolutions of 1848, depicting the defeated nations as oppressed by tyranny and despotism. This understanding of defeated European nations as oppressed paved the way for elite southerners to use international comparisons to dramatize the tensions within their own nation. These international comparisons bridged the partisan divide in the late antebellum South; while Democrats led the way in comparing the woes of the South and defeated European nations, Whigs likewise participated in the internationalization of white southerners' fears of abolition.

The basic formulation of early international comparisons asserted that northern antislavery forces would re-create European-style oppression in the South. Southern politicians, journalists, and other opinion-makers routinely turned to these international comparisons as they argued for the South's right to expand slavery into the new American territories. As early as 1849, for example, a journalist for the Democratic *Macon Telegraph* calling himself "Sylvias" declared that "the northern federal party have left no stone unturned to engender the increase of the spirit of abolitionism," a trend "which if not stayed will . . . reduce the Southern States to the condition of Ireland."[4] Similarly, in the spring of 1850, Virginia politician Robert M. T. Hunter, then a Democratic senator, spoke in Congress on the territorial governance of California, arguing that "the North declared their consciences could not justify their support of a constitution which guaranteed to the slaveholder certain rights," and adding that "this Union, in the hands of a reckless majority—of a sectional majority—would be a curse instead of a blessing. The union of England and Ireland placed all legislative power in England, and England rules Ireland now with greater power, and force, and oppression, with her statute book, than she did when she held her by the sword."[5] For Hunter, the South had both a right and a need to expand its power by expanding its institutions territorially; otherwise, white southerners would be denied their ability to participate equally in government, just as Ireland was denied equal participation in British government.

Elite southerners were so concerned by what they saw as the impending oppression of the South that they began holding meetings and conventions to discuss the future of the South within the United States. International comparisons of oppression were particularly appealing to the delegates at these southern unity and southern rights meetings, which proliferated during the crisis of 1850. These meetings brought together concerned white men to discuss appropriate responses in case the abolitionist elements in government succeeded in blocking slavery in the Mexican territories. In a speech at one such southern meeting held in Mississippi, Whig politician General Felix Huston argued that the separate institutions of the North and South made them as distinct as England

and Ireland, a comparison that prompted him to ask, "Do you suppose that a dominant and overwhelming Northern majority will deal with the Southern slaveholder more leniently than the English have done with the Irish Catholic?" before answering his own question with the claim that "if you do you will find yourselves most egregiously mistaken."[6] The Nashville Convention was the most prominent of these meetings, bringing together delegates from southern states to begin debating unified southern action. James Lyons, who would soon break with the Whig Party and join the Democratic Party, was one of the delegates in Nashville who used the debate over southern unity and the Nashville Convention to express concern not only with the European-style oppression of northern efforts to limit slavery but also with the supposed violation of southerners' rights to meet and assemble in order to discuss the issue of slavery.[7] Felix Huston likewise warned his fellow Nashville Convention delegates that the "obtrusive interference" of the North in the issue of slavery would cause the South to "sink below the miserable state of Ireland" by stripping the white South of its "institutions" as well as its "fixed, separate and distinct character."[8]

If limitation of slavery was the primary threat that would create European-style oppression in the South, elite white southerners during the crisis of 1850 asserted that states' rights, or the primacy of southern states' power over national and federal power, was the solution that would best protect the South from such a threat. North Carolina congressman Thomas Lanier Clingman, a Democrat, declared in Congress that southerners should "assemble in convention and assert their rights" before "the fate of the South" came to resemble that of "Poland, crushed under the foot of Russia, or Hungary . . . overcome and pierced to death by the gigantic strength of Russia."[9] Whig congressman Henry W. Hilliard of Alabama similarly argued that "if we submit, we have examples before our eyes of the condition to which we shall be reduced. Ireland . . . is a picture of what we should be. With her representation in Parliament, she constitutes nominally a portion of the British empire; yet the policy of that empire degrades and ruins her." This example, Hilliard declared, taught that "the Southern States can maintain their position in the Union only by cultivating a spirit which makes their people stand ready to defend their equal claim to the benefits of the Government against every assault."[10] A writer for the *Macon Telegraph* summarized the position of Georgia Democratic and states' rights political candidates David J. Bailey and Zachariah E. Harman more bluntly, stating that they believed "our only possible hope of escape from a doom worse than Poland or Hungary, is to be found in the doctrine of States Rights."[11] To many elite white southerners during the crisis of 1850, northern attempts to block slavery in the territories represented nothing less than an attack against white southerners' self-government, thereby constituting European-style oppression, requiring southerners to embrace states' rights as a solution.

With the passage of the Compromise of 1850 in September, the issue of slavery in the Mexican Cession was technically resolved, but white southerners' fears that a northern abolitionist movement would strip them of participation in self-government persisted. Accordingly, many influential southerners continued to use an international perspective to push for the preservation and expansion of slavery. The *Macon Telegraph* encouraged readers in October 1850 to "let the South take warning from the fate of Ireland, under the misrule and oppression of English majorities. If the compromisers think they can shift the evil hour on to posterity by acquiescing in the aggressions of the late Congress they are most egregiously mistaken." For this author, the compromise did not adequately address the threat to southern self-government, and if white southerners ceased fighting for further protection of slavery, they "will be forced to a solution in less than ten years."[12]

Although territorial slavery was the primary target of white southerners' emerging international perspective, once developed this perspective proved useful for discussing other aspects of slavery as well. For example, Mississippi congressman Albert G. Brown, a Democrat, declared at a rally in Jackson that northern-driven taxes and monetary policies were stripping the South of its slave-produced wealth and, combined with the issues of territorial slavery and the slave trade, making the South "as tributary to the North as Ireland to England, Poland to Russia, and Austria to Hungary."[13] The Central Southern Rights Association of Virginia adopted a similar stance, stating that a northern-oriented economy and northern aggression toward the South meant that "we have become a second Ireland."[14] The proliferation of comparisons between the oppression of European nations and the South, even after passage of the compromise, reveals that southern fears of northern oppression were not resolved even after the conclusion of the crisis of 1850.

The international comparisons between the South and defeated European nations that the southern elite used to process the crisis of 1850 were critical to helping the southern elite reimagine the place of the South within the United States. Comparisons that equated the South with aspiring and defeated nations cast the South as the equivalent of a nation, rather than just a section within a nation, opening the conceptual possibility of the South as a nation. Arguments that claimed that the best course of action for the South was to strengthen the power of the South against the rest of the nation—in other words, to divorce

southern power from the larger federal power—further solidified white southerners' growing sense that their interests were not necessarily served within the
American nation and were better served by some form of southern unity and
independence.

While international comparisons of oppression, equating the South with
defeated nations in Europe, reveal general southern support for European nationalist movements, conservative southern respect for social order and hierarchy nonetheless meant that white southerners were wary of the values such as
equality and freedom associated with those movements, as shown in southern
analysis of the revolutions of 1848. Accordingly, a competing conservative version of the emerging international perspective developed as a minority position
among elite southerners during the crisis of 1850. This conservative variation
expressed white southern fears of northern power by positioning European nationalist movements as a negative, rather than positive, reference point for the
South. Endorsements of this perspective were relatively few in number, and due
to widespread southern political respect for the liberalism of the American Revolution, overlapped significantly with the more mainstream comparison between
the oppressed South and oppressed European nations. Nonetheless, the instrumentalist nature of southerners' international perspective allowed for significant
variation, enabling individuals to respond differently to different themes and
creating diversity within white southerners' thought.

In the more conservative variation of international analysis, the international
similarities were between the extreme radicalism and liberalism of European politics and northern politics, rather than between the oppression of the South and
aspiring nations in Europe. Previewing the conservative arguments that would
emerge during secession, some antebellum southerners blamed what they claimed
was excessively liberal and democratic European ideology for the problematic
antislavery ideas emerging in the North. For example, a speaker at a Virginia
Whig convention in 1851 asserted that the reason the North had initiated sectional conflict and betrayed the previously peaceful union between the sections
was that it had been poisoned by "wild political theories" including communism
and red republicanism from France, Italy, and Germany.[15] Similarly, a writer for
the *Southern Quarterly Review* noted with approval that the author of the book he
was reviewing had "watched, with an intelligent mind, the current events, which
have been crowded in the last few years of revolution and reaction," and had now
"detected in this country symptoms of disease kindred to the fatal maladies which
have infected Europe." The warning this author furnished was particularly important to the reviewer, who added, "Our people have thought themselves out of

reach of the pernicious doctrines that were afloat in the Continental air in 1847 and 1848," and thus were unprepared to combat these ideas.[16]

Proslavery minister Reverend Frederick Augustus Ross of Huntsville, Alabama, provided an explanation for this negative reaction to the liberal doctrines of Europe, focusing on the harms of social equality that might derive from liberal ideals. Ross declared in a critique of abolitionism that "God gives no sanction to the affirmation that he has created all men equal. . . . God has cursed seven times in France since 1793. . . . He has cursed [equality] in Prussia, Austria, Germany, Italy, Spain. He will curse it as long as time."[17] Because of the threat that liberal European political ideals posed to southern conservatism, and in particular slaveholding and white supremacy, for some southerners the northern threat was best illustrated through comparisons between the North and Europe, not the South and Europe. Even while proposing a different relationship between European revolutions and the South, however, once again in this perspective the North stood as the enemy, rather than a cooperative ally united by functional national bonds.

The existence of competing southern international perspectives on the crisis of 1850 reveals just how central the emerging international perspective was to elite southerners' attempts to make sense out of their own nationhood at a moment of national and sectional crisis. Across the political spectrum as early as 1850, white southerners applied their understanding of transatlantic ideas of nationhood to their own nationality in ways that enhanced their sense of division from the North.

Not surprisingly, as international comparisons prepared elite southerners to consider the South a unit that could, intellectually speaking, be separated from the North and directly compared with independent nations, the idea that the South should in fact become a separate nation took hold among more radical white southerners. As southern reaction to the crisis of 1850 created a new sense of the South as opposed to the North in issues of nationality and as a potential national unit equivalent of aspiring European nations, the possibility opened for southerners to begin thinking and speaking of secession from the United States. While the majority of southerners remained committed to the idea of American national unity during the crisis of 1850, fears of northern power did indeed lead a few radical fire-eaters to begin proposing an alternate national future for the southern slaveholding states.[18] As the secession debate commenced, both pro- and antisecession southerners turned to their international perspective to make sense out of the ideas of national unity and disunion, and to make their case for what they believed was the best national future for the South.

For white southerners who saw secession as a valid response to what they feared would be the loss of slave territory, and therefore southern power, at the hands of northern abolitionists, an international perspective supported secession, not only by indicating that the South could be a separate national unit than the North but also by dramatizing the consequences that slaveholding states would experience if they remained in the United States. For example, Mississippi politician Albert G. Brown argued in Congress that any "act of aggression upon slave property" would create "frightful, terrible consequences" for the South. In describing these consequences, Brown urged his listeners to "picture to yourself Hungary, resisting the powers of Austria and Russia. . . . I tell you sir, sooner than submit we would dissolve a thousand such unions as this."[19] Congressman Joseph A. Woodward, a Democrat from South Carolina, concurred in a speech given in Columbia. Despite disagreeing with Woodward and his secessionist ideas, the *Richmond Enquirer* summarized his views as "he knew not one single reason why the South should not separate from the North. The history of the world presents no arguments in favor of a Union. . . . Was the union of Ireland and England a blessing or a curse to the former country? Was it expedient that France and Prussia should be amalgamated, or that Russia should find a helpmate?"[20] Building on the general comparisons that presented the South as equivalent to an oppressed nation in Europe, both in lack of rights and in possibility of nationhood, these secessionists used an international perspective to warn their fellow southerners that only secession would avoid finalizing the oppression that the limitation of slavery would create in the slaveholding South.

As the most radical of southerners proposed secession, the issue of potential war inevitably entered the debate. Indeed, for many prominent southerners, international comparisons were most useful in revealing how southerners would handle any war that might follow an act of disunion. To most of these southerners, an international lens revealed that even the possibility of war did not discredit secession as a viable course of action. Felix Huston was a frequent proponent of this idea, because for him, an international perspective demonstrated that the South would be successful in war against the North. For example, he argued in a speech given in Lexington, Mississippi, that "out of the Union, but one thing could abolish slavery, and that would be the conquest of the Southern States. That we must risk. . . . We were more numerous and far more wealthy than Hungary, which successfully resisted the arms of Austria and Russia, until betrayed by her own generals."[21] Similarly, as Albert Brown warned of the "frightful, terrible" consequences of antislavery, he also declared, "If Hungary, which had never tasted liberty, could make such stout resistance, what may you not anticipate from eight millions of southrons made desperate by your aggression."[22] If Hungary could all but succeed in defending its claim to independence, according to Huston and Brown southern success was guaranteed.

While these men focused on the potential victory that a war would bring to the South, other southern writers instead used international comparisons to criticize the North for forcing a seceding South to engage in such a hypothetical war. For example, the *Macon Telegraph* reprinted a report by the *Columbia Telegraph* which argued that the North's potential use of military force to prevent secession would re-create the oppression of European despotisms that had defeated aspiring nationalities. As the reporter for the *Columbia Telegraph* declared, the entire world would carefully follow a war between a seceding South and the United States, and "a Republican and limited Government, enacting the tragedy of Poland or Hungary, will be a spectacle of which the world will require some explanation."[23] If the South stood to benefit from waging a war with greater passion than that of aspiring European nationalists, the North had much to lose in re-creating the actions of European despots. International comparisons thus bolstered elite southerners' belief that secession could be a viable response to the oppression that antislavery northerners would create.

Even as more radical southerners used international comparisons to argue that secession could be a valid path for escaping northern tyranny, however, the majority of white southerners remained committed to the unity of the American nation, despite their fears of the consequences of limiting the expansion of slavery. These loyal southerners, like their more radical disunionist counterparts, adapted the language of international comparisons not just to dramatize the stakes in the conflict between slavery and free soil but also to argue for the continued unity of the nation despite that conflict. As early as the crisis of 1850, the matter of which form of international comparison most accurately reflected southern reality, and therefore best predicted the southern future, became a debate between southern secessionists and Unionists.

The negative consequences of disunion, as illustrated by European examples, featured prominently in the international comparisons that pro-unity southerners drew in order to refute the nascent secessionist movement. Speaking in the Senate in February 1850, Sam Houston argued that the South should avoid disunion for fear such an action would lead to a Civil War that would destroy southern prosperity. Houston urged his fellow senators to "look at Hungary. Consider the civil war that has raged between Austria and Hungary—one nation," pointing to the horrors of war to illustrate the dangers of national division and disunity.[24] In a similar approach, the Victoria *Texian Advocate* wrote a year later that anyone who should speak "with flippant tongue of the fatal malady of

Disunion" should "look at Poland, Venice, and Genoa, and see the insignificance and obscurity which must follow division."[25] Samuel S. Boyd likewise endorsed this perspective as he celebrated the success of the Compromise of 1850 in warding off disunion and thus war in a speech at an 1851 Jackson, Mississippi, union festival. Boyd urged his audience to "witness the sad scenes of sanguinary strife in glorious Italy, in Germany, Hungary, and indeed throughout central Europe! Behold the melancholy spectacle of France, the so-called Republican France, marching her armies . . . to assist Despotism in crushing" the Roman Republic.[26]

Expanding on the theme that Boyd introduced in his speech, many pro-union southerners identified the harm caused by disunity to be the destruction of liberty and enhancement of tyranny, not just in the nation suffering the division but also in any other nation aspiring to free government. Drawing on the sense of American exceptionalism that led antebellum Americans to claim the American Revolution and American nation as inspirations for the revolutions of 1848, loyal southerners during the crisis of 1850 dramatized the harms of a divided United States by pointing to the negative consequences that such a division would have for the cause of free government in Europe. Frederick A. P. Barnard, a northerner serving as a professor at the University of Alabama, wrote in 1851 of the "sublime mission" of "this majestic Republic" to be an "example and the encouragement . . . and powerful protector of the wretched and oppressed," such as the recently failed republic of Rome and the "gallant [Hungarian] people ground into the dust." With this noble mission, Barnard questioned, how could disunionists seek to "shatter [the United States] into fragments, and give it over to anarchy, confusion, and ruin." In this scenario, not only would the United States suffer the loss of its liberty and strength but so too would aspiring nations such as Italy and Hungary, which looked to the example and protection of the United States.[27] A southerner by the pen name of "Americanus" wrote a letter to the editor of Little Rock's *Arkansas Gazette* endorsing this dire prediction, passionately arguing that "the future happiness of this great nation, and, in a degree, of the world, depends upon the stability of our Union. Let this Union be destroyed and we not only entail on our posterity an inheritance of bloodshed and woe, but we dash to dust the last hope of struggling Republicanism in Europe. We plant a fresh dagger in the bosoms of the Mazzinis, the Garibaldis, and the Kossuths of Italy and Hungary." Even worse, the division of the United States would mean that "the conclusion will be drawn that freemen cannot govern themselves."[28] For commentators including Americanus and Barnard, unity was a critical aspect of American nationhood, not just for the United States but for the cause of liberty worldwide. The stakes were higher than just slavery and southern self-government; the values and glories of the American Revolution granted the United States a critical role within the international conversation on nationalism, one that should not be shirked through national division.

While these pro-union southerners used an international context to dramatize the negative consequences of national division, and thus to overturn the secessionists' arguments that disunion was the correct path for the South, most of them did not directly challenge the exaggerated claims that northern antislavery was a tyrannical force re-creating European despotism over the South. For at least one pro-union southerner, however, an international perspective revealed that disunion was undesirable both because of the harm it would cause and because it was simply unnecessary. William John Grayson, a states'-rights, proslavery, antisecessionist South Carolina politician and journalist, wrote in the *Charleston Courier* under the penname "Curtius" that the South should not secede, as the section had yet to face the oppression suffered by Hungary and Poland, and therefore secession would not be justified. As Grayson assessed, "The orators of the seceders assure us that we are a degraded people—that we are no longer free—that so disgraceful a case of submission to oppression, has never before been known since the beginning of the world." So extreme were the secessionists' claims that Grayson declared, "If we were in the condition of Hungary, or Poland, or Austrian Italy, or Sicily . . . it would be impossible to use more extravagant and unlimited phrases." Despite the passion of the secessionists' rhetoric, however, Grayson did not buy their arguments. In his opinion, the claims of secessionists to such oppression were "midsummer nights dreams, and nothing more—a sort of stereotyped form of expression, unaccompanied with definite ideas—words merely, without any meaning."[29] Directly refuting the widespread southern equation of antislavery forces with the tyrants oppressing aspiring nations in Europe, Grayson declined to exaggerate the actual situation of the early 1850s, noting that white southerners still exercised more than their due share of power within the nation.

Grayson reveals that the usage of international comparisons to describe the situation in the sectionally divided antebellum United States—and to proscribe a future path for the South—was complicated. While the majority of white southerners used these comparisons to draw attention to what they believed to be the oppressive nature of the antislavery movement, particularly its efforts to limit the territorial expansion of slavery, such views were not unanimous. Grayson broke with this position, taking the more realistic stance that an international perspective revealed the South had no reason to break up the nation. The inflamed nature of other southerners' rhetoric did not mean these claims were without impact, however. Showing sharp insight and revealing the importance that even false claims could have in shaping broader southern discourse about nationhood, Grayson pointed out "the effect, however of perpetually repeating the same thing, no matter how absurd that may be, is not without its influence."[30] Even in the early 1850s, secessionists repeated their beliefs that the South was like Hungary or Poland often enough that they wore people down and convinced them that the South must be under threat by the North. As Grayson wisely recognized, his fellow southerners' international perspective on nationhood was based on sentiment rather than reality, but that lack of reality did not matter to many white southerners, who widely used their international perspective nonetheless.

The southern debate over the proper international framing for territorial slavery and potential secession temporarily dissipated as the crisis of 1850 receded. When sectional tensions flared again a decade later, however, white southerners—once again in both secessionist and Unionist camps—would return to the arguments they used to make sense out of the earlier national crisis, now resurrecting and expanding those arguments as crisis turned into war. In the meantime, southerners' use of international comparisons to process the crisis of 1850 and to debate the possibility of secession did, as Grayson predicted, influence the ways in which white southerners thought about their nationhood. By positioning the South as a unit within the international conversation about nationhood, elite southerners applied their international analysis to their own nationality, intensifying their sense that the South could indeed be analyzed as a national entity, which prepared them to consider an independent southern nation.

By the end of 1851, southern analysis of the Compromise of 1850 waned as the issue of slavery in the Mexican territories became a *fait accompli* rather than a matter of debate. While the compromise resolved the issue of the expansion of slavery within the Mexican Cession, however, it did not halt the larger debate over the territorial expansion of slavery elsewhere. Throughout the decade of the 1850s, the idea of American territorial expansion, and the subsequent issue of the expansion of slavery, continued to play a critical role in American political debate. Inspired by Manifest Destiny's argument that God ordained the United States to spread its glorious republican institutions across America, expansionist Americans conquered North America from Atlantic to Pacific, annexing Texas and Oregon and waging war against Mexico to claim most of northern Mexico. Although most Americans were content with such a drastic territorial increase, and indeed many Americans opposed expansion in general, others found this continental domination insufficient. A minority, increasingly centered in the South, argued that the United States should not only spread from sea to sea but also should continue expanding and claim new territory in areas including the now-reduced Mexico, the Caribbean, and Central and South America—and should bring slavery into these territories as well.

Although the antebellum government did not accomplish expansion beyond what became the continental United States, a small number of particularly passionate citizens decided to take the issue of expansion into their own hands, leading so-called filibuster expeditions to locations including Cuba, Nicaragua, and Mexico. In these filibusters, private citizens enlisted for a privately led invasion of the target country, with the goal of setting up a new government led by the filibusters, thereby expanding American influence in the region. Among the most well-publicized filibusters were Narciso López's unsuccessful attempts to take Cuba from Spanish imperial control. After Cuban revolutionary López tried and failed to free Cuba, he fled to the United States in 1848 to escape persecution. In the United States, López gained the support of many Americans and planned and organized a series of filibuster invasions of Cuba before being captured and executed in 1851. William Walker emerged as the next prominent filibuster. An American, Walker organized a filibuster to Nicaragua and succeeded in overthrowing the government in 1855. Walker declared his forces to be the government of Nicaragua and instated a program of Americanization, including reestablishing slavery in order to win the support of white American southerners, before being defeated in 1857 by combined U.S. and Central American forces who were concerned by the precedent of a successful filibuster expedition.[31]

Such filibusters became topics of fierce debate in the Atlantic world, with Americans and even Europeans sharply divided on the issues of whether filibusters were legal, much less deserving of support. Although initially the debate in the United States was largely partisan, with Democrats more supportive of filibuster expeditions and Whigs more critical, throughout the 1850s the debate became increasingly sectional, with southern slaveholders emerging as a leading pro-filibuster voice. Fearful of the growing antislavery and free-soil movements and their attempts to block the expansion of slavery within the United States, southern slaveholders looked further south to find new territory that would allow them to expand and therefore preserve slavery, advancing a proslavery imperialism that sought greater power for southern slaveholders.[32]

Filibustering, dealing as it did with issues of national and imperial expansion, national sovereignty, international relations, and legitimate governance, was yet another issue, much like the revolutions of 1848, that played a role in the larger mid-nineteenth-century Atlantic world debate over the meaning and form of nationhood. Not surprisingly, southern opinion-makers, convinced by their analysis of the crisis of 1850 that international comparisons were useful in understanding issues of American nationhood such as the territorial expansion of slavery, now actively combined analysis of European nationalist movements and American filibustering expeditions, using their understanding of the former to make sense of the latter. As with their interpretation of the revolutions of 1848, the application of this international lens to the issue of filibustering and annexation refined white southern beliefs about nationhood, ultimately helping lead southerners to begin conceiving of the existence of a particularly southern form of nationhood.

Southern application of an international perspective to the filibustering movements highlights the extent to which elite southerners in the 1850s believed in the utility of this perspective but still debated the particulars of how best to utilize it. Even elite white male southerners were not united in their assessment of how filibusters fit into the larger international picture of nationalism, and southern opinion-makers used international comparisons to make their case both for and against filibustering, often debating each other by actively referring to the supposed fallacies of the other side's positions. These positions on filibustering often grew out of larger positions on American expansion and annexation of foreign territories.

In particular, partisan alignment helped shape white southerners' positions on filibustering and on American expansion in general. Providing one example of partisan influence, the pro-annexation Democratic *Richmond Enquirer* and anti-annexation *Richmond Whig* used their partisan viewpoints to debate the international meaning of the annexation of Mexican territories. The *Whig* equated the expansion of the United States into Mexico with the much-reviled partition of Poland, a comparison to which the *Enquirer* objected, asking, "Can party madness farther go than for a journal, in this great nation, shamelessly to denounce the American people, who have thought proper to . . . acquire by treaty California and New Mexico, as equally guilty with the Holy Alliance in their detestable partition of Poland."[33] For these Richmond papers, the well-understood examples of oppressed European nations could be used to make sense out of an expanding American empire, even if the partisan journalists disagreed on the particulars of the comparison. Similarly, the Whig newspaper the Montgomery *Alabama Journal* asserted that one of many problems with the Democratic Party was that it supported annexation in cases including Texas and the Mexican territory, filibustering in places including Cuba, and American intervention in foreign affairs such as the Hungarian nationalist movement.[34] To the editors of the *Alabama Journal,* as for many of their fellow elite white southerners of both parties, official expansion, filibustering, and involvement in nationalist movements abroad were all part of the same larger issue, meaning southerners could draw on knowledge of one to make sense out of the others.

Even as elite southerners differed in their assessment of the appropriateness of filibustering, however, they tended to agree that an international perspective was useful in evaluating filibustering, particularly in assessing the positive values of nationhood that a nation, its citizens, and its representatives should uphold and express. Beyond the issue of expanding slavery, the values that white southerners sought in filibuster expeditions were the same that they had searched for in European revolutions. Southern analysis of the revolutions of 1848 had established that foreign events could be analyzed on the basis of their adherence, or lack thereof, to national values such as republicanism. Building on this tactic for evaluating international affairs, then, antebellum southerners supported filibusters if they assessed them to advance self-government, and criticized them if they failed to meet that standard. This strategy forced them to ignore the reality that filibusters imposed an external government on a nonconsenting population, but elite white southerners, used to excluding certain groups from self-government, made this manipulation easily.

Although filibusters by definition handed political control to outsiders, the popular will of the people being filibustered was nonetheless one of the most frequent values that white southerners looked for to determine the presence of self-government in a filibuster movement and therefore to determine whether that filibuster deserved southern support. Most Americans agreed that popular will was a necessary element of nationalist revolutions—a belief that had been reinforced by southern analysis of the revolutions of 1848. Accordingly, southerners referred to the popular will exhibited by nationalist movements in Europe as they assessed the extent to which filibusters lived up to that standard. If southerners could claim that filibusters were welcomed by the local population, they would be able to support the filibusters in the name of self-government, just as they had supported movements for self-government in Europe.

The Cuban filibuster was of particular interest to southern slaveholders, who had long eyed the slaveholding Spanish colony of Cuba as a potential target for southern expansion; thus, southern writers sought a way to claim the filibuster of Cuba as a legitimate expression of self-government. The *New Orleans Picayune,* for example, interpreted the Cuban filibuster as a justifiable attempt to provide assistance for what they characterized as a popular movement of Cubans engaging in a legitimate struggle against Spanish oppression. To make this case, the *Picayune* declared that López's filibustering expedition to Cuba met the standard of a popular movement and therefore deserved support for advancing self-government. In an 1850 response to European fears that missions to spread republicanism would veer out of control and topple governments in Europe (a fear that the *Picayune* admitted was not entirely unfounded, given recent events in Europe), a *Picayune* editor argued that Americans had withheld their support for López "until they could obtain the assurance, by sufficient acts, that the movement had become a demonstrated revolution of the Cuban Creoles themselves, and that they should be allies to a people struggling openly for its own independence as a nation."[35] This was not a fleeting belief on the part of the *Picayune*'s editors; over a year later, another article stated outright that "the proofs of what is the popular will" were part of the process of "judging of the moral right of . . . a subject people in a struggle to overthrow an oppressive government," adding, "we hold that, with satisfactory evidence, that there is a real and determined effort of the Cuban people to achieve independence of the island." To the *Picayune,* Cuba was a nation seeking freedom from oppression, and filibusters simply provided assistance. Even failure did not negate the nobility of the goals of the Cuban people, as international examples taught that "neither Poland, nor Hungary, nor Rome has lost any thing in the affections of mankind because their heroic children fell at last before the organized hordes of embattled despotism."[36]

The *Picayune* was not alone in its positive assessment of Cuba's display of popular will, nor in using popular will as a standard by which filibusters could be judged. The *Florida Republican,* for example, similarly declared that "we are justified in believing that Cuba herself has started the ball of revolution" and are therefore unable to "withhold our warm sympathy with the patriots in what must resolve itself into a struggle between Republicanism and colonial vassalage." While the author was not yet convinced that filibusters would aid the Cuban cause, he was convinced of the righteousness of the cause itself, going on to argue that "America sympathized with Poland . . . with Hungary, with Ireland; and when her true impulses have play, they will respond the more warmly to Cuba."[37] To the extent that efforts to extract Cuba from Spanish control were, at least in part, the result of popular will, some southerners were willing to support the Cuban revolution on the same basis that they had supported those in aspiring European nations.

Such assessment found applicability beyond the case of Cuba. Continuing its pro–popular will and pro-filibuster stance, the *Picayune* argued in 1856 that William Walker's new Nicaraguan government deserved official diplomatic recognition from the United States, in part because "the war in which they are engaged is, in fact, a war of the people of Nicaragua in the defense of their own right to govern themselves." While the *Picayune* was thus convinced that the Nicaraguan revolt was a popular one, other statements in the article suggest that perhaps the author had lowered the standard of popular will in order to allow Walker's government to meet it. Condemning with faint praise, the author argued that Walker's government "is acquiesced in as completely by the inhabitants as . . . that of King Bomba, of Naples, by his subjects; or that of Pope Pius the IXth, as temporal sovereign of Rome, supported by French and Austrian bayonets. We have not inquired whether either of these monarchs— the pressure of force or foreign help being removed—could keep his throne by the free will of his subjects," but they nonetheless were recognized as the de facto governments. Considering that "Bomba" was usually reviled as one of the worst despots and oppressors of free government in Europe, this was hardly an enthusiastic endorsement of the popular support for Walker. In a slightly more complimentary tone, however, the author did add that "there is less opposition to [Walker's government] among those over whom it rules, than there is in the hearts . . . of Italians against the hateful King of Naples, and the secular sway of the Roman Pontiff."[38] The familiar events in Italy provided a point of comparison for the *Picayune*'s author, serving as a benchmark of popular will.

Given these tepid evaluations of the popular support for the new government of Nicaragua, it is unsurprising that other southerners argued that Nicaragua did not meet the necessary standard of popular will. In an objection to granting diplomatic recognition to Walker's government, the *Columbus Enquirer*, an anti-annexation Whig paper, asked for "evidence . . . that any considerable part of these Nicaraguans . . . have 'freely expressed their approval in the present condition of political affairs,'" pointing out that when Americans evaluated their support for Hungary, the "'expressed approval'—not of Kossuth and his admirers only—but of a 'considerable part' of the citizens of Hungary was absolutely necessary."[39] While the *Picayune* was willing to give Nicaragua the most generous possible definition of popular will that they could support within an international context, the *Columbus Enquirer* turned to another familiar example in Hungary to argue that international context required a much higher level of popular will, one that Nicaragua failed to meet.

In reality, the *Columbus Enquirer*'s assessment was most accurate; almost by definition, filibusters represented an imposition on a people by an external invading force. Even if some local residents came to support the filibuster, supporting the popular will was not the main motivation of a filibustering expedition. Because antebellum southerners, and Americans in general, believed so strongly in the necessity of popular support for a government, however, and because of their desire to expand slavery into the targets of filibusters, some southerners proved willing to manipulate both the reality of the filibuster expeditions and the meaning of popular will in order to support the filibusters.

While popular will was an important value that southerners looked for as they assessed filibustering expeditions, southern analysts also debated the goals that the popular will supported. Echoing their analysis of the European nationalist movements, southerners who supported filibusters generally interpreted the filibusters as fighting against oppression and despotism. In particular, arguing that the Cuban or Nicaraguan people were oppressed in ways similar to the people of Hungary and Poland aided pro-filibuster southerners in making their case that filibuster expeditions were positive forces that extended the desired form of nationality to suffering people. A meeting of citizens in Pass Christian, Mississippi, for example, convening to show support for the failed Cuban filibuster, resolved that "we have approved the repeated manifestations of popular sympathy in our countrymen for the cause of political liberty throughout the world," including "Poland and Hungary, struggling for independence; yet in none of these, or in all together, was power so intense, so sanguinary, so relentless, as that of Spain over Cuba."[40] The *Arkansas Gazette* of Little Rock concurred that López was "a patriot! He had undertaken to free his beloved country—to unrivet the chains of Spanish despotism, which clank louder and gall worse than those of Austrian or Russian despots."[41]

These assessments of the desire of filibusters to free oppressed peoples were not limited to Cuba. The *Columbus Enquirer,* although still wary of filibusters and despite doubting the existence of a popular will supporting Walker's Nicaraguan government, wrote that Walker nonetheless had acted "to overthrow the corrupt system of government" which had foisted "enslavement and degradation" on the people of Nicaragua. Further, the *Enquirer* assessed, Walker's expedition was "remarkably alike" to that of Garibaldi's much-praised Sicilian expedition, with "no essential difference in principle between the Nicaraguan revolution of Walker the filibuster, and the Sicilian revolution of Garibaldi the deliverer."[42] Even southerners who expressed skepticism of filibustering, like the writers for the *Enquirer,* could admit that one movement that sought to end political oppression had at least as much merit as the next, whether it took place in the Americas or in Europe.

If a filibuster sought to overturn oppression and despotism, then it only stood to reason that perhaps that filibuster attempted instead to establish liberty and freedom, at least on the national level (albeit certainly not for the enslaved). The supposed potential to advance liberty, a key issue that southerners had evaluated in European nationalist movements, thus became another standard that southerners could use to evaluate filibusters. As elite southerners looked to the case of Cuba, many of them believed that, just as Cuba had arguably fought against oppression with the support of the people, so too did it fight for liberation from a burdensome Spanish Empire. The writers for the Natchez Democratic paper the *Mississippi Free Trader*, which frequently utilized international comparisons to evaluate current events, were particularly vocal in their support for what they claimed was the Cuban fight for liberty. A correspondent for the *Free Trader* using the pen name "Chat" wrote that "we honor every movement in behalf of liberty," arguing that López and the Cuban filibuster deserved as much sympathy as Kossuth and his Hungarian revolution, as "Lopez was as noble-minded as Kossuth; his cause was equally as sacred."[43] The Little Rock *Arkansas Gazette* agreed, declaring that the failure and execution of López and his men did not undermine "the cause of liberty, in which these men so nobly sacrificed their lives." The *Arkansas Gazette* emphasized its point by asserting that the judges who gave the orders to execute López "would have loaded with infamy and execrations the names of Washington and Tell, Lafayette and Dekalb," adding that "it should not be forgotten that [López's] cause was the same . . . which encircles with a melancholy halo, the names of Kossuth and Bern, of Emmet and Mitchel."[44] In the assessment of these southern journalists, the Cuban filibuster equaled the nationalist movements in Europe in seeking to expand and protect liberty; accordingly, it deserved equal sympathy. Of course, it was understood that this liberty did not apply to enslaved Cubans any more than to enslaved southerners. Regardless, when southern analysts looked at the filibuster expeditions that sought to expand American control, and slavery, abroad, whether they supported these expeditions or not, they used an international perspective to evaluate whether the filibusters fit within the proper mold, established during the revolutions of 1848, of fighting for self-government and popular will in the face of oppression.

Just as an international perspective helped elite southerners analyze the implications of filibusters for the proper values and expressions of nationhood, so too did southern analysis of filibusters shape southern opinions on the proper form, content, role, and powers of a government. The powers of government and the protection of slavery were fundamentally intertwined in white southerners' politics; as long as they could use the federal government to support slavery, white southerners were content to do so, but they vehemently denied that the federal government had power to limit slavery. Extending from white southerners' larger concerns about their own relationship with federal power,

elite southerners used an international perspective to determine if, in their assessment, a government had overstepped its authority in either supporting or
prosecuting a filibuster expedition.

As white southerners debated what filibuster expeditions revealed about the
proper extent of government, they focused on the question of whether intervention in the form of a filibuster was legal and within the bounds of international
law, and therefore should be supported by government, or if filibusters were illegal and therefore should be blocked by government. The answer to this question
was interwoven with southern commentators' analysis of the nationalistic values
of a filibuster movement, although the assessment of these issues did not always
line up neatly; for example, a filibuster could theoretically be legal without representing the popular will, or it could be illegal and yet nonetheless help grant
liberty to an oppressed people. While southerners did not always agree on the
answers to these questions, an international perspective proved useful in helping
southerners on all sides of these debates develop their answers, and in doing so
develop a clearer picture of the proper form of government and nation-building.

As white southerners debated the legality and values of filibusters, and therefore how governments should deal with filibustering expeditions, they trended
over time from the geographically broad to the specific. In general, southern
reporters at the opening of the 1850s focused on the place of filibusters within
international law, while a couple years later emphasis shifted to the United
States, as southerners debated whether the American government was properly handling filibusters. As sectional conflict increased and filibustering became
more of a sectional issue, white southerners began engaging in analysis of how
governmental response to filibusters had sectional, not just national or international, significance, enabling them to reconsider the place of the South within
the United States and the larger international family of nations.

Guided by the question of whether filibustering was a legal or illegal form of
intervention according to international law, elite white southerners opened the
1850s by debating what filibustering revealed about the proper form of international relations. International comparisons to nationalist movements in Europe
proved critical here, especially for pro-expansion southerners trying to make the
case that filibustering was an acceptable form of expansion. In particular, southern reporters pointed to what they claimed were examples of British filibustering
during European revolutions to prove that an accepted precedent for American
filibustering existed. A New York correspondent for the *Alexandria Gazette,* for
example, stated outright that "the United States have no intention of violating
their international duties in regard to Cuba," clarifying what exactly was within

the bounds of "international duties" by explaining that the U.S. government should no more be held accountable for the actions of filibustering citizens than the British were punished for the actions of any of their citizens who "pray[ed] heartily for the success of Hungarians in their late struggle." Although the correspondent did not agree with the actions of the filibusters, he nonetheless believed the filibusters' actions were covered by the precedent of pro-Hungary British citizens, who were "not charged with violating its neutrality." To be sure, "praying" and invading constitute two radically different forms of support and intervention, but the correspondent for the *Gazette* proved willing to conflate the two, using the example of supposed British filibustering to argue that although American filibusters acted "in defiance of our Constitution and laws," they nonetheless acted in defense of a sympathetic cause and did so within the bounds of international precedent, if not international law.[45] The correspondent for the *Gazette* was not alone in stretching the reality of international precedent; in an article reprinted in the *Raleigh Star,* the *Richmond Republican* likewise claimed that European history revealed myriad examples of similar filibustering activities, among them "the subjection of Hungary by Russia . . . the aggressions of Austria in Italy, and bombardment and occupation of Rome by the French," as well as Britain's actions in expanding its empire. Such history illustrated to this author that American filibustering was at least as legitimate as the conquests of European nations.[46] To these southern commentators, international analysis and comparisons proved the assertion of external power to be a valid method of nation-building, or at least of government formation.

As these commentators argued about the legality of filibustering, they continued their analysis of the advance or destruction of national values. Part of why the correspondent for the *Alexandria Gazette* connected filibusters' actions in Cuba with British sentiments regarding Hungary was that he saw both movements as fighting to overthrow oppression.[47] The *Richmond Republican* was more neutral in its assessment of whether filibusters in America or Europe advanced rights but agreed with the *Gazette*'s correspondent that the issue played out similarly in both cases, with American filibusters not doing any more harm to rights than Europeans had.[48] Because the American filibusters fit with elite southerners' interpretation of international precedent, both in form and in treatment of the national values by which they had learned to evaluate nationalist movements, these southerners argued that American filibustering deserved acceptance by the international community.

While southerners focused on international legality of filibustering in the opening of the 1850s, by 1852 and 1853 they increasingly looked closer to home, using their discourse on the filibuster to debate the proper role and exercise of power within the United States. The intensification of filibustering activity, which forced the federal government to respond, opened up new avenues of debate as white southerners sought to determine whether the government's attempts to block and punish filibusters was proper.[49] For a large number of elite southerners, an international perspective revealed that in seeking to block the filibuster and therefore block the expansion of American interests (such as slavery) abroad, the American government was mishandling the issue of the filibuster. In their meeting to discuss the aftermath of the Cuban filibuster, the citizens of Pass Christian, Mississippi, who argued that Cubans sought liberty as did Hungarians and Poles, also resolved that "the part recently enacted by our Government, in paralyzing the effort of General Lopez and his friends, to relieve his fellow country-men of Cuba from the grievances under which they suffer, and the active agency of our Government in aiding the sanguinary Spaniard to maintain his iron rule over the oppressed Cuban, is without vindication by a just rule of neutrality, sound policy, or good morality."[50] To these citizens, the government had overstepped its bounds in allying with the Spanish Empire's desire to block the filibuster, rather than with López and his associates. Similarly, in an article republished in the *Mississippi Free Trader*, the *Louisiana Courier* argued that President Millard Fillmore's actions in aiding Spanish authorities by prosecuting filibusters were "indefensible" and "exhibited his servility to the power of kings, and the doctrines of obsolete Europe."[51] For the *Courier*, filibusters sought to advance liberty in the face of oppression; in blocking filibusters, the U.S. government became an agent of oppression, similar to the oppressive kings of Europe, thereby violating the proper role of government. The Little Rock *Arkansas Gazette* concurred with this assessment in an enthusiastically punctuated statement, exclaiming that in executing López and his supporters, the government "*chimed* in with the despot," initiating a "crusade against those who were anxious . . . to '*extend the area of freedom*'" during which "many of our citizens have been *deprived* of their *liberty, distrained* of their *property,* and *arrested* in their *pursuit of happiness.*" This action was particularly unwarranted in the opinion of the *Gazette*'s writer, given the government's supposedly more sympathetic reaction to Kossuth and his men, who fought for the same cause of liberty in Hungary for which López fought in Cuba.[52] For these southerners, the actions of the U.S. government in prosecuting filibuster expeditions, especially in the face of evincing sympathy for nationalists in Europe, violated the government's commitment to self-government and self-determination.

While many southerners determined that the American government betrayed the values of nationhood and role of government in blocking filibusters, others used an international perspective to argue the opposite position. For these men, evaluating filibusters by the same standards by which they had evaluated the European revolutions revealed that the government acted properly in seeking to stop illegal and harmful filibusters that violated both national values and international law. Sam Houston criticized both filibusters and the idea of foreign intervention in general, including in both Cuba and Hungary, by arguing that it is "the duty of the law-makers, or the executive of our country, to maintain peace," and further that "[peace] is really the duty of every individual; for unlike other countries . . . our sovereignty resides in the people themselves."[53] Houston's assessment, which held that intervention was illegitimate whether in the form of filibustering or providing aid for a European revolution, more closely adhered to antebellum American political norms as well as to reality. The United States had indeed opposed official intervention in the revolutions of 1848, just as it opposed filibustering. Nonetheless, while antebellum southerners did not unanimously agree in their assessment of what filibusters revealed about the proper exercise of American governmental power, southerners on both sides of that debate utilized an international perspective to evaluate how governments should best handle filibusters in a manner that would advance national values.

As filibustering became intertwined with the idea of the expansion of slavery and therefore took on a southern character, elite southerners also assessed the proper governmental response to filibusters through a sectional lens. Returning to their concern over the expansion or limitation of slavery that had driven the crisis of 1850, southern slave interests argued that anti-filibuster governmental action would not just violate norms and values but would also block the spread of slavery, therefore harming white southern interests and potentially oppressing the South. Internationalizing that concern, slaveholding southerners worried that American opposition to filibusters would pave the way for European anti-slavery interests to end slavery in the very same territories that southern filibusters were eyeing as prime targets for the expansion of slavery. In particular, southerners feared that blocking the filibuster of Cuba would enable a supposed European conspiracy to support Spain in abolishing slavery, thereby potentially leading to race riots and race war that could spread to the South.[54] An international perspective, then, increasingly revealed to late antebellum southerners that in opposing filibusters, the U.S. government opposed the South.

Guided by sectional concerns about slavery, pro-filibuster southerners expressed outrage and dismay at the United States' prosecution of filibusters. The pro-filibuster *Louisiana Courier*, for example, in an article picked up by other southern journals, argued that Fillmore's government not only blocked the advance of freedom in prosecuting the Cuban filibuster but also, in not allowing filibusters to intervene in supposed European plans to abolish slavery in Cuba, "commence[d] a war on the institutions of the South."[55] Similarly, the *Mississippi Free Trader* expressed disbelief that the government would sell weapons to Kossuth without regard for the impact of that decision on American relations with Austria, even while blocking the actions of private citizens to free Cuba on the basis that the United States must preserve relations with Spain. Asking "why this difference?" the *Free Trader* then declared, "The answer is obvious. In the Cuban affair the movement was supposed to be Southern in its conception and aims. In the matter of the Kossuth muskets, the Yankee kindred and friends of President Fillmore warmly sympathise."[56] To the *Free Trader*, which was willfully ignoring the lack of official American intervention on behalf of Hungary, only antisouthern hypocrisy explained the government's supposedly divergent reaction to actions in Hungary and Cuba.[57]

For many antebellum southerners, filibusters were critical to the future of slavery and therefore to the future of the South. In blocking filibustering, these southerners claimed, the American government also blocked southern progress. This assessment not only increased sectional tension but also helped prepare white southerners to imagine that, with their greater support of the filibuster and greater belief in its ability to spread values of freedom (as well as the institution of slavery), southerners believed in a different form and expression of government than northerners. With this conclusion, elite white southerners prepared to imagine an independent southern nation.

When these elite white southerners debated the place of filibusters within international law in the mid- to late 1850s, they increasingly used an international perspective to highlight the importance of a specifically southern interpretation of events and of the proper form of government and nationhood. The American government, these southerners argued, might not uphold the proper southern vision of nationhood, but the international community would. Although the overwhelming majority of southerners were not yet ready to seek an independent southern nation, their international analysis of filibustering laid the groundwork for conceiving of a southern nation by convincing slaveholding southerners that not just antislavery northern citizens but the government of the United States itself was hostile to the slavery that they believed was necessary for the preservation of southern self-government.

As white southerners debated the complicated issues raised by filibustering, they used their international perspective to make sense out of issues including what the filibuster meant for national values and the proper role of government.

This conversation over the international meaning of the filibuster helped southerners identify the importance of national values of self-government and define the proper role of government within the international, domestic, and sectional realms. For the large number of white southerners who supported filibustering, their analysis led them to increasingly conclude that the South answered the national questions raised by filibustering differently than did the North, and therefore that the South interpreted national values and proper governmental forms in a specifically southern way, once again paving the way for southerners to conceive of a separate and distinct southern nation.

The 1850s opened with a sectional crisis over slavery in the new western territories and would continue to be shaped by issues of territorial expansion and the expansion of slavery, particularly with the rise of filibusters' attempts to spread American influence—and southern slavery—throughout the hemisphere. As white southerners debated domestic events including the Compromise of 1850 and the American prosecution of filibusterers, they did so through an international lens. Although they had yet to agree on the proper application of an international perspective, elite southerners on all sides of these issues relied on an international context to make their case for their vision of the South. During the crisis of 1850, this international perspective led southerners to begin considering the South as potentially distinct from the rest of the American nation, even to the possibility of secession, through comparisons of the slaveholding South with defeated nations in Europe that aided white southerners in translating concerns about slavery into the internationally supported language of rights. As filibustering posited a different method of territorially expanding slavery and southern power, southerners' international perspective encouraged them to believe that the American national government was not upholding the southern vision of nationhood by preventing slaveholders from using filibuster expeditions to gain slave territory elsewhere. Southerners' usage of an international perspective in the 1850s played a critical role in preparing white southerners to conceive of the South as separate from the North on issues of nationhood, allowing for the possibility of a separate southern nation.

3

A Tool Wherewith to Promote Agitation

EUROPEAN REVOLUTIONARIES
AND SECTIONAL TENSION

John Mitchel led a colorful and eventful life even before he set foot on American soil and entered the debate on the growing issues of late antebellum American sectionalism. Mitchel, an outspoken supporter of Irish independence who fled Ireland after being arrested by the British for treason, subsequently became internationally recognized as a hero of the Irish independence movement. Mitchel arrived in the United States in 1853, setting himself up as a leading newspaperman with his New York paper the *Citizen.* From there he proceeded to confound expectations regarding his position on the sectional conflict embroiling his adopted nation. Instead of equating freedom for aspiring nations with freedom for the enslaved, as northerners in particular expected of exiled revolutionaries, Mitchel loudly proclaimed his support for slavery. In 1853, Mitchel famously declared in the *Citizen* that "we deny that it is a crime, or a wrong, or even a peccadillo, to hold slaves, to buy slaves, to sell slaves, to keep slaves to their work by flogging or other needful coercion," adding that "we wish that we had a good plantation well stocked with healthy Negroes in Alabama."[1] With such a declaration, he rejected the growing antislavery sentiment in the North, instead aligning himself with proslavery white southerners. Critically, because Mitchel as a leading Irish nationalist symbolized the cause of Irish nationalism to many Americans, northerners and white southerners who were divided in their reaction to Mitchel and his proslavery sentiments were also divided in their reactions to the ongoing issues and aftermath of the nationalist revolutions of 1848. With his hyperbolic statement of support for slavery, Mitchel not only intensified sectional divisions but also aided white southerners in connecting their own concerns to the events playing out in Europe.

Mitchel and other exiled revolutionaries who had led the failed European revolutions of 1848, like the filibusterers who later led adventurous expeditions throughout the Americas, garnered much attention from elite white southerners in the 1850s. The defeated revolutions of 1848 had attracted enough attention in the South that even from across an ocean, southern reporters and their audiences were able to use comparisons with these revolutions to navigate the divisive issue of territorial slavery through both the crisis of 1850 and the filibustering expeditions. Not surprisingly, the arrival of Mitchel and other exiled European revolutionaries, particularly Hungarian Lajos Kossuth, in the United States in the early 1850s also featured prominently in white southerners' discussions. In a decade defined largely by sectional tension, and therefore by debate over differing visions of American nationalism, the presence of European nationalists within the United States enhanced southerners' sense that their own national issues were connected to Europeans' national issues.

In particular, as Mitchel illustrates, the presence of exiled European nationalists in the United States facilitated elite white southerners' usage of an international perspective to distance the slaveholding South from the North on issues of nationhood. Although initially the American nation joined together in welcoming these celebrated nationalists, domestic politics quickly interfered, and both northerners and southerners began discussing the famed revolutionaries in terms of sectional issues, values, and concerns.[2] Particularly, antislavery northerners believed that abolition, not the protection of slavery, best replicated European nationalists' desire to advance freedom, and thus they sought to use the arriving nationalists to strengthen their case that freedom must be advanced both for nationalities abroad and for the enslaved at home.[3] While many European revolutionaries, particularly Germans, concurred, a few notable exceptions such as Mitchel instead embraced a more proslavery viewpoint, thereby implicitly validating white southerners' emerging international perspective that asserted their blend of liberalism and slaveholding conservatism was a legitimate expression of the international ideals of nationalism.[4] Americans diverged, then, in their estimation of how foreign nationalists fit with American national values.

As a result of these differing reactions, European revolutionaries stood as a foil on which both sections could project their values. In addition to Mitchel, Hungarian leader Lajos Kossuth played a central role in American discourse on foreign revolutionaries and their connection, or lack thereof, to American ideals. An international perspective enabled white southerners to reject Kossuth and his pleas for intervention on the basis of their proslavery values while still claiming that they, not the North, best represented international values such as republicanism. Even revolutionaries still active in Europe, such as Giuseppe Garibaldi, provided white southerners with opportunities to draw connections between Garibaldi's nationalist values and their own, bolstering the idea of the South as superior to the North in nationalism and as a potential national unit.

The imposition of sectional visions of nationhood onto exiled European revolutionaries thus enhanced sectional division and encouraged white southerners to conceive of southern interpretations of nationalism and national issues as distinct from northern interpretations. Southern awareness of what they saw as their unique response to European revolutionaries also bolstered their growing sense of identification with a unique southern identity on issues of nationhood. White southerners' analysis of European revolutionaries, and the subsequent sense that they held different interpretations of national values of freedom and self-determination than northerners, constituted a critical step in enabling them to envision an independent southern nation.

The first exiled revolutionary to fully catch the attention of Americans, northern and southern alike, was Hungarian nationalist Lajos Kossuth, whose visit to the United States was particularly influential in enhancing elite southerners' perception of the growing distance between them and antislavery northerners on issues of national values and nationalism. Kossuth was the leader of Hungary's defeated 1848 bid for independence from the Austrian Empire and was well-known and widely embraced throughout the Atlantic world as a hero of the cause of Hungarian independence, a cause that Americans had viewed sympathetically. After fleeing Hungary, Kossuth arrived in London to much celebration. In late 1851, Kossuth traveled from London to New York, which likewise embraced him as a hero, and from New York Kossuth set off on a tour of the United States, including an excursion into the South during the spring of 1852. As he toured the United States, he solicited aid for the Hungarian cause from individuals while also seeking official assistance from the federal government, attracting much attention, both positive and negative, throughout the nation.

While the Hungarian Revolution had received widespread support from Americans in all sections, Kossuth himself quickly became a controversial figure within the United States. Despite his best efforts, Kossuth was unable to avoid the issue of slavery, which increasingly defined American politics through the 1850s. Northern abolitionists expected that Kossuth would embrace their cause as equivalent to his own and were sorely disappointed when Kossuth instead hedged his position in a failed attempt to not alienate white southerners. Meanwhile, beyond the controversy over his position on slavery, Kossuth's pleas for official American governmental intervention in the Hungarian cause, rather than just for support from individual Americans, angered Americans, particularly white southerners. White southerners argued that the intervention Kossuth requested violated the key American political value of republicanism. They also feared the potential consequences the idea of intervention would have for their ability to protect the institution of slavery, reinforcing their rejection of the so-called Kossuth doctrine. By the end of his tour, Kossuth would leave the United States once again defeated.[5]

Despite such a discouraging conclusion to Kossuth's tour, when the Hungarian nationalist first arrived in the United States, Americans greeted him with praise and adulation, white southerners included. Many early southern reports on Kossuth's visit emphasized the central themes of southern analysis of 1848, highlighting Kossuth's republican virtue and expressing support for him as a representative of an aspiring nationality for which southerners wished independence. Southern newspapers repeatedly identified Kossuth as being associated with the ideas of republicanism and national self-determination, and thus evinced sympathy for the cause of Hungarian freedom. As a writer using the penname "Chat" declared in the Natchez *Mississippi Free Trader*, for example, Kossuth would be "honored as the representative of a great *idea;* he will be welcomed for his sacrifices, talents, and services."[6] In keeping with this support for the ideals Kossuth represented, the *New Orleans Picayune* informed its readers that the lavish preparations for Kossuth's arrival in America were only befitting the "most dangerous foe of European despotism."[7]

Even while white southerners recognized Kossuth as a representative of a fight against tyranny and cheered the cause of Hungarian nationalism, however, their support for Kossuth was ultimately limited. Southern praise for Kossuth intertwined with criticism of Kossuth's requests for official intervention in Hungary's attempts to gain independence. Kossuth arrived in the United States not just as a refugee but as a lobbyist and fundraiser who attempted to raise money from private citizens and, critically, sought material and financial assistance from the government, as well as direct governmental intervention in the cause of Hungarian freedom. Such appeals for official intervention violated the long-standing republican principle of nonintervention in the affairs of other nations. For the United States, this principle had been central to foreign relations since George Washington's Farewell Address, which urged the new nation to remain independent of foreign issues and entanglements. Thus, despite American sympathy for Kossuth and the Hungarian cause, as well as Kossuth's widespread success in private fundraising, the United States declined to officially intervene and refused to provide material, military, or diplomatic aid to Hungary.[8]

White southerners' absolute rejection of Kossuth's pleas for intervention and refusal to allow for official governmental intervention on behalf of Hungary derived from the importance of nonintervention to republican ideas of governance. To white southerners, the self-government that was critical to republicanism inherently precluded one nation's interference in the governance of another. Drawing on their American value of nonintervention, southerners of both political parties, as well as independents, responded to Kossuth's requests for aid from the federal government as a violation of republicanism, one that would prevent Hungarians from exercising self-government while potentially also giving foreigners a voice in American governance.

Accordingly, throughout late 1851 and early 1852, southerners avowed their sympathy for Kossuth's cause but remained resolute in their absolute rejection of the principle of intervention and of Kossuth's requests for the same. The Democratic *Macon Telegraph,* for example, stated in no uncertain terms that "we do not blame Kossuth for desiring to stir up the world against the oppressors of his country. . . . But while we say this, we do not, cannot, and never will, agree that the Federal Government has a right to involve this country in European wars. . . . We regret to see that Kossuth has overlooked those great and original and essential principles upon which this government is founded." In the same article, the *Telegraph* approvingly included an excerpt from the *Richmond Examiner* that explained, "We can espouse [Hungary's] cause at a distance, and hope for its success against the foe with which it has grappled" but "to join actively forces with it against European Absolutism . . . would be anything but propitious to the purity and permanence of American republicanism."[9] Similarly, a writer for the *Alexandria Gazette* using the penname "Pacificus" wrote that "Kossuth is a great and extraordinary man. I honor his virtues and respect his principles," but, such virtues notwithstanding, Kossuth's request for intervention "attacks virtually the foundation of our government and intimates an opinion that he is wiser than the illustrious men who founded the government, and that its principles ought to be changed. . . . M. Kossuth has gone too far when he professes to be wiser than George Washington, Madison, Jefferson and Jackson, in their doctrine of non-intervention and neutrality."[10] Democrat Jeremiah Clemens of Alabama advocated similar ideas on the floor of Congress in December 1851, arguing that while "the people" of the United States were welcome to fete and celebrate Kossuth, "it is a different matter when the Senate of the United States is asked to take part in it." By asking for this, Kossuth supposedly urged Americans "to abandon the policy of Washington and his successors—forget all the lessons they have transmitted to us."[11] Clearly, these southerners believed that Kossuth's plea violated their American national principles.

Although they used the language of American national values, elite white southerners also had a distinctly sectional motivation underlying their opposition to Hungarian intervention. Southern slaveholders, fearful of the intervention of abolitionists in their own proslavery governments, were particularly motivated to hold fast to ideas of nonintervention in cases such as Hungary, where, unlike in the filibuster movements, intervention would not aid slavery. Accordingly, although elite southerners' main stated objection to intervention would remain its inconsistency with American values, particularly republicanism, at the dawn of the new year in 1852 and with Kossuth's impending arrival in the South, southerners increasingly imposed a sectional lens on their analysis of Kossuth's visit. To begin making a sectional case for nonintervention, elite southerners boldly claimed that they and their fellow southerners best exhibited the ideals of republicanism in their commitment to nonintervention. As they followed news of the continued celebration of Kossuth in the North, southern commentators argued that southerners were distinct from the rest of the nation in the fervency of their desire for nonintervention.

Of course, white southerners' growing support for intervention in the form of filibusters seemingly belies these claims to a unique southern commitment to nonintervention. As was typical in the antebellum South, white southerners' thoughts on slavery provide a likely explanation for these contradictory positions on the issue of intervention. In the case of Hungary, where intervention would not advance the institution of slavery, intervention set a potentially dangerous precedent that could possibly pave the way for intervention in southern slavery. In contrast, filibustering stood to advance slavery and slave interests. The defense of slavery, then, helps explain the divergent southern visions of intervention as well as the southern claim that the South was the true defender of American values through its opposition to intervention in Hungary.

Proving that southerners were unique in their commitment to the national value of republican nonintervention required white southerners to first point out all the supposedly shameful ways in which northerners overstepped the boundaries of American principles in excessively cheering for Kossuth, despite Kossuth's requests for intervention. Doing just that, an article from the *New Orleans Delta* that other southern journals found worthy of republishing criticized "the people at the North, who disgust the great Magyar with their fulsome toadyism."[12] Similarly, Chat wrote to the Democratic *Mississippi Free Trader* to criticize the "humbuggery" of the northern response to Kossuth, asserting that the southern response would be quite different.[13]

Once they established that northerners responded incorrectly to Kossuth, influential southerners were able to assert that, in contrast, southerners' response was more proper and correct. Southern newspapers in the first few months of 1852 reveal a widespread belief among southern journalists, editors, and other opinion-makers that southerners were unique among their fellow Americans in the vehemence of their opposition to intervention and were to be praised for their stance. For example, a Washington correspondent for the independent *New Orleans Picayune* pointed out that "Southern members of Congress have looked coldly upon the Hungarian leader" because they recognized the problems with his pleas.[14] Similarly, the Whig paper the *Alabama Journal* of Montgomery praised southerners for ensuring that "the doctrines of Kossuth," official intervention, were "combatted every where through the South, and repudiated with almost perfect unanimity" in every southern state that Kossuth had visited.[15] A writer for the *Picayune* summarized the critical "manner in which Kossuth has been generally treated by the Southern press," pointing out that "they have preserved a marked distinction between Kossuth the exile and patriot. . . . No men, anywhere, have paid more free tributes to the personal qualities of the Hungarian chief than those who are inflexibly opposed to the policy to which he is urgently inviting this country."[16] Even as elite southerners remained committed to what they saw as the American and republican ideal of nonintervention, they became convinced that the South, distinct from the North, was the only section of the nation that still retained proper adherence to and respect for that value.

Critically, southerners argued that not only was their response more suitable but that it better reflected American national values. In white southerners' analysis, northerners' more positive response to Kossuth revealed that they had veered away from the true ideals of the American Revolution. For example, the *Macon Telegraph* extracted an article from the *Charleston Courier* which declared that when Kossuth visited that city, his requests for intervention "have made no impression on a community whose hearts and minds are too strongly imbued with the wise and paternal lessons of Washington to be led astray by the sophistry or enthusiasm of the gifted foreigner."[17] Similarly, the Montgomery *Alabama Journal* approvingly printed a speech of Democratic Alabama congressman William R. Smith, praising Smith's "spirit of dauntless patriotism and great discernment. When the whole country appeared carried away by enthusiasm—when almost every paper was filled with the speeches and eulogies of Kossuth, and before the South had taken a conservative stand on the doctrine of intervention, Mr. Smith stood up the first and alone in Congress to arrest the progress of the Kossuth excitement."[18] In this view, southerners like Smith were the last bulwark of true American values. The South stood alone in the nation, retaining the national values that the North had corrupted or rejected.

Although southern commentators most frequently referred to national values such as republicanism in their explanations for southern insistence on nonintervention, ultimately, since republicanism was an American, not solely southern, value, additional explanations were necessary to clarify why southerners in particular were vehemently opposed to intervention. Southerners developed a variety of explanations for why, as they claimed, the South alone adhered to the previously American value of republican nonintervention, in doing so hinting at the underlying proslavery motivation.

Southern conservatism provided one possible explanation for the South's supposedly more appropriate response to Kossuth. A writer for the *Alexandria Gazette* who identified as a South Carolinian suggested, for example, that southern conservatism, which stood in contrast to northern radicalism, led southerners to show proper respect for nonintervention. After criticizing the North for advocating for an interventionist policy that would supposedly serve to extract southern wealth and appropriate it according to northern desires, the writer explained that "the present is but another development of the utter dissimilarity existing between the ever restless spirit of rampant democracy prevailing at the North, and that conservative republicanism of the South, which is the citadel of her institutions and the guarantee of her prosperity. It is another incidental proof of the propriety of a political separation of the two sections, where the people are, in almost every leading feature of true and sound republican principles, so utterly opposed to each other."[19] Similarly, although suggesting that the southern response to Kossuth was perhaps a "coincidence," a writer for the *New Orleans Picayune* nonetheless concurred that "the South, it is true, is naturally more conservative . . . is less liable to act or speak under mere impulse. . . . Hence it forms more deliberate judgments."[20]

Of course, the primary factor in antebellum southern conservatism, and southern politics in general, was the desire to protect slavery. Ultimately, fears of northern abolitionist intervention in southern slavery helped drive white southerners' opposition to the principle of intervention. Occasionally, southerners even admitted the central role of slavery in motivating their nonintervention and therefore in creating different interpretations of national values in the North and South. For example, Edward William Johnston, academic and journalist, wrote in the *Richmond Whig* under the penname "Il Segretario" that "I desire to know with what sense . . . Southern men can for an instant, countenance the Kossuth doctrine," stating that the best way for southerners to show their patriotism was to adhere to nonintervention. Johnston explained his opposition to intervention by pointing out that if the American government were granted the ability to intervene in Hungary, abolitionists would be justified in claiming "precisely the same right to intervene" to protect "defeated insurrectionists" such as

Nat Turner.[21] The *Macon Telegraph,* meanwhile, reversed the causation; instead of blaming Kossuth for empowering abolitionists, the *Telegraph* accused free soilers of empowering Kossuth and his loathed doctrine of intervention.[22] Again making the connection between intervention and slavery clear, a correspondent for Montgomery's *Alabama Journal* declared that allowing intervention would have a "vital consequence which urges itself upon the attention of every man interested in the preservation of Southern institutions."[23] To many white southerners, allowing any intervention by one party in the affairs of another set a dangerous precedent, not just for lofty ideas of republicanism but for pragmatic concerns over intervention in the institution of slavery.

These accounts that conflate intervention in Hungary with intervention against slavery, and point to southern conservatism as the necessary corrective, help explain white southerners' rejection of intervention as nonrepublican. As seen in the filibustering movement, many white southerners were perfectly content to impose their will on a foreign people, contrary to the principles of self-government and republicanism, when they believed that doing so would advance white southerners' interests, particularly slavery. In contrast, however, white southerners did not identify any ways in which intervening in Hungary would aid the white South or its protection of slavery; further, by enhancing the power of a federal government that was increasingly influenced by abolitionism, they did believe that Hungarian intervention might ultimately harm the white southern interest of slavery. White southerners' insistence that nonintervention in Hungary was the only way to uphold republicanism ultimately drew on their larger desire to protect slavery and their definition of republicanism as serving only the interests of elite whites.

For all that elite southerners vehemently decried the supposed northern support for intervention on behalf of Kossuth, their interpretation of the southern versus northern response largely ignored the reality that, the enthusiasm of the general population aside, Kossuth did not win enough support from even northern congressmen to achieve official American intervention. Instead, the official stance of the American nation did indeed remain that of nonintervention. Arguing that northerners' enthusiasm for Kossuth violated the American value of republicanism, however, enabled elite southerners to translate their concerns about slavery into the international language of national values, as well as to begin conceiving of the North and South as distinct in their interpretation and enactment of these national values.

Kossuth's requests for intervention dominated white southerners' responses to the American tour of the Hungarian patriot, but the chronological juxtaposition

of the issue of Hungarian nationalism with other events related to ideas of nationhood meant that white southerners also discussed Kossuth in connection
with developments outside the South. In particular, the filibuster movement
was gaining popularity among white southerners, even as support for Kossuth
was waning, and provided an obvious point of connection for debates on foreign intervention and national independence. Despite decrying intervention in
Hungary, filibusterers in the South supported intervention elsewhere, and the
overlapping timing of Kossuth's requests for aid with López's filibustering in
Cuba meant that southern analysts frequently discussed the two issues together.

Whereas white southerners largely rejected intervention as requested by Kossuth, intervention as practiced by filibusterers won much more white southern
support. Here again, the connection between intervention and slavery is clear;
unlike in Hungary, in the case of filibusters, intervention promised to expand
slavery territorially. For pro-filibuster southerners, northern support for Kossuth
provided them with an opportunity to draw parallels between the popular Lajos
Kossuth and the Cuban filibusterer Narciso López in an attempt to translate support for the former into support for the latter. Doing so required southerners to
conflate popular support and sympathy, which was relatively widespread in the
North, with governmental support and intervention, which was never forthcoming, but pro-filibuster southerners proved willing to do just that. The *Mississippi
Free Trader's* correspondent Chat, for example, argued that any northerners who
favored aiding Kossuth and Hungary must also support López and the filibuster
of Cuba. As Chat declared, "There seems a strange inconsistency in the character
of our government. Kossuth is the idol of a resolution, is a creature of universal
sympathy, whilst poor Cuba is forgotten altogether," adding, "A Free-soil administration brands Lopez and his followers as 'pirates' and holds the expedition up
to public execration" but "lauds the struggles of the far-off Hungarians and strews
the way of Kossuth with flowers and honors. Shameful inconsistency!"[24]

Such pro-filibuster southerners did not hesitate to speculate on why exactly
northerners and the U.S. government supposedly supported intervention for Kossuth without supporting southern-favored intervention in Cuba. Once again, slavery stood at the heart of this analysis. As Chat hinted, pro-filibuster southerners
believed that the different reactions to Kossuth and Cuba grew out of antislavery
and even antisouthern sentiment. The *Macon Telegraph* reprinted an article from
the *New Orleans Delta* which concurred that free soilers were to blame for the
hypocritical response, stating that "our people cannot free their minds of the suspicion freesoil purposes are the bottom of this," adding that "[southerners] are not
so blind" as to misinterpret the situation in which northerners opposed López's

Cuban efforts precisely because they stood to "increase southern territory" and give southerners an "augmentation of power" to "resist the innovations . . . of the Northern states."[25] Similarly, an article from the *Louisiana Courier* republished in the *Mississippi Free Trader* declared that the government at least spoke out about oppression in Europe and yet remained silent in the case of Cuba, as the oppression of Cuba would also "commence a war on the institutions of the South."[26] As pro-filibuster southerners assessed what they believed to be differing reactions to intervention in the cases of Kossuth and the Cuban filibuster, they identified sectional differences as the critical issue, confirming the growing white southern belief that northerners and southerners differed in their response to Kossuth due to their varying expressions of national values.

While pro-filibuster southerners used international comparisons to shame the North for supposedly divergent reactions to Kossuth and to Cuba, the adamant noninterventionist stance that most southerners took toward Kossuth meant that these prointerventionists were the minority within discussions of the Hungarian nationalist. Hardline noninterventionists, the majority position, used the association between Kossuth's attempts to create a Hungarian nation and filibusters' attempts to create their own governments abroad to further attack Kossuth, more in keeping with the general southern criticism of the Hungarian nationalist. The *Richmond Whig,* for example, representing the antiannexationist Whig Party, used the term "filibuster" to denounce Kossuth and evinced the belief that "we have the fullest confidence that the cool and patriotic good sense of the great body of the people, of all parties" will reject intervention in all cases.[27] For the *Savannah Daily Republican,* the similarity between Cuba and Hungary was a compelling reason to avoid intervention in both; the author asked his readers to "suppose we [intervene to aid Hungary], our work will have but commenced when Hungary is freed. . . . We must . . . bestow independence upon Cuba." Indeed, as the author imagined it, should the United States intervene in Hungary, then in the name of consistency, the United States must "become a travelling Don Quixote, going up and down among the nations and along the seas to redress the wrongs of outraged humanity." The author added that the only way any Americans could justify such a course of action was because "the people of this country may not have a proper understanding of [nonintervention]. Indeed, it is highly probable, as Kossuth says they have misinterpreted Washington's Farewell Address."[28] Intervention, these southerners argued, was a harmful plan that would violate American principles both in Cuba and in Hungary, leaving Kossuth once again in opposition to these southerners' cherished national values and norms.

As elite southerners analyzed the potential connection between intervention as requested by Kossuth and intervention as practiced by the filibuster expedition to Cuba, they agreed that nothing less than national values were at stake. Underneath the surface of the claims of republicanism and national values, however, white southerners also continued seeking to protect slavery. Inspired by their nonintervention, the majority of white southerners resoundingly rejected Kossuth's pleas for intervention, a position they believed set them apart from more prointerventionist northerners. Southern analysis of Kossuth and his requests for intervention played a central role in southerners' assessment of their own national values, as well as in encouraging southerners to envision the North and South as differing on those national values.

While southern reactions to Kossuth's request for intervention intensified sectional division, created a sense of distinct southern identity, and prepared white southerners to envision a separate southern nation, intervention was not the only issue on which Kossuth divided the nation. The difference between the southern and northern reactions to Kossuth's visit, and the sense of sectional distance that it created, was further increased by northern analysis of Kossuth's position on the questions of slavery and abolition. If nonintervention doomed Kossuth's efforts in the South, Kossuth's unwillingness to commit to abolition similarly crippled his success in the North. For all that Kossuth attempted to ignore slavery in order to keep southern sympathy, however, ultimately Americans of both sections rejected Kossuth on the issue of slavery.[29]

Through the southern press, elite southerners were aware that northerners expected Kossuth to support abolitionism and to speak out against slavery. In one example of southerners' familiarity with northern expectations, the *Savannah Daily Republican* republished an article from the *New York Herald* in which the author enthusiastically tied Hungarian freedom and abolition together as part of a broader international movement toward liberation. Turning to Kossuth's effect in the United States, the *Herald*'s author declared that "the sympathy and the agitation excited by these revolutionary visionaries from the Old World, threaten to drive us headlong to the rescue [of the enslaved]. . . . It is impossible that the South can escape the effects of a universal liberating movement."[30]

Despite this awareness of northern expectations regarding Kossuth and abolition, white southerners claimed to see no connection between Hungarian freedom and antislavery. For example, the *New Orleans Picayune*'s Washington correspondent "Le Diable Boiteux" wrote that "there is no doubt whatever but that the gentlemen inclined toward Free Soil have made an attempt to appropriate Kossuth to themselves; though he has . . . declared his determination not to interfere in any, the most remote manner, with the States rights doctrines of the South." The correspondent added that Kossuth "declared himself a States Rights man even in regard to Hungary."[31] Another writer for the *Picayune* blamed northern politicians for purposefully inciting sectional discord by actively seeking to associate Kossuth with abolitionism, rather than celebrating him for his own cause, thereby drawing a clear line between the two issues.[32] Southern slaveholders had already established, in part through international comparisons with defeated nations such as Hungary, that they believed abolitionists were a tyrannical force seeking to strip the South of its ability to participate in self-government. In this assessment, abolition and Hungarian freedom could have nothing in common, and northerners claiming otherwise only pointed out the growing differences between the North and South.

Despite elite southerners' own convictions that Hungarian freedom did not necessitate freedom for the enslaved, southerners were less convinced that Kossuth himself was open to the white southern position on slavery. The *Mississippi Free Trader* printed a report that the slave state of Kentucky had given far fewer donations to Kossuth than the adjacent free state of Ohio, adding that Kossuth would make a fitting free-soil governor of Ohio.[33] In this author's mind, Kossuth was indeed predisposed to favoring free-soil policies, resulting in the differing responses to Kossuth by free and slave states. Similarly, the *Mobile Alabama Planter* worried that "to the South the Kossuth policy presents this dangerous aspect—that it is lead by all sorts of factions which are hostile to us and our institutions," adding that this Kossuth coalition "is calculated to gather to itself all the elements of military ambition and sentimental freedom, not only in behalf of the negro, but all the world beside."[34]

Ultimately, Kossuth's attempt to avoid the sectional issue of slavery failed in the South just as it had in the North. White southerners, already wary of Kossuth due to the intervention issue, were unwilling to trust him on slavery without an outright declaration of support for the institution. Combined with the problematic nature of his pleas for intervention, the issue of slavery ensured that elite white southerners, while always sympathetic to Kossuth's Hungarian cause, were critical of his presence in the United States. As such, Kossuth's relation to slavery further convinced southerners that the North and South differed in their reactions to European nationalists and therefore to issues of nationhood.

As Kossuth toured the United States, southern discourse about the Hungarian patriot helped to create the sense among southern opinion-makers that the North and South held different interpretations of American national values, if not different national values altogether. Through identifying the differing re-actions of the two sections to Kossuth, his pleas for intervention, and his stance on slavery and freedom, elite southerners developed a sense of national values, such as nonintervention, that they believed the South but no longer the North represented. As they did so, they enhanced their perception that the North and South were fundamentally different on issues of nationhood. Further, because these southerners believed that their nonintervention was tied to American principles such as republicanism, analysis of Kossuth began building the idea among white southerners that the South represented the purest iteration of the ideals of the American Revolution. Such a formulation helped create a sense of southern identity and elevated the South as a unit of analysis equal to nations and aspiring nations, such as the United States and Hungary.

Kossuth was not the only revolutionary whose presence and ideology led white southerners to distinguish themselves from northerners on issues of nationalism in ways that enhanced their sense of regional distinctiveness. John Mitchel, an Irish nationalist and avowed advocate of slavery, also played an important role in highlighting the differing northern and southern interpretations of the international expressions of nationalism. Because of his association with the Irish nationalist movement, southern commentators praised the inspiring nationalistic virtues that Mitchel represented, with southern newspapers referring to Mitchel as a patriot who fought for liberty and freedom and against tyranny and oppression.[35] Other southerners also added their voices to this praise of Mitchel; for example, Richmond citizens gave a dinner for him in order to celebrate his "effort towards the liberation of his country from English tyranny," and the Louisiana General Assembly invited "distinguished patriot" Mitchel to the state because of, among other reasons, his "just and expanded nationalist sentiments."[36] For many white southerners, Mitchel, like Kossuth before him, embodied the same national values that white southerners themselves cherished.

Mitchel and his views became personal to Americans when Mitchel, fleeing persecution like many other revolutionaries, arrived in the United States in 1853. In the United States, Mitchel used his talents as a writer and journalist to continue advocating for Irish independence while also engaging with American issues. As editor of first the *Citizen,* published in New York, and later the *Southern Citizen,* published in Knoxville, Tennessee, Mitchel had a powerful platform from which to spread his views—and his views of the sectional issues in the United States attracted attention in the North and South alike. Unlike most foreign nationalists, Mitchel approached the sectional issues dividing the United

States with sympathy for the white South. In particular, Mitchel was adamantly proslavery, as he made clear in a famous statement that he wished he had his own plantation full of enslaved workers.[37]

Mitchel's support for slavery, while unusual among European revolutionaries as a group, was less uncommon among Irish immigrants. Many Irish Americans viewed slavery as acceptable, if not desirable, due to their association of antislavery ideas with the British, their belief that slavery was the path to advancement in the South, and their desire to be associated with the benefits of whiteness.[38] Accordingly, even Irish immigrants in the North tended to support slavery rather than abolition; although these northern Irish immigrants were fiercely devoted to the Union, many Irish troops reacted negatively when Lincoln's Emancipation Proclamation turned the North's war effort into a war against slavery, for example.[39] Southern Irish troops, meanwhile, joined Mitchel in sympathizing with the South and even viewing the Irish and Confederate causes as connected.[40] While Mitchel was certainly the most outspoken Irish revolutionary to support slavery and the South, he was not alone in his proslavery sentiment.

As the leading pro-southern Irish voice, Mitchel earned praise and support from elite southerners, even beyond what he claimed as a representative of Irish nationalism. Southern journalists celebrated Mitchel's arrival in the South, republished his speeches, and encouraged fellow southerners to subscribe to the proslavery newspaper that Mitchel began in Knoxville.[41] Indeed, so strong was southern support for the Irish nationalist that South Carolina congressman Lawrence M. Keitt used Mitchel to support his pro-immigration stance, arguing that people like Mitchel should be allowed to enter and enrich the nation.[42] As a representative of the best virtues of nationalism who also supported the southern institution of slavery, Mitchel won the support of the southern elite.

Critically, Mitchel's views overlapped with those of many white southerners on the issue of whether the slavery he supported in the American South could fit with the ideas of liberal nationalism that he supported in Ireland. During their analysis of the revolutions of 1848, southern commentators had determined that their vision of proper nationalism could blend liberal ideas such as republicanism with a more hierarchical social order and conservative restriction of the electorate. Mitchel implicitly endorsed this manipulated vision of liberal nationalism with his belief that slavery was not only compatible with more liberal nationalist values such as republicanism but that it strengthened the nation and its values. As Mitchel stated on a southern tour in 1858, "Southern society . . . where slaves are numerous to occupy the fields of toil . . . is the most perfect form of social polity now existing anywhere in the world."[43] For Mitchel, as for the southern elite, slavery created a stronger, more perfect form of society. His embrace of such views created a veneer of international support for elite southerners' defense of slavery as acceptable within the bounds of nationalism as practiced throughout the Atlantic world.

Elite white southerners were aware and vocally appreciative of the fact that, unlike many European revolutionaries, Mitchel's vision of slavery, the South, and nationalism more closely resembled their own. As Louisiana politician Frank H. Hatch explained, slavery was all too often a casualty of overly enthusiastic nationalists, as "men who have been engaged in national struggles for freedom throughout the civilized world, have too frequently abandoned their reason, to the guidance of their feelings, and in their zeal for the distraction of political oppression, have often blindly included useful and necessary social institutions."[44] Demonstrating recognition that Mitchel, unlike most foreign nationalists, did not interpret nationalism and abolitionism as inherently linked, the *Baton Rouge Advocate* cited Mitchel as proof that "the bold assumption that foreigners are Abolitionists" was nothing more than, as the title of the article put it, "a stupid fallacy."[45] Mitchel's proslavery views opened up the possibility in southern minds that their belief in the compatibility of slavery and nineteenth-century nationalism was a legitimate interpretation of the nationalist movements they followed abroad, thereby providing foreign support for the emerging white southern vision of southern national values and enhancing a growing sense of distinct southern identity.

Mitchel did not only seemingly validate white southerners' views of slavery and nationalism, however; he explicitly rejected the vision of freedom shared by abolitionist and antislavery northerners, once again highlighting the differences between North and South. Mitchel's proslavery beliefs confounded northern abolitionists, who wanted Mitchel, like they had wanted Kossuth before him, to support the cause of freedom from slavery due to its similarity to the nationalists' fight for national freedom. As with Kossuth, southern journalists were aware of northern expectations and made a point to report on how northerners reacted differently than did southerners to Mitchel's proslavery beliefs. The *Charleston Courier*'s Boston correspondent, for example, informed his readers that "John Mitchel, the Irish patriot, has been violently assailed by the northern newspapers, for declaring that he 'rather approved of Southern slavery.' . . . The *Tribune* and others of it class can not see how a man can profess to be an Apostle of Irish freedom, and favor Southern slavery." The correspondent made it clear, however, where his own sympathies lay, praising Mitchel for holding strong to his proslavery beliefs.[46] Similarly, the *Richmond Whig* declared that Mitchel's views have "shocked [abolitionists'] sensibilities excessively. Their hopes have been egregiously disappointed. Fanatics and madmen as they are, they expected, when Mitchell [*sic*] arrived in this country, to use him as a tool wherewith to promote agitation and assail the institutions of the South. . . . In this they were mistaken." What is more, Mitchel's commitment to his proslavery position even in the face of northern criticism elevated his stature in the South according to the *Whig*'s author, who added that "if we had a couple of big plantations in the South, John Mitchell should certainly have one. He deserves it for his course upon the slavery question."[47] For all that northerners had expected Mitchel to fall in line with the abolitionist perspective, he maintained his proslavery belief, to the thrill of southern writers who delighted in mocking the North's mistaken perception of Mitchel and in pointing out the increasingly divergent southern and northern interpretations to revolutionaries and the issues of nationhood they represented.

Mitchel's proslavery stance had significant ramifications for northern and southern visions of nationhood. By challenging abolitionists' definition of freedom, Mitchel's views supported the possibility that the more limited, conservative southern definitions of national values, including the embrace of slavery, could be accepted as a legitimate part of the international discussion of the meaning of nationalism.[48] Elite southerners' discussions of Mitchel, then, like their discussions of Kossuth, solidified their belief that their views of nationalism were distinct from those of northerners and that white southern ideas of nationalism were worthy of discussion within the international framework of nationalism.

By the late 1850s, elite white southerners were well-versed in the utility of an international perspective in understanding national issues. Through the crisis of 1850, the filibustering expeditions, and the arrival of revolutionary exiles in the South, southern opinion-makers used an international perspective to clarify their vision of southerners' national values and to distinguish those values from northern national values, helping them envision the South as distinct from the North, even as they retained their American loyalty. As the 1850s came to a close, events in Europe provided southerners with yet another opportunity to analyze the expression of nationalism as exhibited by a famous European revolutionary. With the 1860 joining of the central Italian states and the southern Sicilian states to Piedmont-Sardinia, Italy succeeded in uniting the majority of the Italian peninsula under the governance of one king, allowing for the declaration of a new United Kingdom of Italy in March 1861. Famous nationalist Giuseppe Garibaldi, already revered for his part in establishing the short-lived Roman Republic during the revolutions of 1848, once again played a critical role in this process. In May 1860, Garibaldi, acting on his own authority, marched with one thousand red-shirted volunteers to liberate Sicily from Bourbon rule and attach it to the united Italian nation forming under the king of Sardinia. Garibaldi's dramatic triumph over a rule seen as despotic, and his victory for the cause of united nationalism, received enthusiastic attention throughout the Atlantic world. Although Garibaldi's own previous visit to the United States had been too brief and private to receive much attention in the American press, Garibaldi himself nonetheless featured prominently in American periodicals' foreign news and analysis. As the United States approached the ultimate American national crisis, Garibaldi's success in building the Italian nation provided much encouragement for any people seeking to form a new nation.[49]

Critically, white southerners took the opportunity of Garibaldi's victory to draw connections between the virtues they believed had led to Garibaldi's success and the virtues that they, as southerners, likewise held. Such comparisons prepared elite southerners once again to see the South as part of the international discussions of nationalism, even while they also aided white southerners in praising the specific nationalism that southerners, distinct from northerners, supposedly exhibited, elevating the South as the superior exemplar of nationalism.

White southerners, unknowingly on the brink of their own experiment in nation-building, paid close attention to Garibaldi's latest exploits. Garibaldi had long received praise from the South and elsewhere for his attempts to advance liberal nationalism in Brazil, Uruguay, and Italy. As a military general who fought for national unity or independence on the battlefield, instead of a politician who potentially fought for equality within society, Garibaldi was relatively immune from the charges of radicalism and excess liberalism that white southerners leveled against many of his contemporaries. Accordingly, white southerners watching Garibaldi during the revolutions of 1848 had determined that he fit their emerging vision of proper nationalism. Even after his defeat in Rome in 1848, southerners lauded his nationalistic virtues; a correspondent for the *New Orleans Picayune* explained his support for Garibaldi in 1849, for example, by proclaiming that Garibaldi had "bearded . . . petty South American despots, and planted the banner of popular rights on the capitol of 'Rome, the Eternal.'"[50] If a defeated Garibaldi earned flowery praise from southern commentators in the wake of 1848, it stood to reason that a victorious Garibaldi would win even more acclamations in 1860.

As they sang Garibaldi's praises, late antebellum southern commentators held Garibaldi up as the model of a perfect nationalist, one that the rest of the world would do well to emulate. Many southerners referred to Garibaldi's virtue in glowing, almost hyperbolic terms. For example, a reporter for the *New Orleans Picayune,* after celebrating the Risorgimento's victory against tyranny, enthused that Garibaldi was "the informing spirit" of this movement, going on to say that "he is the sword, too, by which Italians hope to retain and defend the independence they assert," and arguing that to support Garibaldi was to support nothing less than "the right of nationalities to independence."[51] The *New Orleans Daily True Delta* declared that Garibaldi's actions in Lombardy "won for him a distinguished place among historic patriots," further describing Garibaldi as "genuinely patriotic, ardent, fiery, honest," and praising that he "rushed into the war with but one purpose—the liberation of Italy."[52] In the minds of the southern elite, Garibaldi's spirit was synonymous with nationalism at its best and most virtuous.

Although much of this praise substituted enthusiasm for ideological precision and neglected to identify which values and virtues Garibaldi supposedly represented, other accounts of Garibaldi's strengths referred more clearly to particular aspects of liberal nationalism that Garibaldi exhibited. Among these virtues was his dedication to freedom and liberty. As one southern reporter for the *New Orleans Picayune* asserted, "in the history of no one" could be found "such devotion to the cherished cause of freedom" as Garibaldi's.[53] Other southerners lauded the achievements of Garibaldi not just for advancing freedom and liberty but also for doing so in the face of tyranny. Another New Orleans journalist enthused, for example, that Garibaldi's "spirit of liberty" had emancipated the Italian people, who "have meekly bowed for centuries beneath an iron rod of oppression."[54] This victory was not only a triumph over tyranny but a victory for self-determination, as southerners were clear that in fighting for this national freedom, Garibaldi represented the desire of the Italian people. As the *Richmond Daily Dispatch* reported, for example, "in the cause of Italian liberty," Garibaldi "worked wonders, because he represented the popular sentiment and passion of oppressed Italy."[55] To these southerners, Garibaldi's commitment to the proper values of nationalism was worthy of noting.

After a decade of sectional crisis that white southerners had processed through an international lens, Garibaldi's virtues were not limited to just Italy in elite southern minds. Garibaldi's values were so worthy of comment according to southerners in large part because they were the same values that southerners themselves held dear. When white southerners praised Garibaldi's fight for freedom and liberty in the face of tyranny, they did so as fellow proponents of these same values. Southern admiration of Garibaldi's values, so like their own, served a larger purpose for elite white southerners. Taught by their reactions to other European revolutionaries such as Kossuth and Mitchel that analysis of European nationalists could reveal sectional differences, and encouraged by their success in using international perspectives to navigate the crisis of 1850 and the conflict over filibustering, late antebellum southern opinion-makers actively drew connections between Garibaldi's and white southerners' values, using this connection to bring attention to the national values that they sought to encourage in the South.

The first step in connecting Garibaldi to southern values was demonstrating that such a connection was possible and beneficial. Southerners began this process by consciously creating Garibaldi as a symbol, useful as a standard of republicanism and nationalism. As an author for the *Macon Telegraph* declared, the name Garibaldi was a "synonym of daring bravery, military genius and stern virtue."[56] Similarly, the *New Orleans Picayune* asserted that "the name of Garibaldi in Italy is a type of revolution . . . a type of active belligerent republicanism" that was "dreaded" by "authorities" including "Bonapartist France, or the grim despotism of Russia and Austria."[57] Garibaldi represented a standard of nationalism that was recognized not just across the South but throughout the Atlantic world, providing southerners with a well-understood symbol of virtuous nationalism.

Because it exemplified nationalism, the symbol of Garibaldi could also be used to create a sense of connection with the positive aspects of nationalism that he represented. Garibaldi was so strongly associated with positive values of nationalism—both those clearly identified and those given only surface praise— that his unique uniform, characterized by a red shirt, served as a marker of his virtue, transferring this virtue to anyone who wore the red shirt. As the *Richmond Daily Dispatch* informed its readers, "as long as the revolution which he has just accomplished shall be remembered in history," the red shirt would be associated with Garibaldi and with "revolution, unaccompanied by excess," referring to the southern standard of restrained revolution that had emerged through southern discourse on 1848.[58] International sartorial trends led antebellum southerners to adopt aspects of Garibaldi's famous red-shirted costume as a way of associating with the great nationalist. In fact, he garnered such popularity that merchants attached his name to various items of clothing in an attempt to sell more goods, creating items ranging from Garibaldi jackets to Garibaldi hats. These items of clothing became popular among late antebellum southerners who wanted to express their support for the Italian nationalist.[59] With the seemingly innocuous act of donning Garibaldi clothes, late antebellum southerners cemented the connection between themselves and the symbol of Garibaldi.

Elite white southerners politicized this connection to the symbol of Garibaldi by actively drawing comparisons between him and their own southern leaders, right at the moment when many white southerners were beginning to consider the possibility of turning their section into a nation. In an 1859 letter to the editor of the Montgomery, Alabama, *Daily Confederation,* for example, a fire-eater by the penname "Nero" declared leading secessionist William Yancey to be "a Garibaldi in this fight" for southern rights.[60] Another expression of this sentiment was found in a satirical advertisement for an American president, published in the *New Orleans Daily True Delta* in response to the election of Abraham Lincoln in 1860. The farcical ad sought a candidate with not only the virtues of Washington but also the "national spirit and determination" of Garibaldi to heal the sectional tension that was surging due to the hotly contested election.[61] To white southerners concerned with asserting the South's power in its growing conflict with the North, the symbol of Garibaldi was useful in processing their concerns and expressing their beliefs. Although few in number, these comparisons between Garibaldi and desired southern leaders indicate that by the end of the 1850s, southerners were familiar enough with the meaning of the symbol of Garibaldi that they were able to use it to express their beliefs about the South's national values. Such a formulation required these southerners to abandon intellectual rigor and instead deal in vague perceptions of symbols, but well-used to cherry-picking from international affairs to support their own agenda, elite southerners were willing to do just that.

Critically, while these comparisons reveal that white southerners saw their national values and future as in conversation with those of Garibaldi's Italy, these comparisons also helped southerners begin to imagine a future that elevated the South to the same status as Garibaldi's Italy. As white southerners contemplated the solution to what they saw as the violation of southern rights by an abolitionist North, they turned to comparisons between Garibaldi and southern leaders, subconsciously preparing them to see their own sectional leaders as potential nationalists. Comparisons with Garibaldi thus served both to help white southerners clarify their own national values and to begin to see these values as potentially justifying a separate southern nation.

While most of these comparisons remained in the realm of rhetorical platitudes, a few late antebellum southerners were so convinced of what they saw as the connection between Garibaldi's values and their own that they chose to go to Italy to fight in Garibaldi's army during his campaign of 1860. As Garibaldi and his thousand red-shirted soldiers conquered Sicily, a handful of southerners were among his volunteers, many of whom would go on to later fight for the Confederacy. The most famous of these soldiers was Chatham Roberdeau Wheat, an adventurer who served in and distinguished himself in the Mexican-American War, joined the Cuban filibustering expedition, fought for liberal republican Juan Alvarez in his struggle against Santa Anna in Mexico, and traveled to Italy to aid Garibaldi's campaign in Sicily, only to quickly return to his native South to fight for the Confederacy.[62] Southern periodicals resoundingly praised Wheat for his devotion to Garibaldi's cause. For example, a foreign correspondent for the *New Orleans Picayune* reported that the tyrannical Habsburg would soon face another formidable foe when Wheat arrived to join Garibaldi; the author hoped that Wheat's "shadow never decrease" as he fought tyranny in Italy, before adding in a more personal note that "we fear for him among the Neapolitans."[63] This support for Wheat's passionate defense of nationalism transferred to his service for the Confederacy. Upon Wheat's death in June 1862 at the Battle of Gaines's Mill, the *Richmond Daily Dispatch* lauded the soldier as "a martyr in defense of . . . liberties and independence of his dearly beloved South—thus ending a career rendered famous on the battle-fields of Mexico, Nicaraguans, and Italy."[64]

Although Wheat was the most famous of Garibaldi's southern soldiers, southern periodicals during the Civil War additionally praised several other Confederate soldiers for their prior service in Garibaldi's army. Charles Carroll Hicks, a Confederate soldier who had also made a name for himself fighting and filibustering throughout the antebellum period and who, like Wheat, was a veteran of Garibaldi's Italian campaigns, received accolades for exemplifying through his campaigns in Italy and in the South the daring and adventure that supposedly characterized men of the South.[65] A Colonel Adler, another Confederate who had fought for Garibaldi, likewise received praise for turning down northern solicitations for his aid in favor of fighting for the South, which he claimed constituted "a free people" engaged in a "struggle for independence."[66] Southern periodicals made a point to note the service of other southerners in Garibaldi's army, including a Captain Warwick of Richmond, Frank Maney of Nashville, and Alfred van Benthuysen of New Orleans.[67] While few in number, the fact that southerners fought with Garibaldi, combined with the positive press coverage of these men, reveals the connection that many antebellum southerners felt to Garibaldi just as they embarked on their own experiment in nation-building.

At the close of a decade of sectional conflict and the opening of a decade that would see a sectional war, white southerners celebrated Garibaldi as an example of their desired form of nationality. Southern analysis of Garibaldi, as with earlier analysis of the crisis of 1850, filibustering, and exiled revolutionaries, connected sectional issues and southern values to European experiments in nationhood. On the eve of their own experiment in nation-building, Garibaldi provided southerners with a final data-point on the expression of nationalism, giving white southerners an example of a nationalist who was successful in building a new nation and did so while representing the same values that southerners themselves revered. The sense of connection between southern leaders and their values and Garibaldi and his values helped prepare white southerners to see the South as a potential nation. After a decade of using an international perspective to clarify southern national values and distinguish between southern and northern national values, white southerners were increasingly capable of envisioning a southern nation.

Elite white southerners' international analysis of sectional issues throughout the 1850s prepared southerners to think of the South as an individual player on issues of nationhood. Beginning with the crisis of 1850 and continuing through the debate over filibustering, the arrival of European exiles in the South, and the success of Garibaldi's expedition, an international perspective clarified southerners' beliefs about the desired values of nationhood and intensified their growing sense that the North and South had different national values. In a decade of conflict and division, European nationalisms and nationalists provided southerners with examples, models, and representatives of nationalism that they could debate and utilize at will to help them understand their own national issues. This international contextualization of domestic issues, and this growing sense of differing northern and southern values, would be critical to helping white southerners describe and defend their visions of a national future for the South during the secession crisis of 1860–61.

PART III

Secession, 1860–1861

In December 1860, South Carolina seceded from the United States, adding new urgency to white southerners' national self-conception. While the vision of an independent southern nation led secessionist southerners to ultimately prevail in ten other southern states, prompting these states' secession through the early months of 1861, a significant minority of Unionist southerners continued to assert that the southern states should remain within the United States. Accordingly, debates over secession spread throughout the South in the winter and spring of 1860–61 as citizens and politicians alike deliberated the proper form of nationhood for the slaveholding southern states, with the central question asking if remaining in the United States best upheld southerners' national values or if secession and the creation of an independent southern nation created a more fitting form of nationhood for white southerners.

As secessionists and southern Unionists alike made their case for their desired form of southern nationhood, they turned to the international perspective that had guided their beliefs about nationhood throughout the antebellum period. Representing the range of southern political thought, secessionists developed multiple variations on their international perspective, now using this international understanding of their nationhood to claim European nationalist movements as a reference point for the legitimacy of secession and later the new southern nation.

A more liberal international perspective emphasized the central importance of internationally respected principles such as republicanism and self-government, arguing that the South seceded to protect its rights (particularly those related to the preservation of slavery), which were supposedly the same type of rights for which European nationalists fought. In this liberal secessionist perspective, the Confederacy followed in the footsteps of the nationalist movements of Europe and therefore was justified for upholding the internationally popular values of liberal nationalism.

In contrast, a more conservative counterargument agreed that an international perspective validated southern secession and nationhood but claimed that southern conservatism and protection of slavery would purify, rather than emulate, the excessively liberal and radical nationalist movements in Europe. Focusing on the necessity of racial hierarchy to white southerners' preferred form of society, the conservative international perspective rejected European nationalist movements' calls for equality and democracy. To the secessionists utilizing this perspective, the creation of a southern nation was justified because, by preserving a racial hierarchy rather than embracing liberal ideas of equality, the southern revolution would result in a superior form of nationhood.

Secessionists were not alone in justifying their actions through this international perspective. For southern Unionists, an international perspective taught a different lesson, as comparisons with national division and disunion in Europe, combined with the critical role of the United States as a republican model for Europe, demonstrated that national unity was the only way to secure their national values. Critically, this Unionist international perspective directly challenged and undermined those of secessionists, limiting secessionists' ability to use their international perspectives to gain support for their project in nation-building.

Beyond the South, sympathizers of both secession and continued unity, from both the North and Europe, likewise endorsed aspects of southerners' international perspectives, thereby validating white southerners' international comparisons and revealing that southern international perspectives were, at least to some extent, accepted as a legitimate part of the nineteenth-century debate over nationhood. Across the range of white southern thought, and interwoven throughout the fierce debate over southern secession and the international meaning of nationalism, elite southerners of all political persuasions utilized an international perspective to argue for their desired form of southern nationhood.

4

Equal among the Other Nations

SECESSIONISTS' LIBERAL

INTERNATIONAL PERSPECTIVE

On March 4, 1861, Abraham Lincoln was inaugurated as the sixteenth president of the United States of America. The *Richmond Daily Dispatch* had a dramatic response to this momentous occasion. A writer for the *Dispatch* declared that "this day witnesses the inauguration at Washington of a Black Republican President, elected solely by Black Republican votes, having a Black Republican Cabinet, and sustained by a Black Republican Congress." As bad as a "Black Republican" president was, however, the true tragedy of Lincoln's inauguration, according to this writer, was the harms that Lincoln would enact against the South. Turning to international comparisons to make his point, the journalist declared, "This day the South comes under a dominion which has been forced upon her by the North; this day she begins a servitude as involuntary as that of Italy to Austria; this day inaugurates a foreign rule as distinct and complete as if we had been conquered by European bayonets, and annexed to the throne of some continental despot."[1] For this southerner, Lincoln's inauguration was not simply the latest iteration of democratic government; instead, it was tyranny and despotism, a vile European-style oppression of the white South by the North.

The writer for the *Dispatch* was not alone in imagining dire consequences for the South in the wake of Lincoln's inauguration. Despite the realities that Lincoln was elected through a fair democratic process and that he promised to preserve slavery where it existed, for many white southerners Lincoln stood poised to shatter everything they held dear. As slaveholders, of course, the southern elite primarily held slavery dear, and with it the right to a form of self-government that would allow them to use the power of government to protect the institution of slavery. To express their outrage and fear at Lincoln's inauguration, white southerners such as the writer for the *Dispatch* embraced and expanded on the international perspective on nationhood that they had used to assess events both abroad and at home throughout the antebellum era, now using that perspective to dramatize the stakes of Lincoln's presidency for white southerners.

If Lincoln's presidency promised defeat at the hands of "European bayonets" and oppression as severe as that faced by those "annexed to the throne of some continental despot," such a weighty situation required an equally strong response. For many white southerners in the Deep South in the wake of Lincoln's election, and for increasing numbers of Upper South whites after Lincoln's call to arms, the drastic solution was secession from the United States and the creation of a separate southern nation. Only through independence, secessionists argued, could white southerners be free of antislavery northern governmental power.

International comparisons, which had already prepared white southerners to consider the South as a unit worthy of discussion within the international conversation on nationhood, proved useful to secessionists in making this case, as well as in proving just how necessary such a revolutionary action was. Following up on their earlier comparisons, in May 1861, the editors of the *Richmond Daily Dispatch* declared that "the 'struggle for Nationality' . . . abroad, is the identical struggle" of the Confederacy; "it is the struggle of Italy against Austria; of a Confederation of independent States, occupied by a homogeneous people, against foreign oppressors, who have violated the common league into which they have entered, and threaten us with cruelties and barbarism, compared with which, the so-called despotism of Russia is mercy and compassion."[2] To the editors of the *Dispatch,* an independent southern nation was not only necessary to escape Lincoln the tyrant but also justified as the latest example of the fight for national independence that had spread throughout the Atlantic world in the middle of the nineteenth century. In this view, the Confederacy was just one more in a long line of aspiring nations, seeking acceptance to the international community of nations and making its case for independence on the basis of internationally recognized principles such as national self-determination.

The international comparisons that the editors of the *Dispatch* and many other southern nationalists used to explain and justify their actions were more dramatic than accurate; a southern nation based on the defense of slavery did not follow in the footsteps of nationalist movements seeking freedom and liberty, nor did Lincoln or any other antislavery northerners limit white southerners' self-government (or even right to enslaved property), much less do so in a way that equaled the tyranny they perceived abroad. These comparisons were further complicated by the reality that the majority of aspiring European nations had failed to gain their independence, seemingly making them dubious examples of nation-building. Nonetheless, southern nationalists embraced these comparisons throughout the winter of secession and the spring and summer of the creation of the Confederacy. These international comparisons made up in enthusiasm and emotion what they lacked in accuracy and realism, and aided southern nationalists in making their case, to each other and to the world, as to why the South deserved independent nationhood. By utilizing the international language of nationalism, secessionists sought to translate their concerns about slavery into more widely accepted principles of nationality. Tying their attempt at nation-building to well-known nationalist movements in Europe—the same nationalist movements that southern commentators had analyzed and praised throughout the antebellum period—allowed secessionists and early Confederates to justify their actions as a legitimate expression of the same ideas of nationalism found abroad.

Critically, a minority of observers in European nations including Great Britain and France, and even within the United States itself, viewed secessionists' self-comparison with European nationalist movements with approval. As inaccurate as these comparisons were, they nonetheless found favor among Confederate sympathizers outside the South, revealing that these comparisons were not entirely outside the bounds of acceptable discourse in the mid-nineteenth century. As pro-Confederate northerners and Europeans adopted secessionists' international perspective, they granted plausibility to southern nationalists' claims to legitimacy, enhancing white southerners' belief that they could use comparisons between a nascent southern nation and aspiring nations in Europe to win support and legitimacy for an independent southern nation.

Secession, especially from the nineteenth-century world's largest and most long-lived republic, was indeed a dramatic action, requiring secessionists to explain their cause and justify their actions, a task they approached with a willingness to draw from all potential inspirations. While fundamentally the desire to preserve the institution of slavery was the main justification for southerners' secession, secessionists nonetheless attempted to tie this motivation to broader international principles. In particular, some secessionists relied on the Lockean right to revolution, which stated that rebellion against a government was justified if that government were tyrannical. Building on antebellum fears that antislavery northerners would limit and ultimately destroy the institution of slavery, and ignoring the fact that white southerners had exercised disproportionate power within the American nation and government, secessionists claimed that such anticipated harms to slavery constituted a restriction of southern rights, and that white southerners were therefore justified in creating a southern nation that would protect the right to slavery.[3]

Turning to American history, secessionists additionally argued that in rebelling against this imagined oppression, they followed in the footsteps of the American patriots in practicing a legitimate form of nation-building. The U.S. Constitution anchored an alternate variant of this argument, with secessionists declaring that their seceded states were merely reassuming the independent sovereignty that they had won in the American Revolution. In this estimation, the Constitution created a loose compact of sovereign states who could reclaim independence at any moment.[4] With such arguments, secessionists asserted that the tyranny of the growing antislavery movement was significant enough that secessionists' actions were legal according to both the Constitution and international law.

Southern secessionists did not limit themselves to the United States when looking for models of these principles that they claimed justified their actions. Secessionists such as the editors of the *Richmond Daily Dispatch* also looked to the nationalist movements of Europe to situate secession and the subsequent southern nation within the international exchange of ideas of nationhood, and to translate the desire to protect slavery into more internationally acceptable principles in an Atlantic world that had increasingly embraced abolition. The *Dispatch*'s assertions of similarity between the oppression of European nationalities and the anticipated oppression of the South at the hands of Lincoln constituted an example of secessionists' nascent liberal international perspective, which claimed that white southerners followed in the footsteps of aspiring nations abroad in justifiably seeking national independence on the basis of liberal ideas of nationhood. Such a formulation ignored the contradiction between slavery and the ideas of liberal nationalism as they were increasingly understood in the middle of the nineteenth century. Nonetheless, elite white southerners who saw much to celebrate in what they interpreted as European nationalist movements' attempts to create self-government used their positive assessment of revolutions abroad to legitimize their own revolution by asserting that the same values motivated both southern nationalists and nationalists in Europe, by arguing that secessionists' actions followed the models presented by aspiring European nations in seceding from empires, and by declaring that the success of the Italian Risorgimento in creating a new Italian nation heralded similar success for the South.

Although proponents of this liberal international perspective could be found among white southerners of all regions and partisan affiliations, this perspective proved particularly resonant with southern politicians and journalists as they concentrated on southern rights. Independent, nonpartisan newspapers such as the *Richmond Daily Dispatch, New Orleans Picayune,* and especially the

Charleston Mercury, which promoted a southern rather than a partisan (and therefore national) agenda, led the way in advancing secessionists' liberal international perspective. Notably, Democratic newspapers such as the *Macon Telegraph* also joined the independent papers in utilizing the liberal international perspective, as did Democratic politicians including Georgia's David J. Bailey and Zachariah E. Harman. Although Democrats were more likely to endorse this position, some Whigs were vocal proponents of the liberal international perspective too.

The commonality among advocates of the liberal international perspective on secession was their emphasis on southern rights, particularly white southerners' perceived right to preserve slavery. White southerners argued that the government must protect white men's right to property in the form of slaves, manipulating the liberal ideas of governance that elevate the rights of the governed and emphasize the duties of the government to protect those rights. These ideas resonated with southern rights' newspapers such as the *Mercury*, which focused on promoting what they considered to be southern rights, as well as with the Democratic Party, which frequently defended white southerners' vision of a national government that existed to protect their interest in slavery. This focus on southern rights provided a point of perceived connection to a discussion of the rights for which European nationalists fought; although the defense of slavery was not the same as Europeans' fight for the right of self-government, white southerners recognized that conflating the two issues would help them make their case for independent nationhood. To advocates of the liberal international perspective, white southerners' fight for the right to use governmental power to preserve slavery reflected European nationalists' fights for their right to direct their own government. For secessionists who conceived of the conflict between the North and South as one primarily centered on rights and the issue of whether or not the government was adequately protecting rights, comparisons with fights for self-government and against tyranny in Europe helped them draw attention to what they argued were their own violated rights.

The first step in building the liberal international perspective to justify secession was proving that secessionists had a just cause. Freedom from tyranny, long a concern of antebellum Americans as they analyzed events both at home and abroad, promised such a cause. Slaveholding interests in the South had argued throughout the antebellum era that any government action that threatened slavery constituted tyranny. During the crisis of 1850, proslavery advocates in the South had declared that northern attempts to limit the territorial spread of slavery constituted threats to white southerners' ability to participate in the governance of the United States by limiting the power of southern voices and votes. Such a stance stoked fears of oppression at the hands of northern antislavery advocates and led white southerners to claim that any efforts to end slavery were as tyrannical as the actions that European despots used to crush aspiring nationalities. These fears were largely exaggerated in a nation in which white southerners still held more than their share of power in the national government, but nonetheless this fear of northern tyranny only increased in response to the rise of the antislavery Republican Party in the late 1850s and the subsequent election of Republican candidate Abraham Lincoln in 1860.[5]

Freedom from tyranny seemed additionally appealing as a just cause for secession due to the fact that elite white southerners had myriad examples of what they had determined to be fights against tyranny in both the failed and ongoing nationalist struggles in Europe. As the debate over secession raged through 1860 and early 1861, white southerners returned to the comparisons they had crafted during the crisis of 1850, which cast antislavery northerners in the place of European despots. Once again, white southerners used comparisons between tyranny abroad and what they claimed was tyranny at home to dramatize the stakes in the sectional conflict and claim northern oppression of the white South. For example, Clement Clay, a Democratic politician from Alabama, warned as early as June 1860 that if the North succeeded in dictating the national conversation about slavery or recasting southern attempts to protect their rights as disloyal, the South would be "doomed to worse shame, subjugation and vassalage, than Ireland or Hungary now endures," urging white southerners to take care not to allow this to happen.[6] Unsurprisingly, such belief in the oppressive nature of antislavery interests was also evidenced at the secession conventions; judge and diplomat Alexander Mosby Clayton, for example, argued during the Mississippi secession convention that northern attempts to tax slave property, especially aimed at raising funds to make war against the seceded slaveholding states, was so abhorrent that "the most absolute despot in Europe would as soon think of abdicating his throne as to resort to such a course."[7]

Abraham Lincoln and the election of 1860 intensified white southerners' fears of losing slavery, and therefore inspired further usage of international comparisons of tyranny, with Lincoln featuring prominently as a leading tyrant and source of impending northern despotism. William Dennison Porter, writing under the pseudonym "Rutledge," declared the goal of Lincoln and the Republicans in 1860 to be "to inaugurate and establish in the government a policy hostile to the peace and safety of the slave States," a policy that would inevitably "terminate only in subjugation on one hand or disruption on the other!" Porter went on to beseech his readers to imagine the "iron hand of a hostile government" that Lincoln would use against the South, declaring, "Ireland could tell you a tale! And Poland and Italy!"[8] The editors of the *Charleston Mercury* also published this piece in October 1860, demonstrating the resonance and reach of these international comparisons.[9]

Such warnings of the oppression that Lincoln would enact only increased after Lincoln's election became an accomplished fact. As it published the results of the election, the *Nashville Union and American,* for example, informed its readers that with Lincoln's victory, the "Black Republican party" had succeeded in electing "a geographical and sectional President, pledged to pursue hostility against the institutions of the South," adding that "every principle of human nature rebels against a purely sectional rule over a free and independent people." In a critical statement against any war that this sectional government would wage against the South, the author pointed out that "in the case of Austrian rule in Hungary, Transylvania and Italy, the most bloody and desperately contested wars have resulted from the tyranny of Austrian despotism," as a result of which "even Austrian despotism has seen its error, and has learned that bayonets cannot safely and long be used to fortify its power against a spirited . . . people."[10] Similarly, a self-identified "National Democrat" wrote to the *Baton Rouge Advocate* in December that Lincoln's election constituted an assault against the rights of the South, and that the South must therefore follow the example of Italy in throwing off tyranny and monarchy.[11] These white southerners feared that Lincoln would oppress the South more thoroughly than any European despot had oppressed defeated nationalities, spurring them to consider actions that could forestall such a dire situation.

For an increasing number of white southerners in late 1860 and early 1861, that action meant secession and the creation of a separate southern nation. Having established that antislavery interests were oppressive and violated the rights of white southerners, and having learned through their international analysis of the sectional tension of the 1850s that the South could be discussed alongside nations, secessionists were ready to use their international comparisons to declare secession and independent nationhood to be the appropriate, justified plan for preserving the supposed right to slavery. In one early and bold statement of this new policy, in April 1860 John Tyler Jr. exclaimed in *DeBow's Review* that his readers should "remember that Poland has her Russia, Hungary her Austria, Ireland her England" and look to "the positive remedy of SECESSION AND A NEW CONFEDERATION" as the best response to northern threats to southern liberty.[12]

Writing in *DeBow's Review* in October 1860, an A. Roane likewise declared that unless northerners were willing to change their stance on slavery, European fights for liberty demonstrated that southern secession would be necessary for the "deliverance from wrongs, from tyranny, and from injustice."[13] To such secessionists, the common fight against tyranny, shared by white southerners and nationalists in Europe, justified the creation of a separate southern nation.

In order to fully legitimize secession, the liberal international perspective expanded its claims to a just cause beyond the fight against tyranny. Secessionists saw themselves not only as fighting against European-style tyranny but also as fighting for the liberty and self-determination that their much-admired European nationalists had sought but failed to establish. Self-determination, like the fight against tyranny, was a value that southerners had identified as appropriate for a nation through their analysis of the revolutions of 1848; now they used their internationalized understanding of the importance of self-determination to claim that they, like European revolutionaries, sought the right to self-government. For example, a preacher giving a sermon in Jefferson County, Georgia, accused the North of such severe harms to self-government that even Europe would react in disgust.[14] Similarly, in a report on the Louisiana secession convention, the *New Orleans Picayune* declared that Louisiana must follow aspiring nations in Europe who, though defeated, kept pushing for "the principle that communities have the indestructible right to create their own governments, and to throw off those which they find to be intolerable."[15] In an article republished in the *Charleston Mercury,* a New Orleans paper asked, "Why, then, should the South be deterred from re-asserting her independence," given that European nations had historically sought independence and freedom from oppression through war.[16] Even Jefferson Davis claimed in a January 1861 speech in Congress that southerners had the same right to "abrogate and modify their form of Government whenever it did not answer the ends for which it had been established" that had been enacted in the American Revolution and that foreign subjects of Austria had called on in their bids for independence.[17] To secessionists, the similarity between their fight for self-government and European nationalists' fight for self-government justified their actions.

Even as they used international comparisons to establish the legitimacy of their goals, secessionists also began embellishing these international comparisons. In particular, as success seemed within reach, secessionists began using their international perspective to argue that northerners and southerners were distinct and foreign peoples. To secessionists, if the North not only oppressed the South but did so as a foreign power, then white southerners would surely be even more justified in fighting against this foreign power. These claims not only internationalized southern secession but also blended the liberal appeal to self-government with a romantic nationalist vision of culturally based national distinctiveness.[18]

In one such claim to national distinctiveness, prominent Charleston politician Edward McCrady declared in September 1860 that "the utter impracticality of the good government of distinct peoples, diverse in their social characteristics, is most aptly illustrated in the history of . . . Great Britain. There lies Ireland, side by side with the English isle . . . diverse only in social organization: and that in a much less degree than the slaveholding from the non-slaveholding States of this Confederacy." In a warning for the South, McCrady added that despite being more similar than the sections of the United States were, Great Britain's inability to co-govern with Ireland meant that Ireland "still sits in her misery."[19] Similarly, John Townsend directed his listeners at a December 1860 political meeting in St. John's Colleton Parish, South Carolina, to consider how Congress had become characterized by "insult and vituperation;—the vulgar threats of conscious power on the one side, and scorn and defiance on the other," before asking, "Could it be worse if the representatives of France and England, or of Russia and Austria, in their worse days, were forced together into one hall, to legislate *together* for the interests of each kingdom—the representatives of one nation having the decided preponderance in making laws for the other?"[20]

Claims to national distinctiveness increased in both number and intensity as secession, and therefore a separate southern nation, became a reality rather than a mere possibility. The *Richmond Daily Dispatch* led the way in using the distinctiveness of northerners and southerners to justify secession as it made its statement that the "struggle for Nationality" that the South waged against the North "is the struggle of Italy against Austria."[21] Similarly, James M. Mason, Virginia congressman and later diplomat for the Confederacy, declared, "The people of the North . . . have separated themselves from the people of the South, and the government they thus inaugurate will be to us the government of a foreign power. We shall stand to such powers as Italy to Austria, and Poland to Russia. It will be one people governed by another people." To Mason, such a situation necessitated the commencement of a secession convention in Virginia.[22] Despite the actual similarity between white northerners and southerners, claims to regional distinctiveness, similar to the difference between European nationalities, bolstered secessionists' attempts to legitimize their attempt at nation-building.

Of course, the creation of an independent southern nation was unlikely to happen without a serious revolution or war. To secessionists who were inspired by the actions of aspiring European nations, however, even war seemed a small price to pay for the possibility of national freedom that would secure the right to slavery. A writer for *DeBow's Review*, A. Roane, was one southern nationalist who declared secession necessary for the protection of southern liberty, even if it led to war. According to Roane, the over-assertion of northern power had reached the point that "the common government is no longer a shield to protect; but . . . a sword to pierce the vitals of the weaker section." Any war resulting from southern secession, Roane asserted, would thus be an honorable and even necessary one, similar to the American Revolution or to wars in "England, France, Italy, Germany, and Spain." Indeed, such a war might even be welcome, as history showed that "liberty can only be won and maintained at the costly sacrifice of human life."[23] Similarly, the *Charleston Mercury* published in December 1860 that war, the last resort of kings, should not be denied to a people fighting for self-rule, as seen in foreign examples. Accordingly, the author concluded, the South should be able to assert its independence.[24] Having thus decided on their course of action, these men turned their attention to defending and legitimizing the new nation that their secession created.

By the spring of 1861, as secession concluded, southern nationalists utilizing the liberal international perspective had firmly established their premise that northern antislavery constituted European-style tyranny of the South, and that secession was thus justified for the preservation of white southerners' self-government. Critically, secessionists had also achieved their goal of leading the majority of slaveholding states to secede from the United States. With these seeming successes, newly minted Confederates would continue using an international perspective to legitimize their new nation.

As white southerners established the new independent southern nation, developed and elected a government, and prepared for and commenced war against the United States, they remained adamant that the North stood in the place of a European-style tyrant but expanded these comparisons to process the new outright enmity between the United States and the Confederate States. As a writer for *Griffin Confederate States*, republished in the *Macon Telegraph*, declared wearily, for example, if the South did not retain control of its governance and economy, "the Goths and Vandalls of the North will overrun the South . . . the liberty of speech and the liberty of the press will be annihilated and we will live—if we live at all in a state of military subjection more intolerable than that of Poland or Hungary," adding, "This is no fancy sketch. I am too old and too practical to draw on my imagination for my facts."[25]

Indeed, the threat of military rule at the hands of the oppressive North that worried the supposedly unimaginative journalist also fired the imaginations of his fellow southern nationalists. Although war had seemed of little concern during secession, once war was imminent, southern nationalists expanded their international comparisons in order to delegitimize northern efforts to use military force to block secession, furthering the liberal international perspective's concern with white southern rights. Supposed military despotisms in Europe loomed large in post-secession declarations of the tyranny of the North; to new Confederates, any actions on the part of the United States to use military force to block or reverse secession would provide proof that the North was not just a despot but a dreaded military despot, using military force to violate the rights of the governed. For example, as war seemed assured in May 1861, the *Charleston Mercury* bluntly declared that "the government of the United States is now nothing but a military despotism," further arguing that the United States would emerge as the most vicious of oppressors, as the case of Poland proved that "the greater the spirit of liberty . . . the more ruthless and bloody must be the despotism to crush it."[26] Likewise, as William Dennison Porter criticized Lincoln's despotism, he also condemned Stephen Douglas's supposed threats of military coercion in the case of southern secession, coercion that Porter claimed would re-create the oppression of Italy and Poland within the South.[27]

As southern nationalists expanded their international comparisons in the face of looming war, they also refocused their efforts on criticizing not just the military actions of the North but the ideology of northerners as well, portraying northerners as actively desiring to violate white southerners' rights. The North did not just act like a European despot, according to southern nationalists; the northern enemy also shared an ideological kinship with tyrants in Europe. For example, the *New Orleans Picayune* explained the Union government's confidence that the North would receive support from Austria and Russia by declaring that "such empires as Russia and Austria have a natural affinity for the principles of government developed at Washington," adding that the emperors "recognize coarse imitations of themselves in Abraham Lincoln."[28] Similarly, a sermon preached in Jefferson County, Georgia, proclaimed that the actions of the North against the South would cause despots to celebrate and Italy and Hungary to shriek, hinting at an affinity between the North and European despots and the South and aspiring European nations.[29]

Irish nationalist John Mitchel helped advance southern criticism of northern values and actions by chastising his fellow Irish for enlisting to fight for the United States. Writing as the Paris correspondent for the *Charleston Mercury*, Mitchel provided southern readers with analysis of news in Europe, frequently incorporating the critical issues of the American Civil War into his dispatches.

During the opening stages of the Civil War, the Irish in the North stood out as one area of concern to Mitchel. In June 1861, for example, Mitchel declared that the actions of the United States were "the regular European style. This is the very way the Emperor of Russia obliges the Poles to participate in the advantages of his paternal rule," adding that the contest was one of "the healthy sovereignty of Independent States against centralizing, stifling Imperialism." Accordingly, to Mitchel, "all that is to be regretted is, that such large numbers of [Irishmen in the North] having lost their own country through an 'Union' which England maintains by force, have now adopted a country which seeks to maintain by force another 'Union' which those who were suffering by it have in a happy hour repealed."[30] Repeating this concern in August, Mitchel followed up by lamenting "as for my unfortunate Irish fellow countrymen at the North, who have volunteered to march against rebels and crush rebellions—as if the very idea of rebels and rebellion were the thought most abhorrent in Irish nature—I know not what is to become of them," adding, "Truly it seems a hard fate that attends my poor countrymen—that they should find themselves so often in anomalous and absurd situations. . . . I blame them not too much; but congratulate most earnestly those Irishmen who have chosen the South for their home and are, by accident, identified in feeling and in interest with the righteous cause."[31] For Mitchel, the cause of the Confederacy was that for which the Irish contested in Europe; by fighting for the United States, northern Irishmen fought for the same despotism that Great Britain exercised over Ireland. Such emphasis on the destructive values supposedly shared by the U.S. government and despotic governments in Europe aided southern nationalists in drawing a connection between the abuses of European tyrants and the supposed abuses of the North. If these new Confederates were to be believed that northerners equaled the worst and most depraved of European tyrants, then they were justified in waging war against such an abusive foe. These comparisons, of course, disregarded the actual lack of oppression of white southerners and absence of tyranny in the North; nonetheless, secessionists were willing and even eager to manipulate reality and ideology in order to justify their actions.

From the early stirrings of secessionist activity in 1860 through the establishment of the Confederacy in early 1861, secessionists thus justified their actions through an international perspective that painted northerners as tyrannical for seeking to end slavery, and in doing so violating the rights of white southerners. With that principle established, secessionists were able to develop a liberal international perspective that legitimized secession by translating concerns about slavery into concerns about broader international values. To do this, they focused on rights and supposed abuses thereof to argue that the cause of their secession—a fight against northern tyranny and for southern self-government—echoed the causes that inspired European nationalist movements. This formulation ignored the reality that white southerners' secession from a republic in order to preserve slavery did not actually emulate movements for self-government abroad; nonetheless, secessionists widely utilized their liberal international perspective in order to defend their actions.

Although secessionists initially focused on proving that a common goal and common type of enemy inspired southern and European nationalists, as the new Confederacy was formed, they expanded these comparisons beyond ideology to also claim similar methods of nation-building in the South and in aspiring European nations. Secessionists believed that if they could prove that not only their values and their cause but also their methods followed the model of nation-building presented by foreign nationalist movements, such an argument would further strengthen their case for nationhood. Accordingly, secessionists using the liberal international perspective looked abroad to find a new nation that they could claim had been formed through actions similar to their own.

Italy, which unlike the many defeated nationalities of the revolutions of 1848 had recently succeeded in gaining unity and independence, proved particularly critical to these comparisons. Beyond the fact of its success, the new nation of Italy enjoyed widespread international sympathy and support, further enhancing its appeal as a model of nation-building.[32] Because Italy provided such a compelling model of the process of claiming nationhood, secessionists sought to draw parallels between their actions and those of Italian nationalists.

One promise that Italy offered secessionists was that if the various southern states united together, as the Italian states had done, they would be successful in building a nation. For example, a reporter for the *New Orleans Picayune* worried that "separate State action" among the slaveholding states, particularly if the cotton Deep South were to divide from the more diversified Upper South, would re-create the "same fate for the South" that divided Italy had suffered for centuries. The only way for a seceded South to avoid that fate and achieve success, according to this author, was to follow Italy's "reunion of her people under one government," which "is hailed by the civilized world as the regeneration of that country." As such, unity in the form of "a new Confederacy . . . is a necessity" for the future of the South.[33] Similarly, lawyer, politician, and military officer Samuel McGowan declared in the South Carolina legislature that "the South had everything to unite her, and it would be the height of madness not to unite," pointing to "the history of Poland [and] modern Italy" as examples of the necessity of unification."[34] The unification of Italy proved to elite southerners that unity among the southern states would lead to a successful process of nation-building.

While southern unity was important, Italy provided an even more tantalizing promise of success if the Risorgimento could be interpreted as a separatist movement rather than a unification movement. Indeed, in the winter and spring of 1861, as the southern states debated and began the process of secession, southern opinion-makers advanced the argument that Italy, like the aspiring southern nation, had been formed through secession. To these southerners, the Italian nation had been created through secession from the Austrian Empire, with, for example, the *Augusta Daily Constitutionalist* approvingly printing a French report that declared, "We do not see why South Carolina should not have the right to secede from the Union as well as several States of Italy have done with their government."[35] Another correspondent for the *Charleston Courier* reported on the creation and future of the Italian nation as dependent on "the Secession of Italy from the Papacy."[36] Corroborating the idea of Italy as having been formed through secession, the *Charleston Mercury* reported that Italian secession had inspired other separation movements, such as Ireland's struggle for independence from Great Britain.[37] In providing such a successful model of nation-building through secession, the example of Italy seemed to herald a great future for the southern nation.

The success of the new nation of Italy also granted critical insight into which methods of nation-building would be accepted as legitimate by the international community. Indeed, secessionists not only believed that they followed Italy in their method of nation-building; they also believed that they equaled Italy in independence and legitimacy—and they expected the world to take note, agree, and act accordingly. In one expression of this sentiment, Democratic lieutenant governor Thomas Reynolds of Missouri, future governor of the would-be Confederate government in Missouri, declared in the Missouri senate, "Let us go boldly before the nations of the earth claiming not to be a Southern Confederacy . . . but as the old United States." To Reynolds, the emerging southern nation, having contributed to the project of making the United States from the beginning, had equally legitimate claims as the North to be the true United States. Critically, Reynolds also recognized that the true settling of the matter had international as well as domestic implications, implications that would play out in the realm of international diplomacy. As Reynolds asserted, "Foreign nations will have to decide between us and Mr. Lincoln's envoys, just as we have to decide whether King Bomba or Victor Emmanuel is King of Naples."[38]

This mention of official diplomatic recognition was not coincidental. While unity and separatism provided models for achieving national success, the official diplomatic recognition of the new Italian nation by European powers created even more promise of success for secessionists seeking indications that their actions would successfully lead to an independent nation. Italy gained recognition from European powers including Great Britain and France, as well as from the United States, in the spring of 1861. Such diplomatic recognition was a key goal of the Confederacy, even as Confederates were just beginning the process of creating a nation. Gaining the recognition of France and especially Great Britain, a major trading partner of the United States and the South, would have benefited the Confederacy immensely, through both public opinion as well as actual aid and legitimacy. Accordingly, in the fall of 1861, the new Confederate government sent James M. Mason to London and John Slidell to Paris, charged with the mission of winning foreign support for the new southern nation. Initially, Confederates were confident that these efforts would quickly bear fruit. Although Confederates were fully aware of the benefits that diplomatic relations could bring them, however, and despite some European pro-Confederate sentiment that encouraged southern hopes, the Confederacy never succeeded in gaining recognition from foreign nations, in part due to the proslavery orientation of the Confederacy.[39] Later Confederates would be forced to deal with the lack of foreign recognition, but in the spring of 1861, fresh off the success of secession, hopes of recognition still flourished throughout the Confederacy.

As new Confederates sought diplomatic recognition, they turned to international comparisons to bolster their case that they were an independent nation and deserved to be recognized as such. While Confederate politicians and diplomats and their European targets spent relatively little time debating comparisons between the Confederacy and Italy, domestic discourse on the new southern nation's place in the international community of nations devoted much attention to arguing that the Confederacy, which supposedly fought for the same values and rights as Italy, deserved the same international diplomatic recognition that Italy merited.[40] As early as November 1860, for example, John Mitchel, writing as the *Charleston Mercury*'s foreign correspondent, characterized Europeans' reactions to the news of South Carolina's secession as fundamentally tied to their reactions to Italy. As Mitchel imagined it, on learning of southern secession, Europeans immediately asked, "Is it not enough that Italy starts up in those days as a new European power, but are we to have a new American power also?"[41] Although the comparison Mitchel placed in the mouths of Europeans was not overly complimentary toward the Confederacy (a realistic assessment, given many Europeans' desires to avoid getting entangled in a complicated and bloody war in America), it did take as granted that the Confederacy would, like Italy, succeed in establishing itself as a new power.

Such conviction in the Confederacy's equality with Italy increased as rumors spread throughout the South that Italy had been granted the diplomatic recognition the Confederacy sought. In particular, news of France's impending recognition of the Kingdom of Italy sparked excitement among southerners. In July 1861, the *Richmond Daily Dispatch* approvingly published a report by the *New Orleans Picayune*'s Paris correspondent that France's plans to recognize Italy boded well for the Confederacy, as Italy and the Confederacy were both "creatures of the same god, *vox populi*," and therefore to recognize one was to recognize the other.[42] Such a claim was not just a passing fancy; the same paper expanded two days later that "we are happy to see it announced that the French Government will soon recognize the independence of Italy, to be followed, it is predicted, by a speedy recognition of the Confederate States. Both of these Governments have been brought into existence by the popular voice, and both have bravely established in the field their claims to independence."[43] Similarly, a southerner calling himself "Gamma," writing from Europe, reminded readers that recognition of the Confederacy was linked to that of Italy, and as France had recognized Italy, recognition of the Confederacy was assured.[44] The similarity between the Italian and Confederate nations, in terms of both values and models of nation-building, was so compelling in Confederates' minds that recognition of the Confederacy necessarily would follow recognition of Italy. To early Confederates, an international perspective taught that secession was not only justified and legitimate; it was a viable model of nation-building. Secessionists' liberal international perspective enabled them to translate their concerns into the international language of nationhood, leaving them confident that, because they followed in the footsteps of new and aspiring European nations, the Confederacy would soon achieve the same success enjoyed by Italy.

Ultimately, the Confederate effort to gain diplomatic recognition would fail, as would the larger project in southern nation-building. Through the summer of 1861, however, secessionists and early Confederates remained confident that the similarity between the values and methods of southern secessionists and European, especially Italian, nationalists would inevitably lead to the success of the southern nation. These secessionists were not alone in interpreting their actions through an international perspective, or even in using international comparisons to claim legitimacy and impending success for the Confederacy. Although the Confederacy never gained official support from abroad, it did win sympathy from a minority of individual citizens and even politicians in Great Britain and France. These pro-Confederate Europeans, along with a small minority of northerners who shared their views, embraced and utilized secessionists' liberal international perspective to express their support for southern secession, bolstering the hopes of secessionists that their international comparisons were aiding them in public opinion abroad and therefore in establishing the legitimacy of their actions.

Northern and European views of southern secession and the Confederacy were complex. While support for unity and the United States predominated in both the North and Europe, a minority of northerners and Europeans nonetheless favored the Confederacy. Among Europeans, more conservative observers cheered the possibility of the downfall of the United States and republicanism. Northerners obviously did not share that desire, but a minority of northerners, particularly Copperhead Democrats, opposed the war and sought immediate peace with the South, even at the cost of a permanent division of the formerly United States.[45] These observers in Europe and the North, while not necessarily pro-secession or pro-Confederate, nonetheless variously supported some of the aims, goals, and methods of southern nationalists, or were at least willing to accept some of their concerns and aspirations as legitimate. As they sought to understand secessionists' goals and actions, they shared secessionists' conviction that international comparisons provided support for white southern slaveholders' right to create a separate southern nation. Continuing to draw on the liberal focus on rights, secessionists using the liberal international perspective and their nonsouthern supporters particularly shared the beliefs that northern and abolitionist attempts to end slavery and the Confederacy were creating a European-style despotism in America, with the oppressed South cast in the role of defeated European nations.

Comparisons between the fate of oppressed nations such as Poland and Hungary and a supposedly oppressed South were particularly widespread among northerners who shared some southern wariness about excessive assertions of power by the federal government and about what the government's policies meant for the rights of the governed. As reported by the *Staunton Spectator,* for example, the *New York Herald* argued that the U.S. government had no sympathizers except "Russia and Austria—the two most detestable despotisms of Europe," adding that "the invasion of the South is upon a par with the invasion of Hungary by Austria and Russia," two nations who would be relieved that Lincoln now shared that "oppressive odium" of despotism with them.[46] As early as the election of 1860, Charles O'Conor expressed concerns that antislavery would limit the rights of slaveholders, declaring in a speech at the Cooper Institute in New York that the success of a northern antislavery political party would oppress southerners just as the British oppressed the Irish.[47]

For supporters of secession from outside the South, the end result of this northern despotism was the limitation of the southern right to self-govern, just as it was in the minds of southern secessionists. A self-styled "Anglo-Californian," for example, wrote that "the right of nations to choose . . . their own form of government . . . has become a fundamental law . . . of civilized nations," asserting that international context revealed southerners should be able to exercise this right. Among other examples of this right of self-government such as the "Garibaldian war," the author singled out Belgium in 1830 as "a forcible example, and a notable precedent in this present crisis."[48] Similarly, George W. Bassett made his views clear in a pamphlet he pointedly titled *A Northern Plea for the Right of Secession,* exclaiming, "We propose to govern a State without her consent!" and colorfully explaining that "coerce South Carolina to submit to a foreign government, and you tear the well-earned laurels from the brow of the brave and unconquerable Garibaldi." Building on the theme that it would be a northern despotism which created such a terrible fate, Bassett furthered that "the doctrine of the coercion of an unwilling people, is an antiquated doctrine," adding, "I will even invoke Imperial Russia . . . to rebuke the recreancy of the American Republic" in taking away southerners' right to self-govern.[49]

Such a view was not limited to northerners. Some Europeans concurred with Bassett on the horrors of the North's violation of southern self-government, with Irishman William Smith O'Brien, for example, arguing that northerners, in perpetrating war against the Confederacy, violated the same right to self-government that they applied in Ireland, Hungary, Venice, and Greece. While the southern states might "act very unwisely" in seceding, "no one can now doubt that such is their deliberate choice," making any effort to block their secession "tyranny."[50] A German minister named L. Muller expressed similar sentiments in a speech to his countrymen in Charleston, claiming that in blocking secession, the North was acting like a European monarch, and asking if his audience wished to become a Poland or a Hungary.[51] Similarly, as the *Richmond Daily Dispatch* reported, the *London Weekly Dispatch* declared, "The principle involved in this quarrel is that which is put in issue in Naples, in Italy, in Hungary, in Poland," adding, "What is right in Europe cannot be wrong in America."[52] For some observers outside the South, secessionists and Confederates fought for the same rights and cause that had motivated aspiring nations in Europe. As some northerners and Europeans evaluated southern nationhood, secession, and the Civil War, an international perspective demonstrated to them, as to southern secessionists, that the North re-created European-style despotism in ending slavery and waging war against the South, in doing so limiting southern self-government and therefore providing potential legitimacy to an independent southern nation.

This belief that the North limited southern self-government by establishing a tyranny was also widely evidenced among foreign soldiers and revolutionaries who fought for the Confederacy. The voices of these European Confederates lent a guise of credence to southern-crafted self-comparisons with European nationalism. Irishman O. A. Lochrane, for example, stated outright that Irishmen fighting for the North had "abandoned their principles of Republican liberty" because the South fought against the same "coercion" that Ireland "resisted with all her genius, energy and manhood."[53] Similarly, Polish revolutionary Gaspar Tochman, who emigrated to the United States after being exiled from partitioned Poland and who then raised an immigrant regiment for the Confederacy, informed fellow immigrants that the consolidation of powers in the federal government violated the ideal of self-government on which the American nation was founded. To Tochman, the United States was "a despotism precisely similar to those of Europe, which we had so indignantly abandoned," leading him to urge his fellow Europeans to "unite yourselves with me in the defense of these same principles of self-government and of state sovereignty" that were fought for in the American and European revolutions.[54] Irish nationalist John Mitchel, of course, was among the most famous of these revolutionaries to support the Confederacy and equate its struggles with those of his home nation.

Having established that the Confederacy fought for the same values and goals as more popular aspiring nations in Europe, it was an easy leap for some Europeans to follow Confederates in claiming that Confederate national legitimacy should be recognized with official diplomatic recognition. In a move that had emboldened and encouraged Confederates' claims, some British and French officials and members of the press echoed Confederates' stance that a similarity to Italy in particular meant that if Italy gained official recognition, so too should the Confederacy. Perhaps most encouraging for Confederates' hopes were reports of French officials, including Napoleon III, equating the southern right to recognition with that of Italy and asserting that as soon as France recognized Italy, it would recognize the Confederacy as well. As the *Richmond Daily Dispatch* reported, for example, "A most significant article is published simultaneously in the Paris Patrie and Moniteur. It evidently foreshadows the coming recognition of the Confederate States of America. The Emperor of France announces for himself and other European powers that the Southern Confederacy has the same claims for its acknowledgment as a new kingdom that Italy had."[55] Such predictions worked best before France had actually recognized Italy, when officials like French minister of foreign affairs Edouard Thouvenel could still explain away a lack of recognition for the Confederacy by pointing out that France also had yet to recognize Italy.[56]

These encouraging reports were bolstered by positive attention from the London press, which, drawing on pro-Confederacy British sentiment, also endorsed the similarity between the Confederate and Italian claims to recognition. A widely republished article from the *London Press* opened with the bold declaration that "the hour is at hand when a new power will take its place among the States of Christendom." Explaining that Confederate diplomats were on their way to Europe to seek official recognition, the author concluded that "the Southern States are confident as to the success of their mission, and their confidence is well founded. The principle of the British Government is to recognize every *de facto* government, and the government of the Southern Confederacy is as much an accomplished fact as is the kingdom of Italy."[57] Similarly, the *Richmond Examiner* informed its audience that the *London Herald* declared that the Confederacy actually had greater claims to legitimacy and independence than had nations like Greece and Italy at the moments that they had received recognition.[58] Pro-Confederacy British citizens, such as those in the Southern Independence Association of London, which supported the Confederacy, likewise concurred that an international perspective taught that the Confederacy was a legitimate nation deserving recognition.[59] For a range of British observers, Confederates were correct in their assessment that Confederate similarity to Italy warranted recognition of the Confederacy.

One of the leading British voices advocating for the Confederacy was James Spence, a wealthy merchant and Confederate propagandist and financial agent. Spence shared Confederates' concerns with the radicalism of northern political ideology and therefore took it on himself to produce pro-Confederate literature.[60] As he pushed for recognition of the Confederacy, Spence, like his allies in the Confederacy, used an international perspective to make his case. Spence opened his book *On the Recognition of the Southern Confederation* with a statement reminiscent of the article in the *London Press,* declaring, "The time has arrived when it becomes the duty of the governments of Europe to acknowledge that another power is added to the family of nations." He quickly went on to explain that Britain could not deny recognition to the Confederacy "on the plea that the new government ought not to have come into being. . . . Few governments, if any, exist in the world, whose origin was perfectly legitimate." As evidence, Spence pointed out that "we acknowledged as *de facto* governments the Netherlands in their revolt from Spain, Portugal also from Spain, Greece from Turkey, Belgium from Holland, the Italian duchies from the family of Austria, the Legations and other provinces from the Pope."[61] Anticipating the concerns of Britons that establishing secession as a precedent would pave the way for Irish separation, Spence also argued that it was the existence of a functioning government, rather than simply a desire for nationhood as existed in Ireland, that granted the Confederacy legitimacy.[62] For Spence and like-minded Europeans, an international context helped them make a case for the recognition of the Confederacy. Despite the relatively widespread nature of these comparisons, however, recognition never came. For Confederate allies in the North and abroad, an international perspective facilitated their support for the Confederacy but was no more successful in assuring Confederate victory than it was when used by Confederates themselves.

While Confederates' international allies proved no more successful than Confederates at convincing a broader audience that the new southern nation deserved independence because it followed in the footsteps of aspiring nations in Europe, the support of these international allies nonetheless bolstered Confederates' own belief in their international comparisons. The resonance of southerners' liberal international perspective outside the white South, even among a minority of northerners and Europeans, reveals that white southerners' self-comparisons with aspiring European nations were not entirely outside the bounds of nineteenth-century thought on nationalism. As southern nationalists sought to prove that their international perspective on southern nationhood revealed the necessity and legitimacy of secession and southern independence, support from outside the South seemed to confirm their self-image as one of many new nations legitimately seeking independence in the middle of the nineteenth century. Especially when Europeans, whether government officials, members of the press, or foreign-born soldiers, endorsed these comparisons, southern nationalists reaffirmed their belief that the Confederacy was one of many new nations aspiring to acceptance among the international family of nations.

Through the international comparisons that constituted secessionists' liberal international perspective, southern nationalists and their allies sought to justify secession and therefore guarantee the success of the southern experiment in nation-building. This perspective focused on the rights of white southerners, both to preserve slavery and to create a government that would protect this supposed right to enslave African Americans, arguing that white southerners followed in the footsteps of European nationalists in seeking to protect their rights and self-government in the face of tyranny. Of course, such claims were factually and ideologically inaccurate, as white southerners were not oppressed and the supposed right to slavery did not equal larger claims to liberty and self-government. Nonetheless, claiming European nationalist movements as a precedent for their own attempt at nation-building aided secessionists in arguing that the South deserved the same chance at national self-determination as aspiring European nations, as well as in placing the aspiring southern nation within the mainstream of nineteenth-century nationalism. These comparisons also helped secessionists and southern nationalists deal with the problem that slavery created for their claim to nationhood by cloaking concerns about slavery within broader liberal principles, thereby focusing attention on the similarities that they supposedly shared with more widely supported nationalist movements in Europe while seeking to obscure the differences. In the debate over the rightness of secession and the establishment of an independent southern nation, secessionists' liberal international perspective was critical to secessionists' attempts to create an image of a new southern nation that properly upheld what they believed to be the correct form of southern nationhood.

5

Without a Parallel and Without a Rival

SECESSIONISTS' CONSERVATIVE

INTERNATIONAL PERSPECTIVE

In January 1861, Leonidas W. Spratt, editor of the states'-rights *Charleston Mercury*, penned a lengthy response to Louisiana politician John Perkins's views on the provisional constitution of the Confederate States. As Spratt made his case for his vision of the nascent southern nation, he elevated slavery as the primary institution, not just for Confederate national identity and success but for its place within the international community of nations as well. Spratt passionately asserted that "if you shall elect slavery, avow it and affirm it . . . assert its right . . . to extension and to political recognition among the nations of the earth. If . . . you shall own slavery as the source of your authority . . . the work will be accomplished." Not only would slavery ensure success for the Confederacy, however; Spratt further declared that, should the Confederacy thus affirm slavery, "your Republic will not require the pruning process of another revolution; but poised upon its institutions, will move on to a career of greatness and of glory unapproached by any other nation in the world." With such a bold statement, Spratt advanced a vision of the Confederacy not as one of many aspiring nations seeking independence but instead as a unique nation, set apart and superior to all others, distinguished through its reliance on slavery. To Spratt, other revolutions required "pruning," but the slavery of the Confederacy would purify that process, avoiding the problems of other revolutions and instead achieving "greatness." Accordingly, Spratt declared, with the creation of the Confederacy, "we are entering at last upon a daring innovation upon the social constitutions of the world."[1] With his vision of a unique, proslavery nation, Spratt elucidated a conservative international perspective on the Confederacy, one that justified a southern nation due not to its similarity to nations abroad but to its dissimilarity and superiority, granted through the South's special commitment to slavery and conservatism. This perspective sought to legitimize and defend the Confederacy by claiming the global superiority of the conservative nation to be created by the seceding southern states.

Such a vision of a uniquely conservative southern nation, set apart from the world, challenged the more liberal international comparisons that predominated through secession and the creation of the Confederacy. While secessionists who focused on the potential loss of their rights, such as self-government, saw themselves as emulating Europeans' attempts to secure their rights, their counterparts who instead emphasized the necessity of a society built on racial hierarchy viewed the European revolutions' calls for greater equality with wariness and disdain. Elite white southerners had always blended liberal respect for republicanism with a conservative desire for social order and even limited democracy, which had shaped southern analysis of European nationalist movements throughout the antebellum era, particularly by limiting support for what white southerners saw as the excessively liberal enactment of the otherwise desirable goals of the revolutions of 1848. During the secession debates, this conservative fear of the consequences of excess liberalism gave rise to an alternative vision of the place of the new southern nation within the international community. In the more conservative vision, elite southerners such as Spratt argued that secession was justified not because it emulated aspiring nations in Europe but because the nation it created would purify the doctrines of nationalism of the extremism that had doomed the revolutions of 1848 and now threatened the United States via northern abolitionism. Conservatism would set the aspiring southern nation apart from all the other nations of the world, placing an independent southern nation in a position of superiority.

While this conservative international perspective was not as widespread as its more liberal counterpart, and was manifestly incorrect in its claims that slavery would create greatness, its recognition of the differences between southern nationalism and the European nationalist movements more closely reflected political reality than the more liberal perspective. Secessionists' assertions of equivalency with aspiring nations abroad, both in values and therefore in legitimacy, always fit uneasily with even the contemporary understanding of revolutions and nationalism. For most observers in the Atlantic world, the nationalist revolutions of Europe were associated with liberalism, including liberal ideals such as equality and freedom. Many Americans and Europeans alike also increasingly associated these ideals with the international abolition movement.[2] White southern conservatism, especially based as it was on slaveholding, had debatable connection to nationalist movements seeking to expand, rather than deny, rights.

The conservative international perspective was also more realistic than its liberal counterpart in its recognition of the success, or lack thereof, of European nationalist movements. Especially in the revolutions of 1848, most aspiring European nations had indeed failed to establish independent nationhood, making them dubious examples of nation-building for future aspiring nations. Additionally, the success of monarchy and empire in defeating these revolutions meant that existing forms of government in Europe likewise failed to provide positive models of republican nationhood.[3] Secessionists claiming that southern conservatism purified European-style nationalism acknowledged the failure of nationalist movements in Europe, even as the liberal perspective largely ignored the fact that the movements they claimed to follow had rarely resulted in independent nations.

The conservative international perspective further reflected the reality that conservatism had constituted a major force in southern politics throughout the antebellum and Civil War eras. While white southerners, like other Americans, were influenced by the Enlightenment philosophies that had shaped the United States, and thus held republicanism as the ultimate form of government, white southern respect for the liberal institutions of the United States was always tempered by conservative desires for such principles as a hierarchical social order and limited democracy. The necessity of defending slavery in particular fueled white southerners' fears of the implications of such ideals as freedom and equality.[4] For white southerners, restricting democracy and citizenship to white men was critical for the success of the republic, particularly as the southern defense of slavery intensified in the antebellum period, emphasizing the importance of the protection of property to liberty and republicanism, and even arguing that slavery allowed for a stronger, more advanced form of republicanism by protecting white men's republican independence and virtue.[5] Not surprisingly, these conservative visions of race and politics influenced secessionists' estimations of not only the values and goals but also the international meaning of their new nation.

Thanks to the centrality of conservatism to southern values, the conservative international perspective, like its more liberal counterpart, emerged relatively organically out of antebellum southern thought. Notably, neither perspective was directed by a clear leader; rather, the building blocks of elite white southerners' analysis of the place of the South within the international world, including knowledge of European nationalist movements and the white southern respect for republicanism and demand for the preservation of slavery, were well-known and widespread enough that they were available for southern commentators of all political persuasions to adopt and adapt at will. Consequently, southerners across the political spectrum did indeed use these elements to make their case for their desired visions of southern nationhood, without requiring elaborate explanations of the issues or needing a specific leader to originate an international vision of the South.

The secessionists who used the conservative international perspective to defend secession thus had much in common, politically and in their values, with their counterparts who had adopted the more liberal perspective. All of these secessionists most obviously shared a belief that ending slavery, as antislavery northerners sought to do, violated the necessary political and social values of white southerners, thereby violating their desired form of nationhood.[6] As they evaluated those desired national values, secessionists in both groups retained elements of their liberal heritage but tempered them with conservative ideas, for example preserving the traditional American desire for self-government even while requiring that self-government would be limited to the white race through the institution of slavery.[7] By definition, secessionists of all political persuasions also agreed that secession and the creation of an independent southern nation was the best way to uphold and preserve white southerners' visions of nationhood. And these secessionists, both liberal and conservative, concurred that placing their actions within an international context would be helpful in explaining their national values and in justifying their attempt at nation-building.

Because of their shared political and social context, national values, and assumptions about forms of nationhood, the elite white southerners utilizing the conservative and liberal international perspectives overlapped significantly; no clear division existed between the southern nationalists who adopted the two perspectives, other than their differing preferences on how best to position the new southern nation relative to the rest of the world.[8] Some Democrats and some Whigs, some fire-eating radicals and some more restrained traditionalists, some politicians and some cultural commentators advocated for each of the perspectives, liberal and conservative. Indeed, some influential southern periodicals, including the *Richmond Examiner*, edited by John Moncure Daniel, who served as an American diplomat in Sardinia during the unification of Italy, printed both liberal and conservative analyses of the southern nation's place within an international community of nations.[9] Occasionally, individual speakers also endorsed both liberal and conservative international perspectives, either in the same speech or during the course of their careers.[10] To many elite white southerners, the liberal and conservative international perspectives were not mutually exclusive. Both perspectives could be used depending on the need at hand. Accordingly, it is more appropriate to refer to secessionists who used a liberal versus a conservative perspective, rather than referring to southern liberals versus southern conservatives.

Despite the significant overlap in usage of these two international perspectives, some trends did emerge that suggest explanations for why one perspective might have resonated more with a particular secessionist or group of secession-ists. While nonpartisan, southern-nationalist newspapers such as the *Charleston Mercury* were some of the leading proponents of the liberal argument that the southern nation resembled aspiring nations abroad, the more cultural-analysis-oriented southern magazines, including the *Southern Literary Messenger* and particularly *DeBow's Review,* frequently advanced arguments that the South's conservatism set it apart from other nations. Analysts focused on the preserva-tion of white southerners' rights were drawn to the vision of the South as one of many aspiring nations of the nineteenth-century Atlantic world, while those focused on southern culture and society instead turned to the values that set the South apart from the rest of the world, particularly by emphasizing the racial hierarchy that defined southern society.[11]

Indeed, the most significant difference between secessionists who used the liberal versus conservative international perspectives was that they responded to different themes in white southern political thought. While the liberal perspec-tive drew primarily on the southern reverence for republicanism and focused on creating a government that preserved white southerners' rights, the conservative perspective was primarily motivated by fears of excess democracy and social equality and the potential implications of these ideas for a society built on racial hierarchy. Southern magazines such as *DeBow's Review* and the *Southern Lit-erary Messenger,* focused as they were on creating, preserving, and advancing a white southern culture, thus provided natural outlets for secessionists who were focused on the social consequences of the politics of slavery and nationalism. Rather than emphasizing white southerners' supposed right to self-govern in a way that would protect slavery, these cultural commentators centered their international analysis on the evils of social equality that could result from the diminished political power of enslavers. Accordingly, while the secessionists who adopted the liberal international perspective drew attention to liberal concerns with rights and self-government, secessionists utilizing the conservative inter-national perspective emphasized the conservation of the inequality of the races and the supremacy of the white race, drawing on the conservative traditions of hierarchy and social order.

For the secessionists advancing the conservative international perspective, European nationalist movements stood as warnings of loss of social order and even of potential loss of racial hierarchy, should the liberal ideas of democracy be taken to an extreme. For example, George Fitzhugh proposed in *DeBow's Review* in 1860, "Let us have ideas, thoughts, opinions, laws, manners, and customs of our own, for we can find none adapted to our social relations in Europe or the

North." Accordingly, he suggested, "Let us show to the world that we, slaveholders, are the only conservatives . . . that Liberty everywhere needs more legal regulation and restrictions," adding that "the drama of free society has been acted out in France. It runs into anarchy and anarchy issues into military despotism."[12] To conservatives, "free society" threatened to destroy southern "social relations" and overthrow the more worthy white race from its position of authority by ending slavery, leading to the anarchy of violent racial conflict and uprisings. As another author in *DeBow's Review* warned sarcastically, "As fruitful as has been the doctrine of 'perfect equality' of all mankind of every color in bringing about in other countries anarchy, civil war, and general ruin," the egalitarian racial ideas of the Republican Party were "still more false and wicked, and cannot succeed without causing more bloodshed and more lasting ruin than all other fallacies of the time."[13] When southern conservatives argued that the limitation of liberty would create a purer form of nationhood, they were ultimately making the case for a white nationalism based on slavery that they claimed would be superior to a more inclusive nationalism as supposedly enacted in Europe.

The conservative international position was thus built on an understanding of nationalism and nationhood in Europe as flawed or failed. While the liberal perspective sought to emulate what it saw as the positive values of the European nationalism movements, regardless of their lack of material success, the conservative perspective instead emphasized not only the failure of the revolutions but, more critically, the reason for that failure, which the conservative international perspective claimed was their excess liberalism. Without this vision of the weaknesses of European nationalism, conservatives would have no case for claiming that they were fixing what was broken abroad. Building on their desire to conserve racial inequality and their belief that excess equality had doomed revolutions abroad, secessionists used a conservative international perspective to justify secession by arguing that the southern nation would use its slave-centered conservatism to create a new and stronger form of nationhood, providing the world with a truly successful model of nation-building that would avoid the excess liberalism that had led to the defeat of nationalist movements abroad.

In the conservative international perspective, aspiring European nations stood as negative reference points, useful in highlighting the contrast presented by the supposedly pure conservative southern values. Thus, the first step to building the conservative international perspective was to recast the European nationalist movements as harmful and threatening, rather than as a positive model to be emulated. The failure of most revolutions proved useful here, and secessionists using the conservative international perspective quickly began arguing that the European revolutions had not just failed but failed due to dangerous liberalism.

White southerners utilizing the conservative international perspective particularly interpreted European revolutions as warnings against the dangers of excess democracy, social equality, and even mob rule and anarchy. In this they returned to the wariness that their predecessors had evinced during the revolutions of 1848, sometimes even rejecting the revolutions outright, rather than merely lamenting their tragic failures. For example, a Captain Cuthbert declared at the presentation of colors to the Palmetto Guard that the seceding South would not be harmed by the "wild Utopian dreams" of European revolutionary leaders such as Giuseppe Mazzini and Lajos Kossuth, which would have led to "riot and confusion . . . and Anarchy, with torch, stake, and scaffold—blood, barricade and guillotine would have driven her blood-stained chariot wheels over the ruins of the Confederacy."[14] As one A. Featherman wrote in *DeBow's Review,* the revolutions of 1848 created "a government instituted on the principle of 'liberty, fraternity and equality,'" which "became the stepping-stone of an adventurer for the usurpation of imperial power." In this analyst's estimation, new nations seeking to enshrine equality ultimately ended in failure.[15] Similarly, the *Charleston Mercury* chose to reprint an article in which the *London Times* stated that "as a general rule, the most successful revolutions in Europe must pass through a phase of anarchy. There was anarchy in Sicily and Naples when Garibaldi invaded them," before excusing the southern revolution from this rule, declaring, "Far different is the case of the Seceded States."[16]

As this statement reveals, the conservative international perspective sought to distance the potential southern nation from the recent European examples of harmful excess. For example, an author in *DeBow's Review* lamented that the French Revolution of 1848 was doomed without a "breakwater against the violence of democratic impulse," and that at the same time Hungary, Ireland, and Poland lost their "proud nationality" and self-government by submitting to "servitude." The author then celebrated the fact that "Southern society presents an anomaly in the history of civilization" which would protect it against such woeful outcomes.[17] To these authors, southern society was superior to those that the revolutions had sought to create abroad. Instead of claiming similarity with European nationalist movements, the conservative international perspective drew attention to the different values held by European nationalists and white southerners, using that contrast to highlight what they viewed as illegitimate, or at least undesirable, examples of nation-building abroad.

With the South cast as being in opposition to, rather than emulation of, the European nationalist movements, new possibilities arose for understanding how the European framework applied to sectional issues within the United States. In particular, the conservative formulation necessarily recast both the North's and South's roles in the international metaphor for American conflict. If the European revolutions represented a violation of the proper values and expressions of nationhood and would ultimately destroy southern society, then secessionists' international comparisons should equate aspiring European nations with the North rather than the South.

The vision of the North as emulating the problems of failed nationalities abroad built off of broader secessionist arguments about the American nation. In particular, this aspect of the conservative international perspective emerged out of the secessionist argument that northerners had corrupted the original principles of the United States and that a southern nation would restore the intent of the founders. According to secessionists, the North had betrayed the original American national compact by embracing antislavery perspectives and, worse, liberal notions of social equality.[18] If the North had corrupted American nationalism in this viewpoint, southern conservatism stood as the corrective.[19] In one expression of this widespread idea, Confederate vice president Alexander Stephens cited the elevation of white supremacy as one of the main improvements that the Confederate States made on the United States in his famed "Cornerstone Speech."[20] Similarly, fellow white southerners argued that southern conservatism had kept northern liberalism in check until the recent growth of northern power. According to the *Richmond Examiner,* without the stabilizing influence of southern conservatism, "the debased Yankee, drunk with delight, dances with joy over the grave of his liberties," while Lincoln accomplished in "three months" what "a long line of French despots required ten centuries to accomplish."[21] The idea of a debased North that stood in violation of national principles was useful in justifying the creation of an independent nation as it happened and remained popular throughout the war; as South Carolina conservative and Confederate congressman Robert Barnwell Rhett said in an 1862 speech, "History has no such record, of the reckless and voluntary abasement of a people from a free government to a despotism. . . . The great cause of free government [northerners] have thrown back, perhaps, for centuries, and have left its preservation, on this continent at least, alone to the Confederate States."[22]

This broader understanding of the North as violating the ideals of the American republic paved the way for secessionists endorsing the conservative international perspective to use comparisons between what they saw as harmful nationalist movements in Europe and dangerous liberal ideas in the North to justify southern secession from the United States.[23] These arguments frequently focused on comparisons between the "red republicans" in Europe, particularly France, and the "black republicans" in the North. "Red republicanism" referred to extreme liberal radicals and was much reviled even by secessionists adopting the more liberal perspective. "Black republicanism," meanwhile, was a pejorative term that white southerners used to criticize northern liberals for supposedly favoring the interests of black Americans over white Americans. Tying these two destructive forces together, John Tyler Jr. relied on the conservative international perspective to equate northern antislavery liberals with liberal forces in France, claiming that "the Radical or Red-republican democracy of France . . . struck down all morals and property-rights in that nation. In the United States they have ruthlessly grasped the territories, and now uplift the red hand against the South. Property-robbery and political power . . . always have been . . . the impelling motives of their conduct, whether the Protean shape assumed be that of the 'Roundhead,' the 'Sans-culotte,' 'Red Republican,' or 'Black Republican.'"[24] Of course, slavery was the main form of property with which southern slaveholding interests were concerned. Similarly, as the *Richmond Enquirer* declared in an article that was republished in other southern journals, "There can be no doubt on the mind of any one who has spent any portion of his life in Europe, that the anti-slavery sentiment there, especially in France, and most especially in England, bears about the same relation even to the fanaticism prevalent in New England."[25] Moving beyond just antislavery, Senator C. C. Clay of Alabama declared in a speech excerpted by a correspondent for the *Alexandria Gazette* that northern attempts to democratize the political process in general equated "sheer radicalism" and "the Red republicanism of revolutionary France."[26]

For secessionists who endorsed a conservative international perspective, northern abolitionists and European nationalists did not just share ideas by coincidence. Conservatives actively blamed the liberalism of Europeans for corrupting northerners. For example, R. L. Gibson wrote in *DeBow's Review* that "the central idea of Northern society . . . is the absolute equality—the political, civil and social equality of all the races of man." To Gibson, such an idea had "originat[ed] in France" and was "entirely opposite" of the ideals of southern society. Tying such a comparison to the more recent events in France, Gibson soon clarified that not just postrevolutionary France but also the contemporary government of France was the "most despotic" of all current governments.[27] Similarly, William H. Holcombe explained in the *Southern Literary Messenger* that antislavery sentiment derived in part from the "radical influence" of France on the "fanatics" in the North, adding that "it is almost impossible at present to disabuse the public mind of Europe and of the North" of such antislavery sentiment.[28] To these southerners, the liberal doctrines poisoning the North and threatening southern society were the same that had poisoned Europeans.

Such a connection boded poorly for the future of the United States according to the conservative international perspective. Secessionists feared that as the North increasingly embraced European "fanaticism," the status of the American nation would continue to decline, suffering from the same excess of liberalism that had weakened and doomed European nations. As a writer for the *Southern Literary Messenger* explained, if antislavery New England were "left to herself, in fifty years nothing can keep her from anarchy and red-republicanism but some Louis Napoleon, with plenty of bayonets."[29] In the conservative international perspective, the negative liberalism of Europe was responsible for the negative liberalism in the North that had violated the original, more conservative form of the American nation. The North, not the South, followed in the footsteps of European revolutionaries, footsteps that threatened the foundations of society rather than promised national independence. Such a formulation cast the South in a very different international context than that of the liberal international perspective; now the South stood apart from, rather than in emulation of, European attempts at nation-building. The conservative international perspective asserted that secession was necessary to protect white southerners from the harmful liberalism threatening the North and Europe alike.

Having established that the North had corrupted the desired values of nationhood due to the dangerous influence of liberal European ideals, secessionists expanded their conservative international perspective to justify secession and an independent southern nation by arguing that a conservative southern revolution and nation would purify nationalism of such undesirable excesses, internationally as well as domestically, by creating an alternate model of a supposedly more stable nation. Indeed, a southern nation, secessionists argued, would create the most virtuous nation in history, which would then stand as an exemplar of nationhood, alone among the world's nations in properly organizing its government and society around principles of conservatism and slavery. Certainly they were incorrect in their calculation that slavery would purify and enhance the values of nations, particularly those such as the American nation, which revered the principles of self-government and freedom; nonetheless, the vision of a conservative nationalism appealed to many secessionists, who claimed that because white southerners' values set them apart from the North and Europeans, secession and the subsequent creation of a southern nation were imperative as well as legitimate and justified.

As secessionists used an international perspective to argue that the South deserved independent nationhood because it alone represented a pure and conservative expression of nationhood, they began by analyzing the necessary political values they believed a southern nation would uniquely preserve. Although not as focused on political rights as were secessionists using the liberal international perspective, those endorsing the conservative perspective were still well-versed in the language of political rights, which they used to argue for the limitation of democratic rights to white men only. Indeed, the primary conservative value that secessionists claimed a southern nation alone would uphold was limited democracy, which they believed was necessary for preserving the racial hierarchy necessary for their ideal society. Drawing on their vision of European revolutions as having created violence and chaos through excess democracy, secessionists asserted that the racially limited democracy of the southern nation would create a more stable, virtuous society and therefore form of nationhood.

Although the idea of a racially limited electorate and citizenry had been accepted throughout the Atlantic world at the founding of the United States, the rise of the international abolition movement in the first half of the nineteenth century had opened new possibilities for rights and citizenship. As they strengthened their defense of slavery in response, antebellum white southerners had long feared that even granting black Americans the minimal equality of emancipation would lead to widespread race rebellion and race wars, obviously undermining the social order of white supremacy and toppling white men's political authority.[30] Creating a whites'-only nation by limiting democracy and participation in the nation to the white race seemed, to these white southerners, to be the only possibility for preventing such a dire scenario, and their international perspective bolstered this case. As a writer for the *Southern Literary Messenger* declared, "While we have slavery, we shall never have universal suffrage," but such limitation of citizenship to the white race would grant the southern nation the "greatest opportunity ever vouchsafed to any people, of establishing free republican institutions."[31] An author in *DeBow's Review* similarly wrote that "sufficient intelligence" of the electorate was necessary for the enjoyment of "the right of self-government," but that "none of the colored races have, in any age or country, proved . . . that they were worthy of . . . the high privilege of governing themselves." The author then turned to international examples ranging from ancient Greece to the contemporary British Empire as proof that a franchise limited to the most intelligent was necessary for national success.[32] For these white southerners, the South's slave-based politics prevented the establishment of full democracy, but that absence created a purer, stronger form of government and nationhood, free of the harmful effects of excess democracy and racial equality.

If these secessionists viewed democracy with suspicion, they likewise questioned the benefits of full liberty. Looking abroad, secessionists using a conservative international perspective built off of their belief that excess liberty had doomed the European nationalist movements to make the case for why the South must secede from an American nation making the same mistakes. In a typical expression of conservative fear of unrestrained liberty, for example, John Pratt wrote in *DeBow's Review* that radicalism had doomed the "unfortunate struggle for rational liberty" in Europe in 1848.[33] Tying this to the South, George Fitzhugh urged fellow southerners to join secessionists, stating, "Let us show to the world that we, slaveholders, are the only conservatives . . . that Liberty everywhere needs more legal regulation and restrictions."[34]

Once again, such concerns centered on the white southern conviction that liberty and freedom must be limited to the white race. For example, "A Mississippian" declared that the South's "perfect labor system" would ensure "every element of moral and political success" for an independent southern nation, in part by ensuring liberty remained "the sole heritage of the white race."[35] Similarly, P. R. G., a self-proclaimed Virginian who, although still seeking unity in December 1860, nonetheless was willing to engage in a discussion of secession, wrote to the *Richmond Whig* that Virginians should evaluate the secession question through the lens of which option best preserved their freedom, clarifying, "I speak not of freedom in the social sense—in the sense which distinguishes the free white man from the African slave. I speak of freedom in its political sense." Making his commitment to political, not social, freedom clear, P. R. G. went on to list examples abroad of nations destroyed by excess social freedom and lack of political freedom, including France, Italy, and Ireland.[36] Limiting liberty to the white race, these southerners argued, would uphold the conservative values necessary for the success of the southern nation.

As with P. R. G., these southerners were clear in their analysis that such restrictions of political rights and implementation of conservative political values would indeed benefit southern society, not just governance. In particular, they claimed that limitation of democracy and liberty along racial lines would preserve republicanism and create necessary social order and stability along both race and class lines. Further, by providing a stable and permanent bottom level of society, slavery, slaveholders believed, controlled not only the black race but also lower-class white southerners, who benefited from avoiding the degradation of enslavement.

Using European nations as examples of how following the supposed natural social hierarchy benefits a nation, the *Richmond Examiner* argued that the South's natural order of racial inequality would lead to a "perfect social order which shall produce peace on earth and good will towards men."[37] As an author for the *Southern Literary Messenger* declared, because of slavery, "the angry strifes which agitate and destroy other nations, are not known with us."[38] Specifying the source of such strife, *DeBow's Review* summarized J. H. Van Evrie's statement that "in free society the conflict of labor and capital is an enormous and growing evil, which threatens to subvert the whole social system of Europe. . . . No such conflict exists, or can exist, in the South," extending Van Evrie's criticism of labor conflict to highlight the particular problems of the North.[39]

Labor and capital showed up repeatedly in white southerners' discourse about the benefits of southern conservatism, with the South always standing as the corrective to the supposedly oppressive labor arrangements in the industrializing North and Europe.[40] The white southern critique of capitalism was thus readily available for elite southerners to incorporate into their developing conservative international perspective. A writer for a Richmond newspaper, for example, declared in a statement republished in the *Charleston Mercury* that "free society in Europe and America rests upon the substratum of slavery," as he expanded on the many benefits of slavery. One such key benefit of slavery, the author declared, was that "white labor at the South is elevated by having beneath it the substratum of negro slavery."[41] Tying this issue to the integrity of democracy, J. Randolph Tucker explained that "in all free democracies the social struggle between labour and capital" corrupted the vote and threatened property rights, problems for which southern slavery provided a "happy solution."[42] Free of the violence and discord that weakened revolutions and existing nations abroad, southerners argued, the racial social order of the South, created through limited democracy and liberty as well as through a rigid hierarchy, would ensure unique stability for a white southern nation, purifying nationalism of the dangerous equality and excesses that subverted revolutions and weakened nations abroad.

Secessionists adopting the conservative international perspective viewed their conservative southern nation as having enormous historic and international significance. These secessionists were explicit in claiming that a conservative white man's nation in the South would not just create a good nation but would also create a stronger, purer, and more desirable form of nationhood, one that would elevate the southern nation above all other nations of the world. For example, the "Mississippian" who thought that liberty was strengthened by being limited to white men predicted that the formation of a southern nation would create nothing less than "an era . . . the like of which the world has not before seen," because such a southern nation would be "peculiarly circumstanced" with "advantages . . . no nation has heretofore been favored with."[43] J. Quitman Moore, in an impassioned plea for secession, explained that slavery would correct for the "arbitrary power" dooming attempts at reform in Russia and France. As Moore grandly declared, "This system of labor, this peculiar domestic institution, these distinct elements of social and political organization, mark out for the States of the South a fixed, independent, and inevitable destiny—a destiny embracing, if followed, a solution of all the disturbing problems, social, political, ethical, and economical, that are convulsing the bosom of modern society—a destiny pointing to the topmost peaks of human advancement, and giving promise of a splendid course of political empire."[44]

Other secessionists were even more explicit in tying their exaggerated praise of the supposed status of the southern nation to the values that would so elevate it. Bold claims directly asserted that the southern nation would not just stand above all others but that it would do so due to its protection of the very republicanism that the United States and aspiring nations in Europe were supposedly failing to preserve. For example, J. S. L., writing for the *Southern Field and Fireside* in an article that was picked up by other southern publications, enthusiastically endorsed secession and southern superiority by claiming that secession "affords the strongest assurance of the efficiency of republican government, and of the perpetuity of democratical institutions," because with conservative ideals, "democracy contains the elements of its own regeneration." J. S. L. concluded by stating, "This Southern confederacy may reasonably and calmly anticipate a career of prosperity and greatness without a parallel and without a rival."[45] L. W. Spratt's hyperbolic statements of slavery leading the South to a revolution free of "the pruning process of another revolution" and then a "career of greatness" through "a daring innovation upon the social constitutions of the world" similarly praised the aspiring southern nation as superior in its institutions.[46] As these statements made clear, to southern conservatives the conservatism and slavery of the South set it apart from other nations and revolutions, with the southern nation standing above the rest as a better exemplar of the very values the aspiring nations abroad had failed to achieve.

For southerners who endorsed a conservative international perspective, their international analysis taught that the South deserved independence due to its dissimilarity, not similarity, with European nationalisms. The desire to preserve a society built on racial inequality, rather than an emphasis on the political rights of white men, drove secessionists using the conservative international perspective to focus on the characteristics that set the southern nationalist project apart from its more liberal counterparts abroad. By purifying nationalism of the excesses found in European revolutions, they claimed, the southern nation would usher in a new and improved form of nationhood, superior to any the world had seen.

For conservative southerners, an international perspective confirmed their broader belief that southern conservatism was superior to the liberalism found among European nationalists and northern abolitionists. While the South was more conservative than these groups, however, the U.S. South was not the only conservative region in the nineteenth-century Atlantic world. On the contrary, more conservative governments such as monarchies, aristocracies, and empires appeared to be consolidating their power throughout Europe and even the Americas, first with the defeat of the revolutions of 1848 and then with the division of the United States. The seeming failure of liberal republics in the face of powerful monarchs and emperors suggested that liberal ideals of governance might be in retreat throughout the world. With liberalism potentially declining, the more conservative forms of government such as monarchy and aristocracy appeared to be growing in strength and influence.[47] For the most conservative of southerners, an international context corroborated their conviction that conservatism created a more stable, successful form of government.

While southerners' American heritage was strong enough that the majority of even conservative white slaveholding southerners retained their desire for some form of republican governance, a few conservative secessionists took their respect for conservatism to the extreme and supported the inclusion of elements of nonrepublican governments in the new southern nation.[48] Drawing inspiration from the governments that had successfully opposed the European revolutions allowed southerners to cast themselves in the role of the victor, rather than the vanquished. Such a path also supported conservative secessionists' desire to avoid the feared excesses of revolutions. As they debated the best form of nationhood for the South, an international context taught a small minority of the most extreme of conservatives that the South should temper its republicanism with aristocracy, or even forgo democracy and republicanism altogether and adopt a monarchical government.

Southern willingness to consider aristocratic or monarchical forms of government derived once again from the longstanding white southern concern with the full implications of democracy.[49] Although the idea of emulating European aristocracies was extreme in the context of American republicanism, it did provide an option for achieving the limitation of democracy and liberty that more conservative secessionists believed would be the defining characteristics of the southern nation. J. S. L. argued in the *Southern Field and Fireside,* for example, that the "South to-day exhibits the only perpetual democratic government possible—that is, a democratic aristocracy—an aristocracy of race, with a democracy of power," which would protect against "revolutions from within, and tyranny from without." The *Augusta Daily Constitutionalist* found this statement worthy of republication.[50] Similarly, an author for *DeBow's Review* asserted that "aristocracy is the only safeguard of liberty."[51] A European-style aristocracy potentially provided protection for the power of the white citizens of the southern nation, protection that would be necessary for the South to fulfill its self-proclaimed mission in creating the best form of nationalism.

While aristocracy had typically been anathema to the idea of republicanism, for conservative secessionists the racial hierarchy of the South nonetheless meant that aristocracy felt familiar, comfortable, and like a natural fit for a people who defined themselves through social inequality. Conservative secessionists already believed that the South benefited from many of the advantages of a racially divided social structure, which could be described as a form of aristocracy. For example, a Scotchman living in Mobile, Alabama, quoted in an article from the *Liverpool Post* that was republished throughout the South, characterized the South as a "republican aristocracy."[52] The author for *DeBow's Review* who had declared aristocracy the safeguard of liberty even went so far as to claim that southerners were "the most aristocratic people in the world," because "pride of caste, and color, and privilege, makes every white man an aristocrat in feeling."[53] A different author for *DeBow's Review* similarly asserted that a "permanent aristocracy, founded upon the natural diversity of races," gave the South a "vital strength and energy."[54] The hierarchical racial structure of the South lent it the form of aristocracy that conservative southerners believed only benefited the South.

If the South's racial aristocracy provided some of the necessary protection of conservative ideals that would be critical for the elevation of the southern nation, formalizing an aristocracy in emulation of European aristocracies promised even greater benefits to the most extreme of secessionists. Observations of conservative governments in Europe helped to convince some conservatives that the informal southern aristocracy should be made official. For example, George Fitzhugh, writing in *DeBow's Review,* looked to France's many revolutions, and to the turmoil that still plagued the French nation in the wake of the revolutions, to argue that France's attempts to eliminate aristocracy had ended in failure and chaos not once but twice, suggesting the potential superiority of a formal aristocracy. He concluded by pondering whether the informal southern aristocracy, despite being "sufficiently patriotic and conservative in its feelings," held the "powers, privileges, and prerogatives" necessary to "give stability, durability, and good order, to society."[55]

While aristocracy provided one model of a government influenced or tempered by conservatism, monarchy provided a more extreme example of a government that might be free of the liberal impulses that supposedly threatened stability within a republic. A letter to the editor of Little Rock's *Arkansas Gazette* declared, for example, that "I am much surprised to see that you oppose a constitutional Monarchy for the South," largely because "republics are unstable. History proves it beyond a question or a doubt. What Republic ever withstood any intense shock? Was it those of Greece or Rome? Did not that of France go down in anarchy?"[56] If France revealed the harms of lack of monarchy, Italy, which had gained national independence and unity under a monarch, provided a particularly appealing example of the benefits of monarchy. A writer for the *Augusta Chronicle and Sentinel* pointed out that "even now, while we are in danger of losing our Republican institutions, Italy is regaining her liberty under a constitutional king. The fact proves that royalty is not always incompatible with liberty."[57] Similarly, the Scotchman living in Mobile suggested that "sooner than allow the country to be destroyed by emancipation of the negro, we boldly look to a strong government" such as one headed by Queen Victoria or her family (an ironic statement, given Britain's long history of abolition).[58] Analysis of nations abroad proved to some conservative southerners that democracy was neither necessary nor desirable for the southern nation, and that more hierarchical forms of power could provide it with better governance.

As they debated the relative merits of aristocracy and monarchy, not all conservatives or secessionists were convinced that these systems of government should be implemented immediately, however. Some southerners praised the benefits of aristocracy and monarchy both in theory and as enacted abroad but argued that these undemocratic forms of government should be a last resort for the South. For example, one southerner wrote to the editor of the *Augusta Chronicle and Sentinel* that "I am pleased to see you discussing the new form of our government. . . . You are right about a monarchy, if Democracy cannot be made strong enough to protect person, property, and itself. None has yet been made to answer these objects. For person and property have been more insecure in this country than any monarchy of which I have any knowledge." If the United States failed this southerner's qualifications for good governance, the monarchy of Great Britain, in contrast, met his expectations, as "she protects person and property with more fidelity than any Government in the world." Of course, the property with which this southerner was primarily concerned was slavery, made clear through his praise that monarchy's "good faith is so well established that I would feel the institution of slavery under her flag—if she would engage to protect it—was safer than in or out of the American Union."[59] Such a statement willfully ignored the robust tradition of abolition within Great Britain, but the author was willing to engage in such ignorance in order to criticize what he saw as the failure of American democracy to safeguard property. While this author was willing to consider the benefits of monarchy, however, he also held out hope that the strength of democracy would prevail. Although even this moderated monarchism was a minority position among conservative southerners, it reveals the extent to which some secessionists were willing to engage in extreme thought experiments about potential forms of government for the new southern nation. The most conservative of secessionists used an international perspective to argue that more formally conservative governments could be an option, if an option of last resort, for strengthening the South's form of nationalism.

Even as a few conservatives suggested experimentation with monarchy and aristocracy, however, the majority of white southerners remained committed to republicanism. Indeed, for most southern nationalists, an international perspective taught that aristocracy and monarchy were not the desired or necessary forms of governance for the South. For example, the *Augusta Daily Constitutionalist* rebutted its fellow Augusta newspaper, the *Augusta Chronicle and Sentinel,* for supporting monarchy, suggesting divided and defeated Poland as a model for the harms of monarchy. The *Constitutionalist* admitted to problems within the American government but blamed the "weakness" on "violation on the part of the North," such as "the faithlessness of a section hostile in its insane fanaticism to the southern portion of the Republic," meaning that northern abuses of the system, rather than the American system of government itself, required reform.[60] Similarly, even while praising aristocracy, *DeBow's Review* assured readers that "there is no danger that we shall run into monarchy."[61]

Such variations in opinion reveal the centrality of an international perspective to secessionists' conceptions of an independent southern nation. Although a minority, as they debated the formation of a new southern nation the most conservative of southerners found inspiration in the more conservative forms of government they saw abroad. The benefits of limited participation in government would supposedly preserve white liberty, property, and supremacy, building off of a southern heritage of racial aristocracy. Ultimately, however, even these conservatives were not fully convinced that monarchy or aristocracy was the best form of government for the South.

Even if the conservative ideas from Europe were never enacted, an international context helped elite white southerners explore different forms for the southern nation as they undertook the process of creating a new nation. A southern nation, conservatives argued, should avoid the unrestrained liberalism that had spread from Europe to the North and caused the North to betray the original principles of the American nation. While ultimately retaining the republican ideal, conservatives also suggested that monarchies and aristocracies in Europe provided potential models for a more conservative southern nation. Through 1861, an international context helped conservative southerners justify an independent southern nation, as well as develop the political form of that new nation.

An international perspective proved useful for helping white southerners with a wide range of political beliefs support their visions of what the southern nation should be. Responding to concerns with racial hierarchy rather than rights, elite southerners on the most conservative end of the spectrum sought to create a new, conservative form of nationhood that would set the southern nation apart from the unrestrained liberalism that they believed had corrupted nations in Europe as well as national values in the North. Their interpretation of the international context taught these southerners that liberalism, as seen in Europe and the North, was dangerous and that in contrast, conservative ideals strengthened a nation. As conservative southerners sought to explain why the South seceded and what the Confederacy represented, contrasts between the racial hierarchy of southern society and the relative freedom and equality sought in Europe defined the southern effort in nation-building. Building on these comparisons, conservative southerners further deployed an international perspective to argue that southern conservative values created the superior form of nationhood, stripping nationalism of the liberal excesses seen in Europe and purifying it with a more stable, orderly, even aristocratic society and form of republicanism. As conservative southerners made their case for a secession justified by and a southern nationhood premised on conservative values, an international perspective proved critical to their attempts to promote their national vision.

6

Disunion . . . Is Fatal in the End

SOUTHERN UNIONISTS'

INTERNATIONAL PERSPECTIVE

In June 1857, an antislavery advocate from North Carolina self-funded the publication of his new book attacking slavery. Focusing on the ways in which slavery harmed the economy of the South, *The Impending Crisis of the South* by Hinton Rowan Helper helped ignite the growing conflict between the North and South. The widely circulated compendium form, a shortened version of the work that was published in 1859, especially became a center point of the growing debate between proslavery and antislavery interests in the sectionally divided late antebellum United States. With its threats of class warfare by poor whites and of a South subjugated by slavery to an economically stronger North, Helper's book helped set the terms of the intensifying sectional debate that would soon lead to secession. Celebrated by abolitionists such as Horace Greeley for exposing the harms of slavery, and excoriated by southern slaveholders for threatening class war, *The Impending Crisis* exemplified and intensified the growing gulf between the North and South. Demonstrating these extremes, while the new Republican Party adopted Helper's book as campaign material, the book was outlawed throughout the South, with possession of it amounting to a criminal offense.[1] By fueling the rancor between North and South, Helper inadvertently helped push his fellow southerners to secede.

Just as Helper's book intensified the larger debate between North and South, so too did it shape the debate over the proper application of an international perspective to the sectional issues facing the United States. As part of his larger argument that the continuation of slavery would weaken the southern economy and pave the way for northern domination, Helper turned to an international perspective to dramatize the consequences of the preservation of slavery for the South. In the popular compendium version of his work, Helper argued that with slavery out of the way, it would not require the non-slaveholders of the South more than a quarter of a century to bring her up, in all respects, to a glorious equality with the North; nor would it take them much longer to surpass the latter, which is the most vigorous and honorable rival that they have in the world. Three-quarters of a century hence, if slavery is abolished within the next ten years, as it ought to be, the South will, we believe, be as much greater than the North, as the North is now greater than the South. Three-quarters of a century hence, if the South retains slavery, which God forbid! she will be to the North much the same that Poland is to Russia, that Cuba is to Spain, or that Ireland is to England.[2]

With such an incendiary statement, Helper added new fuel to the passionate debate about what an international context predicted about the future of the South within the nation while also proposing an alternative international perspective, one that could be used to oppose the interests of southern slaveholders.

By the time Helper's book became widely read in 1859, the southern elite was well-versed in their preferred method of comparing the South to defeated European nations; since the crisis of 1850, southern opinion-makers had been arguing that the South had to protect slavery at all costs or risk becoming oppressed like defeated peoples such as the Hungarians and Irish, prevented from directing their own national governments. Liberal secessionists expanded on these comparisons by claiming that the new southern nation followed in the footsteps of aspiring but oppressed European nations in seeking self-determination from tyrannical powers. Conservative secessionists created their own international vision of the Confederacy, arguing that the influence of European liberalism led to the growth of abolitionism and therefore the oppression of the South at the hands of the North, and that southern conservatism would purify the doctrines of nationalism from dangerous liberalism. For all these white southerners, however, an international understanding of the South highlighted the importance of preserving slavery, particularly through an independent future for the South. Helper completely subverted these southern comparisons, claiming that it was the continuation, not elimination, of slavery that would create European-style oppression for the South.

Southern nationalists' responses to Helper reveal the extent to which they were deeply invested in their own international visions of the South. Indeed, some southerners pointed to Helper's book, including his international comparison, as an important factor fueling southern secession. For example,

Mississippi writer H. C. Clarke published in his *Confederate States Almanac* a section of Henry Wikoff's letter to Henry John Temple, Lord Palmerston, in which Wikoff attempted to explain the South's secession. Clarke included Wikoff's identification of Helper's book as one of the events causing sectional tension and secession, singling out Helper's claims about the South's becoming Poland or Ireland as one of the most offensive lines that would best allow the "reader to form a correct opinion of the character and object of the work" and its attempt to "inflame the mind of the North against the South."[3] South Carolina politician William D. Porter, using the name "Rutledge," also refuted Helper's international comparison, arguing that Helper was incorrect and that Lincoln's election and the rise of the antislavery Republican Party, not slavery, would create a government worse than the ones oppressing Ireland, Poland, and Italy.[4] For southern secessionists, then, not just Helper's book in general but more specifically his particular accusation that slavery, rather than the limitation thereof, would turn the South into an oppressed Poland or Ireland was nothing less than a key cause of the sectional conflict that had necessitated southern independence.

As Helper's book indicates, secessionists, whether liberal or conservative, were part of a larger debate between white southerners over how best to apply an international context to the sectional conflict and potential nationhood of the South. Although Helper's work was among the more widely distributed examples of a southerner using international comparisons to challenge the prevailing claims of European-style oppression in the South, Helper was not alone among white southerners in developing international comparisons and perspectives that opposed secessionist southerners' views of southern nationhood.

In particular, Unionist southerners, many of whom, unlike Helper, remained committed to slavery even as they retained their loyalty to the United States, joined Helper in pushing back against secessionists' claims that comparisons between the South and aspiring nations in Europe justified secession. As debates about secession raged, southern Unionists sought a solution to the sectional conflict that would avoid secession and allow the South to remain a part of the United States. An international perspective proved as helpful for these Unionists as it did for their secessionist counterparts. For southern Unionists, an international perspective highlighted the horrors of national division and confirmed their overall position that the white South was not oppressed by the North, undermining secessionists' claims to legitimacy. Additionally, southern Unionists' international perspective affirmed that secession would lead to ruin for not only the South and the United States but also the aspiring nations abroad that depended on the United States as a model of republicanism. Thus, southern Unionists' international perspective bolstered their argument that the South should remain in or, after secession, return to the United States.

Significantly, northerners and their allies in Europe likewise participated in the debate over the international meaning of secessionists' actions. The questions of the age, centered on competing meanings of governance and nationhood, stirred men in the North and in Europe as well as in the South, and many of them shared southern Unionists' perspective that the United States must remain united, on the basis of ideology as well as self-interest and national interest. Pro-unity analysts and speakers from within and without the South created an alternative international perspective on southern nationhood, one which argued that an international context taught the necessity of an American national future for the South.

As was the case for secessionists, international comparisons proliferated among southern Unionists during the secession winter of 1860–61, as white southerners sought to make sense out of the crisis of their nationhood. Although secessionists ultimately prevailed in the eleven states of the Confederacy, they faced opposition and criticism, sometimes significant, from white southern Unionists who believed that secession was not the appropriate path for the South and that the South should instead remain within the United States. Southern Unionists occupied challenging political ground, caught between their desire to preserve white southern interests, frequently including slavery, and their conviction that the United States must remain united. The white southerners who struggled with this dilemma and adopted the Unionist perspective were a diverse group with frequently shifting philosophies. In general, nonslaveholders such as Helper were overrepresented in Unionist ranks, as were former Whigs. Many of these southern Unionists still self-consciously shared values and a vision of the nation with northerners, not just with fellow southerners. As such, leading southern Unionists were willing to keep working with the North to seek compromise, a rejection of secessionists' stance that northern antislavery had already made the South a permanent oppressed minority in the nation. Despite this willingness to compromise with a northern vision of the nation, however, southern Unionists also shared many values with their secessionist counterparts, including conservatism, antityranny, and, for many Unionists, a desire to protect slavery. In particular, for all but the most adamant of southern Unionists, ensuring that the North did not coerce the South in the enduring union of the sections was paramount.[5] As southern Unionists evaluated the South during the secession crisis, then, they drew different conclusions than did secessionists, but did so as fellow southerners, seeking what they believed to be the best future for their native region.

Southern Unionists' international comparisons helped them advance their vision of the South's future by supporting their case for the continued unity of the nation, leading them to differ from secessionists on the lessons taught by nation-formation abroad. Resuming the strategies that loyal southerners had used during the crisis of 1850, southern Unionists responded to the crisis of 1860 by pointing to the harms that secession and disunion had created in Europe, and the weakness of the nations and regions that remained after national division. In particular, southern Unionists were concerned that small states lacked the strength to protect themselves against coercion or oppression, either from within or without. For example, the Unionist newspaper the *Fayetteville Observer* approvingly reprinted in March 1861 a speech given by Edward Everett during the crisis of 1850 in which Everett called on his audience to "let Germany teach us" of the harms of disunion which, in Germany, had created hundreds of principalities that "[lay] at the mercy of the nearest despot and strongest army."[6] Furthering this strategy, Waitman Willey, in a letter to the *Clarksville Guard* that the Wheeling, Virginia, *Daily Intelligencer* excerpted, "shudder[ed] whenever I think of disunion," in part due to the "struggles of the Italian states" in the years before they achieved national unity. Such struggles, according to Willey, included the harms of "abject humiliation and political slavery," which forced Italians to "fight their way through the ranks of despots and tyrants to the re-establishment of their ancient national unity and freedom." Given that struggle, Willey despaired that "we are treading the downward road which they are ascending. God help us!"[7] The division of European nations such as Italy and Germany taught southern Unionists that a divided nation was weak, lacking in the ability to self-govern, and vulnerable to tyranny and despotism, bolstering their argument that the South should not secede.

Southern Unionists seeking to use an international perspective in 1860, however, had a benefit that pro-Union southerners of 1850 did not. By 1860, Unionists not only had examples of the harms caused by national division in European nations but also had an example of a new European nation that had benefited from national unification. The new nation of Italy, which united various Italian provinces under the Piedmont king, leading to the declaration of the United Kingdom of Italy in the spring of 1861, provided a powerful and timely example for Unionists as they developed arguments against southern secession and in favor of continued national unity. Even as secessionists were using Italy as an example of a nation formed by secession from multinational empires, their

Unionist counterparts drew the more obvious parallel to the unification of many of the provinces of Italy under one government.

To southern Unionists, Italy's unity had driven out foreign powers such as Austria, granting Italians protection against foreign control of their government and thereby providing strength and stability. Such an example taught that the United States must likewise remain united. For example, North Carolinian Bedford Brown pointed out in the North Carolina legislature that "it was remarkable, as [Italy] was emerging from a long night of bloodshed, disaster and misfortune into a more stable and united government that we were now menaced with the same calamity."[8] Similarly, drawing on examples of both defeated and successful unification attempts in Europe, a citizen of Cecil County, Maryland, with the initials O. P. Q. wrote in the *Cecil Whig* of the ongoing lamentations of Poland after that nation was divided. The writer contrasted Poland's suffering with the victory that a united Italy achieved despite centuries of oppression in order to make the case that Cecil County should stand strong for union.[9] This question of why southerners would want to invite the harms of disunion was particularly resonant to Unionist observers from across the Atlantic; an Italian correspondent for the *Fayetteville Observer* asked, for example, "What but insanity could inspire [South Carolina] *single-handed* to attempt to pull down the noble fabric of our Union," pointing out that "while the Italians are pouring out blood and treasure to *re-unite* their long-severed provinces, the Americans seem preparing for a similar outlay, to dismember their Union. God forbid!"[10] For southern Unionists, Italy provided a firm example of the strength and stability granted by national unity, one that sat in clear juxtaposition with the harms suffered by divided nations such as Germany and Poland and one that therefore undermined the case for secession.

Although southern Unionists drew different conclusions than secessionists about the lessons of unity and disunion abroad, they nonetheless shared a similar political outlook and worldview, as well as mutual national values of liberty, republicanism, and freedom from tyranny. Unionists thus evaluated nationhood, at home and abroad, through the same values as secessionists. They differed, however, in their assessment of how the South and European nationalist movements related to those values. Accordingly, another key difference between secessionists' and southern Unionists' usage of international context was their estimation of how exactly to preserve liberty and self-government, and what exactly constituted the biggest threat of despotism.

Beginning with their reverence for liberty, southern Unionists argued that an international context proved that American unity was necessary for the preservation of liberty, long a cherished southern and American value. For example, Alexander Stephens, a Unionist before he became vice president of the Confederacy, in a widely circulated speech given in the Georgia House of Representatives in November 1860, warned that if secessionists were to destroy the institutions created by the founding fathers, international history taught that such an experiment was doomed to failure, and further, that once the failure was complete, liberty would be destroyed and never returned.[11] Stephens's warning found support among fellow Unionists, who highlighted the despotism that would replace liberty if the South were to succeed in dividing the United States. Indeed, Unionists' discussions of the loss of rights suffered by small, divided states and the protection for rights that unity provided reveal southern Unionists' reliance on these principles to help them build their international case for American unity.

This concern that secession would crush liberty not only echoed the broader southern and American concern with despotism but also revealed another of the major differences between secessionists' and Unionists' applications of an international context to the sectional issues roiling the nation. While many secessionists equated northerners and abolitionists with European-style tyrants, for southern Unionists the secessionists themselves destroyed liberty and created the looming threat of despotism and tyranny at home and abroad. In an expression of this sentiment, a writer using the penname "Shenandoah," writing in to Wheeling's Unionist newspaper the *Daily Intelligencer,* warned his fellow citizens of western Virginia that "if we heedlessly follow in the mad career of the seceding states—link our destiny with theirs, we are doomed to submit to tyranny and oppression, equal to, if not worse than that of any government of Europe."[12] North Carolina state senator David Outlaw likewise "believed that a dissolution of the Union would bring about a most desolating and bloody war, unequalled in history, and that this bleeding country would finally seek repose in the arms of a military despot."[13] Singling out a specific model despot, James S. Clark argued at the Alabama secession convention that if the South were to become a small, independent nation, southerners would be "oppressed to the earth by a system of taxation more intolerable than that of despotic Austria."[14] In the estimation of Unionists, by ignoring the voices of Unionist southerners and bringing about the destruction of war, secessionists, not northerners, would ultimately create European-style oppression throughout the South.

While southern Unionists believed that American unity was necessary for the preservation of liberty and avoidance of secession-created despotism in the United States, they equally believed that protecting the American nation was critical for strengthening and securing liberty abroad, a belief that drew on the American exceptionalism that had led antebellum Americans to see their revolution and republic as models for aspiring republics in Europe. James H. Bell of the Texas Supreme Court, for example, spoke on this belief in a speech delivered at the U.S. Capitol, imploring his audience, "Let us not cast away our glorious inheritance of freedom" because "we have already exerted an immense influence for good in the world. . . . Our example has animated the nations of Europe to contend for their liberties. Let us not now put into the mouths of the friends of arbitrary government, an argument more powerful than a hundred thousand bayonets." To Bell, maintaining the American example was particularly important at this moment, since despots were conferencing in Poland and "asserters of the doctrine of the divine right of Kings, appear to be preparing for a last struggle with the nations who are longing to be free."[15]

The Unionist newspaper the *Staunton Spectator* was a particularly outspoken advocate of the idea that the United States must be preserved as the last hope of self-government, not only at home but also in Europe. A December 1860 letter to the editor of the *Staunton Spectator* expressed such sentiments, with the author asking if sectional strife in the United States would force freedom to fall and liberty to flee elsewhere. The writer, going by the penname "Union," worried that disunion would not only "leave us to struggle with . . . evils of anarchy, or offer up our worship at a despot's throne instead of the altar of freedom," but would also end the "hope of the down trodden millions of Europe."[16] It is little surprise that Union's words were well-received by the editors of the *Spectator*, given that the paper, edited by staunch antisecessionist Richard Mauzy, had already expressed similar concerns. In a report on the assembling of Congress, an editor for the *Spectator* lamented in December that "if this Government be destroyed, the star of hope to the friends of freedom throughout the world will be extinguished. Those nations now striving to establish free Governments will be disheartened and paralyzed. . . . If this Government be perpetuated, it will, by its example, crumble every throne in Europe."[17] Once again in January, the *Spectator* returned to this theme, criticizing disunionists who would "thoughtlessly pull down the pillars of the Temple of Liberty" and "cause the downfall of this Republic, which is the hope of the world." As part of this article, the *Staunton Spectator* approvingly republished a speech by a Judge Story that also described the United States as the "last experiment of self-government by the people."[18] For the editors of the *Staunton Spectator* and other similar-minded southern Unionists, the unity of the United States was necessary for liberty, not just for southerners and Americans but for Europeans as well.

The consequences of disunion according to southern Unionists were grave, limiting liberty and empowering tyranny not only in the South and the United States but also in Europe. Secession, in this perspective, weakened nations and made them easy prey for despotism, as had happened in Germany and Poland; unity, in contrast, as seen in Italy, strengthened nations and their values. Meanwhile, the United States, the model republic, stood as a necessary inspiration for spreading the positive values of nationhood abroad as well as at home. Throughout the debate over secession, southern Unionists utilized an international perspective to claim that the South must remain in the United States in order to protect and uphold white southerners', and Americans', national values, both domestically and internationally.

The opening of the Civil War significantly altered southern Unionists' position. With Lincoln's call to arms following the battle of Fort Sumter, even the previously Unionist-majority Upper South states of Virginia, North Carolina, and Tennessee rapidly embraced secession, convinced that Lincoln's actions did indeed constitute northern violation of the rights of the seceded southern states. Former Unionists became Confederates, including many of the previous leaders of the Unionist movement. With the creation of a functioning Confederate government, the loss of much of their leadership and organizational capacities, and significant community opposition, the minority of white southerners who remained loyal to the United States faced a much more difficult task in advocating for a reunited nation.[19] Despite these challenges, some southern Unionists did not abandon their international perspective, even once their original mission failed. Instead, they turned their attention to developing an explanation for why the Confederate government should be overturned, the political division healed, and national unity restored. An international perspective helped them make this case through the opening months of the Civil War.

In particular, southern Unionists used an international perspective to explain why the now-divided Union was worth reuniting and preserving, particularly through continuing to praise the many virtues of the American republic. In a spring 1861 speech to the Kentucky legislature that was approvingly republished in the *Fayetteville Observer*, John Crittenden exclaimed that "all experience has taught us that we have the best Government in the world," asking, "Where else does liberty appear as she does here?" before pointing to the "little Republics of the old world" as examples of liberty in "tatters and rags," contrasted with the "splendor" of American liberty.[20] Similarly, to emphasize the importance of American institutions abroad as well as at home, "Rover," writing for the *New*

Orleans Picayune, asked, "Does it not seem like 'casting bread into the fire,' to see thus sacrificed by the interests and emotions of the hour, those institutions which it has cost rivers of blood to found in Italy, and for which Venetia, Poland, and Hungary, are still languishing?"[21] The Wheeling *Daily Intelligencer* praised a speech by New Yorker Robert Walker in which Walker echoed the theme that the United States was the last best hope for democracy, stating that the nascent war was "not a question which concerns our country, but all mankind. It is this: shall we by a noble and united effort sustain here republican institutions, or shall we have secession and anarchy to be succeeded by despotism, and extinguish forever the hopes of freedom throughout the world?"[22]

Even as southern Unionists during the opening months of the war pointed to the critical importance of the continued existence of the United States for the future of liberty and republicanism, they also expanded their analysis of the threat of despotism and tyranny that the southern nation created. Southern Unionists had been convinced, as far back as the crisis of 1850, that disunion paved the way for the harms of tyranny. Now, faced with the reality of that disunion, they took the logical step of arguing that the European-style tyranny they feared disunion would bring had, in fact, been established by the Confederacy.

In particular, prominent Tennessee Unionist William Brownlow embraced the theme of the Confederacy as not only a tyrant but the worst tyrant in history. Editor of the Unionist *Brownlow's Knoxville Whig,* Brownlow was one of the leaders of the southern Unionist cause and remained staunchly committed to the United States throughout the war. He translated his leadership into a career in politics that led him to become the first post-Confederacy governor of Tennessee.[23] As Brownlow used his considerable platform to advocate for unionism, he endorsed international comparisons of the tyranny enacted by the Confederacy. Such comparisons focused on what Unionists saw as the illegitimate nature of Confederate power, which derived from the support of only a portion of the white southern electorate. Accordingly, to Unionists such as Brownlow, the tyrannical Confederacy stripped southern Unionists of their self-government. In one expression of this sentiment, a March 1861 advertisement for Brownlow's campaign for governor (a race from which he later withdrew) explained that the Confederate States was "not a *government of the people,* and it will not long be tolerated by the people. The people, *who ought to be the source of power,* have been refused the privilege of passing upon any one of their ordinances of Secession, and now they are to be refused the privilege of passing upon their Constitution. I would sooner go into the worst form of European monarchy than into this *bogus* Confederacy."[24] To Brownlow, the secessionists were a minority, and rule by a minority was as illegitimate and oppressive as rule by a European monarch.

Brownlow returned to this theme throughout his career and the war, adding new rights violations to his list of tyrannical actions carried out by the Confederacy. In August 1861, an editor for *Knoxville Whig,* likely Brownlow himself, exclaimed that Jefferson Davis's proclamation urging non-Confederate citizens to leave the state of Tennessee constituted a "species of despotism and tyranny, more hateful, and more infamous, than ever disgraced the Government of un-principled Russia."[25] When Confederate occupation forced him to close the *Whig* in October 1861, Brownlow railed against the tyranny of limiting freedom of the press, calling on his patrons to "bear me witness . . . that I have yielded to a military despotism" which created harms worse than the "wrongs" and "out-rages" that produced the French Revolution.[26] Not only was the Confederacy tyrannical in Brownlow's estimation, however; so too was it corrupt. In a May 1861 letter to a Marylander he identified only as a Breckinridge Democrat with the initials L. M. E., Brownlow argued that the real cause of secession, the Civil War, and the creation of the Confederacy was that "corrupt politicians and bad men in the South, who had long controlled the Government" wanted to reverse what they saw as "the loss of the offices, power, and patronage of the Govern-ment." With this corruption at the root of the secession, Brownlow asserted that he could never support such a cause, pointing to the anarchy that had resulted when similar men with similar motives had gained power abroad.[27] This com-parison clearly shows that to Brownlow, the Confederacy was not an expression of the will of the people; instead, it was a tyrannical government forced on the people from above by a corrupt elite seizing power for themselves and therefore subverting the true principle of self-government.

Following Brownlow's lead, the idea that the Confederacy was the worst des-pot in history became widespread as southern Unionists sought to contextualize their new status during the opening months of the Civil War. John Carlile, speak-ing at the West Virginia secession convention in May 1861, asked, "When has there ever been in the whole records of the past such an utter contempt, on the part of any despot, for the people, as has been exhibited here in what was once free Virginia, by the Richmond Convention?"[28] Echoing this concern with the despotic nature of Virginia's decision to secede, "Grafton" wrote to the Whee-ling *Daily Intelligencer* that the "Virginia Convention have all along professed great horror at the thought of invasion by 'Black Republicans' from the North; but they say not a word against invasion by the disunionists and traitors from the South," adding that "such despotism was never heard of before in a civilized nation."[29] By forcing disunion on the South and the nation, and disregarding the desires of pro-Union southerners, southern Unionists argued, the Confederacy inaugurated a despotism worse than any the world had previously seen.

While the equation of Confederates with international and historical despotic powers, along with the celebration of the glorious virtues of the United States as compared to the rest of the world, created fairly straightforward international comparisons for southern Unionists to use, the adoption of an international perspective was not always this straightforward for Unionists. Being a Unionist was, in itself, often a complicated position for white southerners, as some southern Unionists found themselves torn between their desire to preserve both slavery and the United States, while others struggled to reconcile their loyalty to their hometowns and states with their loyalty to the nation. Such contradictions were reflected in the ways that southern Unionists adopted an international perspective to help them make sense out of a shifting southern nationhood.

Southern Unionists' usage of an international perspective reveals in particular that while they supported a restored United States, they did not always support all actions taken by the wartime U.S. government. Specifically, southern Unionists frequently evinced concern that, while the South should not have seceded, forceful subjugation by the North would not achieve the Unionists' goal of a reunited nation and instead would create even greater harm than disunion had. Turning to their international perspective, southern Unionists argued that for the United States to overextend its power would re-create the oppression faced by defeated European nations.

Pamphleteer Anna Ella Carroll, a former slaveholder and antisecessionist from Maryland, was one southern Unionist who believed that potential northern violation of white southerners' rights created the possibility that the North would, in seeking to reunite the nation, subjugate the South. In her pamphlet *The War Powers of the General Government,* Carroll focused on the right to property, writing that "the proposed general confiscation of Southern property is as repugnant to the rules of expediency as it is to that of constitutional power. . . . It is a proposal to make the Southern States forever what Ireland is to England, what Italy has been to Austria, what Poland has been to Russia."[30] Of course, slavery was the most common form of property that white southerners sought to protect against northern interference.

More commonly, southerners who remained loyal to the United States spoke of concern that military force, wielded by the United States to control the South, would ultimately crush liberty. Lazarus W. Powell of Kentucky, a U.S. senator and outspoken critic of the Lincoln administration despite his policy of neutrality regarding secession, in a July 1861 speech in the Senate, praised Stephen Douglas's argument that military tyrants throughout history justified their despotism by relying on their claim to governmental authority. Powell quoted Douglas, saying, "When, in 1848, the people rose upon their tyrants all over Europe and demanded guarantees for their rights, every crowned head exclaimed, 'Have we a government?' and appealed to the army to vindicate their authority and enforce the law," and yet "history does not record an example where any human government has been strong enough to crush ten million people into subjection when they believed their rights and liberties were imperiled without first converting the government itself into a despotism, and destroying the last vestige of freedom." Powell went on to make clear that such a statement "fully meets my approval."[31] Similarly, Colonel Benjamin Gratz Brown, a leading voice for union in the border state of Missouri, argued in a speech that

> if the [United States] is determined to found its dominion over subjugated states not in the name of a principle that shall assimilate its conquests and assure their liberties, but of simple power—then will it place itself, by its own action, in the attitude of other and equally gigantic powers that have attempted the same work and failed. . . . Does not Poland, as fully alive to-day, after ninety years of forcible suppression, as on the morning of the first partition, convince us that this thing of the dominion of power . . . can only continue upon condition of an ever-recurring application of those forces that achieved the first reduction? Does not the uprising and cry for a united Italy, after five hundred years . . . of continuous conflict, tell . . . how faithful to freedom are peoples, and how certain the retribution [against government policies]?[32]

Although men like Powell and Brown opposed the division of the United States, they also opposed any actions by the United States that would subjugate the South with military force, as such military subjugation inherently limited the rights and self-government of the people. Furthermore, as Brown predicted, such subjugation would be ineffective, as European examples proved that the spirit of freedom would remain strong, even among oppressed and defeated southerners. As southern Unionists at the outbreak of the Civil War grappled with the tension between supporting the United States and challenging its actions, an international context provided useful perspective for understanding even the thorniest issues of American nationhood.

For southern Unionists, as for secessionists, an international perspective was an invaluable tool for navigating secession, the creation of the Confederacy, and the beginning of a civil war. Even though southern Unionists sometimes held complicated views of the government they sought to preserve, international comparisons provided them with a language for expressing their concerns. Looking abroad helped southern Unionists affirm their beliefs that unity was a critical national value and that disunion led to harmful consequences, particularly the loss of liberty and the rise of despotism, thereby helping these southern Unionists make their case that the South belonged within the American nation.

While elite southerners, both secessionist and Unionist, fiercely debated each other over the best form of southern nationhood and what an international perspective revealed about that question, they were not alone in their discussions. Northerners shared a desire to preserve the unity of the United States, as did many Europeans. Just as secessionists using a liberal international perspective had received support from pro-secession northerners and Europeans, so too did southern Unionists share ideas and beliefs with the majority of northerners and Europeans who sought or supported the preservation and reunion of the American nation. As pro-Union northerners and Europeans analyzed the issues presented by the American Civil War, they, like southern Unionists, used international comparisons to criticize the action of secession, explain the Confederacy's failure to represent a legitimate form of national government, and celebrate the proper national values exhibited by the United States.[33] In doing so, these northerners and Europeans granted legitimacy, or at least support, to southern Unionists' own vision of the proper national future for the South, one that had the South remaining within the United States.

Sharing southern Unionists' conviction that an international context pointed to the harms of national disunion, pro-Union Europeans drew on their own history to make a case for unity as a critical national value.[34] For pro-Union Europeans, the developing norms of nation-building in the nineteenth century precluded the possibility of forming a valid nation through the illegitimate means of national division. In speeches and open letters, European leaders including British prime minister Lord Palmerston and Italian general Giuseppe Garibaldi drew attention to the suffering Italy had experienced while divided, contrasted with the benefits that newly united Italy now enjoyed.[35] National division would not only harm the United States, however; taking such a comparison even further, Chevalier Joseph Bertinatti, the foreign minister from the new Italian nation, worried that disunion in the United States would reverse any progress toward national unity and freedom in Europe by causing disunion to spread, potentially even destroying the new Italian unity.[36] Similarly, German immigrant Elias Peissner extolled the virtues of unity both abroad and in his new American homeland, arguing that even secessionists "can not . . . remain blind to the immeasurable advantages of a common Union, and the unavoidable injuries and calamities arising from Disunion," turning to an international perspective to support his case. "Germany," Peissner pointed out, "is panting for unity, and had made the preparatory steps for its accomplishment. Italy has inaugurated a more poetical and radical method of reaching the same." Not only did new and aspiring nations in Europe prove the benefits of unity, however; to Peissner, the international context also "clearly shows that Disunion of parts that properly belong together, is fatal in the end. There is Holland, formerly so powerful, and Belgium . . . and the Italian republics."[37] For many Europeans who examined the threat of southern secession through the lens of their own history, secession and national disunion created only harm and therefore should not constitute a valid method of nation-building.

Many northerners shared these Europeans' concerns that national division led to dire consequences. Union general John E. Wool argued as early as the fall of 1860 that South Carolina's threats of secession must indicate an ignorance of the age of progress being created by nationalists such as Garibaldi.[38] Prominent abolitionist Henry Ward Beecher shared this conviction. For Beecher, the South's constant demands for political power and protection of slavery promised to prevent the abolitionist North from entering the emerging "age of liberty," raising such questions as, "While France and Italy, Germany and Russia, are advancing toward the dawn, shall we recede toward midnight? From this grand procession of nations, with faces lightened by liberty, shall we be missing?"[39] This was not a one-time thought for Beecher; he returned to the topic again at a meeting in Glasgow, arguing passionately that the tyranny of slavery, secession, and war worked to destroy the liberty sought in Italy, Poland, and even the United States.[40] To Beecher and like-minded northerners, secession harmed not just the United States but, more importantly, the larger age of progress and liberty.

While Wool and Beecher were concerned with the retreat of liberty caused by national disunity, other northerners focused on what would be left in the wake of that retreat, echoing southern Unionists' concerns that as secession and slavery caused liberty to recede, they would leave despotism in their place. Edward Everett, for example, pointed to the despotism that thrived in the many small principalities of divided Germany.[41] The *New York Times* similarly argued in an article republished in the Wheeling, Virginia, *Daily Intelligencer* that southern secession destroyed democracy and re-created European-style despotism.[42] For these men, the nineteenth century was a period defined by questions about nationhood, rights, and citizenship; when they viewed secession through that lens, they believed that an international context proved southern secession to be on the wrong side of history in an era of increasing efforts to establish freedom and democracy.

Expanding this argument, many pro-Union Europeans and northerners believed that, contrary to Confederate claims, secessionists were not only following an illegitimate path to nationhood but that their national cause likewise failed to adhere to the proper model exhibited by aspiring nations in Europe. Even as secessionists argued that they deserved legitimacy because they fought for the same causes as those of aspiring European nations, many observers outside the South disavowed such a similarity, pointing out instead that the southern revolution did not resemble European nationalist revolutions. Getting at the heart of the ideological problem that threatened secessionists' comparisons, many Europeans recognized that the South had no true claim or cause that would justify an independent southern nation, as the defense of slavery was incompatible with the ideology of freedom and liberty that inspired European revolutions.

Recognizing the clear difference between the cause of slavery and the cause of freedom fought for by aspiring European nations, William L. Hodge, for example, published an article from the *London Economist* that exclaimed,

> There is something truly astounding in the infatuations which seem to possess the politicians in the Southern States of America. They have not only persuaded themselves into something that has all the *strength,* if not the intellectual *weight* of a moral conviction, that the cause of Slavery is a holy and sacred cause in which they who suffer loss are heroes and martyrs,— but they also have fully persuaded themselves that all who differ from them are the unfortunate subjects of a mere fanciful hallucination which the slightest pressure of real self-interest will dissipate at once. They seem to really believe that *England is as ready to support them, if they can but offer her sufficient interested motive for doing so,* as she would be, for similar inducements, to sustain Italy against Austria or Prussia against France.[43]

The *Economist* was not alone in its belief in the lack of similarity between the Confederate cause and that of other aspiring nations. A translation of a German newspaper article printed in the *Charleston Mercury* declared of the South, "We observe very little of the convulsions of a wounded nationality—such for instance as vibrate to this day in the heart of Poland. . . . To be sure, there is no lack of animosity and passion, but it is an animosity more like that existing between quarrelling partners in business."[44] While secessionists, Confederates, and their foreign and northern supporters deluded themselves into claiming that the cause of the southern nation was the same as that which had inspired nations such as Italy to seek independence, many Europeans clearly saw the reality of the incompatibility of the causes and the dissimilarity between the southern and European nationalist movements, using an international perspective to argue that the Confederacy did not meet the international standards of nationhood.

To further make their case that the Confederacy did not meet the standard of nationhood, pro-Union northerners and Europeans explicitly disavowed the right to revolution in the southern case. This argument drew in part on precedence; the model of Ireland's unsuccessful attempts to remove itself from Great Britain proved particularly useful for northerners and Europeans seeking to explain why southerners could not simply decide to divide the nation. For example, A. J. Cline argued that if each state had the right to follow its own "self-willed presumption" in leaving the nation, "such a doctrine would leave us without law, without authority, and without a government. It would reduce us to a pitiful association of petty independent sovereignties, where there would be no order, because there would be no controlling influence—where there would be no strength, because there would be no union." Cline then urged his readers to "take the United Kingdom of Great Britain for instance. . . . Supposing that Ireland should express a determination to secede . . . and should take up with arms the view to accomplish this purpose, and to form a separate government on her own. Would this be tolerated by the other parties to the compact? Would not the whole world pronounce such a movement rebellious and unconstitutional?"[45] Similarly, English minister and abolitionist Christopher Newman Hall made a clear distinction between the right to rebellion, which he accepted as an international principle, and the right to secession, which he viewed as invalid. As Newman Hall explained, a "right to *rebellion*" could exist "in case of glaring abuse of power" which created "gross injustice" and tyranny that was "unendurable," with Italy standing as an example of a nation that had successfully exercised that right. For Newman Hall, however, there was no "constitutional right of *secession*," and the South did not meet the standards of the right to rebellion, as "the South were not oppressed, were not unrepresented."[46] As these Unionist northerners and Europeans recognized, no right to secession existed in the United States, and the South was not oppressed and therefore not justified in claiming a right to rebellion.

Northerners and Europeans who opposed the southern nation by arguing that the Confederacy did not meet the qualifications of nationhood did not stop with their criticism of secession and the Confederate cause of slavery. As southern Unionists had after the outbreak of war, northerners and Europeans likewise shifted their argumentation to more directly attack the Confederacy and Confederates themselves. Deviating slightly from the position of southern Unionists, who were after all still white southerners, pro-Union northerners and Europeans focused their criticism on what they saw as the aristocratic and therefore inherently harmful nature of the Confederacy and of slaveholding southern society. Thomas Shepard Goodwin, for example, stated that "slaveholders at home and monarchists abroad united by a felt sympathy and oneness of interest in their desire to assault and ruin democracy wherever it presented itself."[47] August Willich, a German veteran of the revolutions of 1848 and an officer for the army of the United States, likewise equated the aristocracy of the Confederacy with the aristocrats he had fought in Germany.[48] Because aristocracy violated the principles of governance sought by the United States and aspiring European nations, these northerners and Europeans argued, the Confederacy presented an illegitimate expression of nationhood.

Drawing the logical political conclusions from the illegitimacy of the Confederacy, pro-Union Europeans also used an international perspective to argue against international diplomatic recognition of the new southern nation. Indeed, the majority position in Europe opposed intervention in the American Civil War, and no European nation granted diplomatic recognition to the Confederacy. Although the primary concerns that prevented European nations from recognizing the Confederacy centered on desire to avoid war, many British citizens in particular also opposed the centrality of slavery to the Confederacy. By pointing out the contradiction between the defense of slavery and broader international liberal principles, an international perspective proved useful to Europeans seeking to explain their opposition to recognizing the Confederacy. Frenchman Agenor de Gasparin, for example, declared that while there were some cases, such as Italy, in which a new nation deserved independence from foreign powers, the Confederacy, "which proposes to break up a great, free nation, and to compensate the human race by presenting to it an ideal State based on slavery," was not one of those cases, and thus the idea of recognition of the Confederacy was a "pretension which Europe owes it to herself to repulse with indignation."[49] For men like Gasparin, the Confederacy's defense of slavery automatically disqualified it from representing the same causes of liberal nationalism that had led to success in nations such as Italy, and thus the new southern nation did not deserve international recognition.

Despite secessionists' claims that they deserved legitimacy and recognition because they followed in the footsteps of new and aspiring European nations, significant numbers of northerners and Europeans were not fooled. For Confederates and their supporters who asserted that the southern nation was legitimate in part because it followed the model of nation-building exhibited by more liberal aspiring nations in Europe, such conclusions by pro-Union Europeans were deeply damaging. Confederate success depended in part on white southerners' ability to convince an international audience of the legitimacy of the new southern nation. For northerners and Europeans to use the same model of international comparisons and context to delegitimize, rather than support, the Confederacy directly invalidated Confederates' own international perspectives.

Even as anti-Confederate northerners and Europeans used an international perspective to criticize and delegitimize the Confederacy, they also deployed this perspective to defend the unity and legitimacy of the United States itself, endorsing the arguments that southern Unionists used to praise the national values of the United States and thus defend its national unity. In particular, the image of the United States as a critical beacon of liberty to the rest of the world echoed as powerfully in the North as it did among southern Unionists. Charles Sumner evoked the glory of a forward-looking United States in the aftermath of the election of 1860, celebrating that "persons everywhere who are struggling for rights, who are vindicating liberal ideas, who are seeking human improvement, will be encouraged when they hear of [Lincoln's victory]. It will be good news to Garibaldi in Italy; it will be good news to the French, who are now suffering under despotic power; and it will be, my friends, good news to all of us."[50] With the United States constituting such a critical aspect of democracy worldwide, it only stood to reason that the destruction of that nation would likewise destroy democracy abroad. Author, minister, and politician Daniel C. Eddy explained this worst-case scenario, declaring, "Destroy this government, and you destroy the grandest hope of liberty; you extinguish the light which is beckoning on the enslaved millions of Italy, Hungary, Turkey and Poland to constitutional freedom."[51] While an international perspective taught many northerners that secession and the Confederacy were contrary to the liberal nationalism being established throughout Europe, this perspective also taught that the United States exemplified the same values sought in Europe, to the point that the unity of the United States was necessary for the advance of these virtues abroad.

Among the most frequent northern and foreign voices joining with southern Unionists to use an international perspective to celebrate the proper American expression of nationhood were those of foreign-born Union soldiers. Foreign-born soldiers, particularly from Germany and Ireland, along with their sons, constituted over 40 percent of U.S. troops during the Civil War.[52] Speaking from experience in both Europe and the United States, these men used their personal international perspectives to actively compare the national values they had fought for, or at least desired, in their homelands and the national values they fought for in defending the United States. As German revolutionary and Union recruiter Franz Sigel stated, "When I saw that the same great principles to whose defense I had devoted my life were at stake here, I did not hesitate to embrace the cause of the Union with all the power of my soul."[53] Leading Irish patriot Thomas Meagher evinced similar beliefs, urging his fellow Irishmen to join the fight for the United States, as the Irish "aspire to establish a similar form of government in our native land."[54] Less well-known foreign-born Union soldiers shared this conviction that they fought for the same cause in the United States as they had abroad, with Irish immigrant Peter Welsh, for example, exclaiming that "when we are fighting for America we are fighting in the interest of irland striking a double blow cutting with a two edged sword for while we strike in defence of the rights of Irishmen here we are striking a blow at irlands enemy and oppressor."[55] Indeed, historians have identified such comparisons as one of the common sources of motivation for foreign-born soldiers to fight for the United States.[56]

Building on their belief in the similarity between the values of the United States and the values of their defeated nations at home, these Union soldiers expanded the discourse on the United States as the "last best hope" of democracy for the world by arguing that fighting for the United States would directly protect and expand the values of liberty and freedom in their homelands. Even as Sigel equated the values of the United States with the values of Germany, for example, he also argued that "this great republic is the last refuge of liberty . . . for free men of Europe."[57] The Irish took this argument the furthest, with members of the radical nationalist organization the Fenians claiming that the military experience they gained in the Civil War would enable them to defeat Great Britain and achieve Irish independence after the conclusion of the American Civil War. In a succinct summary of this belief, James McKay Rorty stated that "the military knowledge or skill which I may acquire . . . might thereafter be turned to account in the sacred cause of my native land."[58] As with the idea that the United States fought for the same values as nationalists in Europe had, historians have identified this belief in the Civil War as a military training ground as a major motivation for Irish to join the U.S. Army.[59]

Many of the immigrant soldiers who fought for the North had experienced firsthand the kind of oppression, tyranny, and defeat that Americans—secessionist, Unionist, and northern alike—feared. Based on that experience, combined with their knowledge of liberty in their new nation of the United States, foreign-born Union soldiers used their international perspective to argue forcefully that the United States, not the Confederacy, represented the desired national values of liberty and freedom, and therefore must be preserved. In doing so, they joined their voices with those of Unionist southerners to claim that an international perspective indicated that the only way to preserve southerners' cherished values was through the national unity of the United States.

In the debate over the meaning of nationhood and the proper form of nationhood for the South, pro-Union northerners and foreigners, including foreign-born soldiers, shared the international perspective that southern Unionists utilized to defend the United States. These northerners and Europeans argued that the Confederacy failed to reach the necessary standards of nationhood due to the harms of secession and the lack of justifying oppression, and that the United States instead represented the world's best example of and hope for the liberty and democracy sought in Europe. Furthermore, many of these northern and European speakers made it clear that beyond any general harms created by national division, the Confederacy's specific defense of slavery disqualified the aspiring southern nation from following in the footsteps of liberal nationalist movements in Europe. This Unionist international perspective thwarted Confederate claims to legitimacy and advanced an alternate view of the war in which the United States was the only legitimate nation. In adopting this perspective, pro-Union northerners and Europeans helped legitimize and spread the same international perspective that southern Unionists used to push for a national future for the South that preserved the South's place within the American nation.

As white southerners debated secession and the creation of the new southern nation in 1860 and 1861, both sides developed and deployed international perspectives to support their visions of the proper form of nationhood for the South. Unionist southerners, aided by their allies in the North and Europe, argued that an international context taught that secession was harmful for liberty, and that national unity was necessary for the preservation of liberty and prevention of tyranny. With this formulation established, secessionists and Confederates became tyrants, subverting not only American and southern national values at home and abroad but also utilizing an illegitimate path to and form of nationhood. As southern Unionists and their supporters sought to strengthen their case for continued national unity, an international perspective proved critical to their attempts to define and defend their position.

The universality of an international perspective on secession and southern nationalism, deployed by southern Unionists and pro-Union northerners and Europeans as well as secessionists and Confederates and their allies, reveals the centrality of an international context to southerners' and Americans' understanding of their nationhood through the winter of secession and the early months of the Civil War. While white southerners deployed a variety of international perspectives, however, not all perspectives were equally valid or as widely popular. The national visions promoted by these perspectives were often mutually exclusive; not all groups of white southerners could be successful in using an international perspective to build their ideal southern nation. As the war wore on, many elite white southerners would increasingly be faced with this reality and forced to deal with the challenges that threatened their international perspectives.

PART IV

Wartime Realities, 1861–1865

Wartime changed the realities shaping white southerners' international perspectives. Secession was a *fait accompli* instead of a topic of debate. The southern nation had ceased being a hypothetical on which any number of hopes or national visions could be projected and was now an existing entity, defined by its actions rather than solely by the dreams and desires of its creators. Fighting and winning a war, rather than winning support for the idea of disunion, became the primary focus of the new southern nation. Meanwhile, southern Unionists faced actual, rather than merely possible, national disunion. As both United States and Confederate States turned to military action to defend their vision of the nation, the endless possibilities of late 1860 through mid-1861 gave way to the sobering reality of war.

In this new reality, the actual shape, characteristics, and actions of the southern nation, as well as the reception it received internationally, challenged the visions of nationhood that white southerners had been promoting through their international perspectives during the secession debates and creation of the Confederacy. Most notably, southern Unionists' vision of a South still joined to the United States was destroyed, at least temporarily. With the nation divided, southern Unionists feared the United States would indeed suffer the harms of disunion faced by defeated nations abroad and could no longer serve as a beacon of republicanism to the international community. The suffering of war additionally provided support for southern Unionists' claims that the Confederacy created a European-style tyranny.

Despite their success in achieving their goal of an independent southern nation, secessionists—now Confederates—likewise confronted a wartime reality that did not necessarily follow from their prewar national vision. Confederates who adopted the liberal international perspective were faced with an actual southern nation that did not, in fact, follow the model of nationhood and nation-building presented by European nationalist movements. In particular, the Confederacy's failure to achieve the diplomatic recognition that the liberal international perspective had predicted, combined with the possibility of Italian nationalist Giuseppe Garibaldi fighting for the United States, disproved Confederates' self-comparisons with Garibaldi and Italy, which had received diplomatic recognition. Instead of rejecting their international perspective as invalid or of no utility, however, Confederates recommitted themselves to manipulating the ideals of nationalism, as well as its symbols such as Garibaldi, in order to continue their attempts to reconcile southern slavery with liberal nationalism.

Confederates who adopted the conservative international perspective found that the actual Confederacy better upheld the slavery-based conservatism they had predicted during secession, and yet they were equally thwarted by lack of Confederate success. Having received no international appreciation for their supposedly glorious new form of nationhood, conservative Confederates turned to conservative European nations, increasingly putting their desperate hopes on the pope and empires such as Austria to provide the recognition that was not forthcoming from more liberal European nations. Ultimately, however, even this effort fell through, and looming national defeat disproved the claim that the Confederacy would be the purest, most ideal nation in the world.

Moving from the hypothetical into reality thus forced elite white southerners to respond in order to defend the international perspectives that they had used to advocate for their vision of the South's national future during secession and the creation of the Confederacy. Despite the fact that wartime developments fundamentally threatened the foundations of all three international perspectives, however, white southerners proved remarkably loyal to the international visions they had developed in 1860 and early 1861. Instead of accepting that their international perspectives were flawed, white southerners redoubled their defense of their international visions. Making whatever ideological manipulations were necessary, these southerners remained committed to using their international perspectives to define and defend their visions of the South's nationhood throughout the Civil War, revealing the critical importance of an international context to white southerners' ongoing and evolving conceptions of southern nationhood.

7

Of What Avail Are the Appeals of the South

THE EVOLUTION OF THE LIBERAL CONFEDERATE INTERNATIONAL PERSPECTIVE

In the spring of 1861, even as southern nationalists constructed the Confederate States of America, rumors began spreading throughout the Atlantic world about a possible alliance between the United States and leading Italian nationalist Giuseppe Garibaldi. Anticipating war between the United States and the Confederacy, these rumors suggested that Garibaldi, who white southerners had long admired as an exemplar of their own national values, would come lead the Union's fight against the national independence of the South. Given Garibaldi's long career as an adventurer and nationalist in Brazil and Uruguay as well as in Italy, such rumors seemed plausible—at least, to observers outside the nascent Confederacy.[1] To Confederates, however, particularly those who had used the liberal international perspective to claim that the new southern nation followed in the footsteps of Garibaldi's own Italy, the rumors were of great concern. Unless white southerners could somehow disprove a connection between Garibaldi and the United States, that connection threatened the southern self-image of the Confederacy as the latest example of a new nation, similar to Italy, aspiring to membership in the international community of nations.

Journalist and Irish nationalist John Mitchel, now actively supporting the Confederacy, helped set the tone for southern commentators' responses to the Garibaldi rumor. In April 1861, Mitchel, writing as a foreign correspondent for the *Charleston Mercury*, stated bluntly of Garibaldi, "I trust he will not go." Instead of basing this belief on an analysis of the very real issues facing Confederate diplomacy and claims to Italian-style nationalism alike, however, Mitchel chose to mock Garibaldi, the very man that his white southern audience had long admired and respected. Marking a sharp shift away from that positive vision of Garibaldi, Mitchel purported that "one would sincerely regret to hear of our gallant Italian being locked up in a Southern calaboose, as he certainly would be—or summarily lynched by Carolinian citizens. Should he really go, however, I venture to beg for his life—for the sake of what he has elsewhere done; do not hang him, but, after having given him four dozen, send him back to us . . . a sadder and wiser man."[2] In Mitchel's view, although Garibaldi's previous career was still noble and deserved esteem, a Garibaldi willing to consider an alliance with the United States became a target of ridicule and even violence rather than respect. And while elite southerners had long seen Garibaldi as effective as well as virtuous in the cause of nationalism, should Garibaldi fight against the Confederacy, Mitchel hypothesized, he would finally find the limit to his military abilities as well; he was so inferior to South Carolinians that the latter would humiliate and destroy the hitherto-great military general.

With this remaking of the image of Garibaldi, Mitchel represented a broader shift in the ways that elite white southerners utilized their international perspectives as the excitement of secession gave way to the discouraging realities of war. Self-comparisons, such as those praising the positive virtues supposedly shared by Garibaldi and southern leaders, became more complicated as wartime developments disproved these connections. Garibaldi's willingness to fight for the United States against the Confederacy represented one such complication, but Confederates' issues went beyond just Garibaldi. The liberal international perspective that secessionists had developed in order to justify a southern nation as following in the footsteps of aspiring nations in Europe was fundamentally premised on the idea that the new southern nation would share its values and methods of nation-building with nationalist movements in Europe. As such, the liberal international perspective was built on a falsehood. A nation conceived to preserve slavery, even one purporting to establish a republic, did not share the same values of equality and freedom that had motivated European nationalists. Further, secession from a republic, especially over the results of a fair, democratic election, was certainly not the same method of nation-building as a rebellion against a multinational empire controlled by a foreign monarch. Political and ideological reality disproved the fantasy advocated by proponents of the liberal international perspective.

Despite the fact that the Confederacy's illiberal emphasis on slavery and limited democracy was ideologically dissimilar from liberal nationalism's emphasis on natural rights, liberty, and freedom, however, for Confederates who had endorsed the liberal international perspective, the vision of the Confederacy as an equal among the family of nations was a key aspect of their new national identity. In order to preserve this sense of the Confederacy as part of a larger trend of liberal nationalism, Confederates were forced to manipulate not only the definition of liberal nationalism, as they had proven willing to do at least since their analysis of the revolutions of 1848, but also the contemporary symbols and ideals that represented liberal nationalism to both domestic and foreign audiences during the years of the Civil War. As Mitchel's response to the Garibaldi rumors reveals, Confederates did just that. In the face of opposition, instead of changing tactics, Confederates redefined and remade the ideals and symbols of nationalism in order to continue defending the Confederacy as the newest member of the international community of nations.

Wartime brought new realities and pressing needs to the new southern nation, leading Confederates who had previously defended secession by claiming that a southern nation would emulate aspiring European nations to now use the same international comparisons to defend and legitimize the Confederacy itself. As during secession, such comparisons focused on the supposedly tyrannical nature of the North, oppressing the Confederacy just as European empires had oppressed aspiring nationalities. Demonstrating the continued resonance of international comparisons, for example, the idea that the North was as tyrannical as European despots was so well-known by 1864 that even the Confederate Congress could assume that these comparisons were understood, as when they informed their citizens that "the past, or foreign countries, need not be sought unto to furnish illustrations" of the "shame" and tyranny that would result should the United States prevail.[3]

Having reaffirmed that their enemy was the worst tyrant the world had witnessed, wartime Confederates likewise continued to argue that the Confederacy, in contrast with the United States and in emulation of aspiring nations in Europe, best upheld the national values that white southerners had identified as desirable during the revolutions of 1848. Liberty and self-government—narrowly defined as synonymous with national independence in order to avoid the implications of radical liberty for a slave society—remained among the values Confederates claimed they, like aspiring European nations, represented. For example, the *Richmond Daily Dispatch* reported in 1862 that because the South fought for its freedom, it would be "enshrined in the sympathies and respect of all lovers of liberty and national independence by the side of chivalric Hungary and heroic Poland."[4] John L. O'Sullivan, the journalist who originated the term "Manifest Destiny," also embraced this idea. Despite long being entrenched in antebellum northern politics, O'Sullivan supported the Confederacy after the outbreak of war. He utilized his wartime residency in Lisbon and London and his background as a journalist to publish pro-Confederate pamphlets in London in an effort to spread southern propaganda throughout

Europe. Supporting the values of the Confederacy, O'Sullivan declared that to deny white southerners the choice of their government was to "blaspheme our very Declaration of Independence . . . to sanction all the despotisms . . . to justify the tenure of writhing and bleeding Poland, by Russia, at this very moment."[5] Throughout the war, Confederates and their supporters continued to use international comparisons of national values to claim that the Confederacy deserved independence, not only because it fought against a European-style despot but also because it exhibited the same values of liberty, self-government, and republicanism admired in new and aspiring European nations.

Although many Confederates remained convinced that their project in nation-building followed the model presented by nationalist movements in Europe, however, the majority of the rest of the world assessed the place of the Confederacy within the international community of nations differently, thereby implicitly disproving Confederates' international comparisons and forcing Confederates to adjust their strategy. Among the earliest and most difficult of these wartime events for Confederates to process within their more liberal international vision of the Confederacy was the invitation for Garibaldi to come fight for the United States.

Garibaldi had always been particularly appealing to elite southerners looking for a heroic model of nationalism abroad, from his romanticized defeat in the revolutions of 1848 to his glorious victory in uniting Sicily to Italy in 1860. The international acclaim he enjoyed for his role in spreading nationalism made him even more attractive as an example of an ideal nationalist.[6] Indeed, before they became aware of Garibaldi's potential alliance with the United States, early Confederate opinion-makers continued their antebellum reverence for the Italian nationalist by drawing comparisons between Garibaldi and Confederates in order to attach the popularity of Garibaldi and his cause to the cause of southern nationalism. Typically these comparisons focused on southern leaders, equating Confederate leaders with the celebrated revolutionary and thereby attributing the positive virtues that Garibaldi represented to these southern men. For example, the *Richmond Daily Dispatch* declared in May 1861 that General Benjamin McCullough "resemble[s] the far-famed and invincible Garibaldi more than any other man in the world . . . and . . . is not a whit behind that celebrated Italian patriot, in courage, skill and ability as a . . . commander."[7] Similarly, in April, southern publisher J. D. B. DeBow endorsed a pamphlet by a Richmond lawyer entitled "Four Essays, on the Right and Propriety of Secession by Southern States," quoting the author's declaration that "if the spirit of Garibaldi could free Italy, the South can never be conquered while her sons are faithful, and have

Lee [and other Confederate generals] to lead them."[8] Garibaldi himself, and not just his nation of Italy, was central to the liberal international perspective that claimed equivalency between the Confederacy and aspiring nations abroad.

These Confederate-crafted comparisons failed, however, to take into account the deep divide between the ideals of liberal nationalism as the larger Atlantic world increasingly understood them and the ideals of liberal nationalism as white southerners had revised them. While Confederates had largely rejected values like equality as irrelevant to their project in nation-building, and indeed, while slavery had not disqualified nations including the United States from independent nationhood, the rise of the transatlantic abolition movement meant that increasing numbers of observers, including Garibaldi, recognized the incompatibility of slavery and ideas such as freedom and equality.[9]

White southerners' reverence for Garibaldi began to erode in the late spring of 1861 when rumors reached the South that Garibaldi would come fight for the United States and against the Confederacy. The initial rumors, encouraged in part by Garibaldi and his supporters, led James W. Quiggle, the U.S. consul in Antwerp, to act on his own authority in inviting Garibaldi to join the Union's fight. This invitation, while unofficial, forced the hand of Secretary of State William Seward. Seward needed positive press after the defeat at Bull Run and formalized the invitation in an attempt to gain that positive attention. Garibaldi's response to the invitation was not an outright yes but nonetheless provided support for the ideals of the North; Garibaldi replied that if he was not needed in Italy, he would indeed come fight for the United States but only on the condition that he be appointed commander in chief of the U.S. Army and granted power to emancipate the slaves. The emancipation in particular would prove to Garibaldi that the American Civil War was not merely "a civil war in which the world at large could have little interest or sympathy" but a war against slavery, thereby elevating the war to Garibaldi's standards of a nationalist conflict and making it worth his while to fight.[10]

This deal never came to pass, and Garibaldi never actually arrived to fight for the United States, in part due to the fact that the United States was unable to grant Garibaldi's demands. Nonetheless, his expressed support for the Confederacy's sworn enemy angered many Confederates. Even more problematic for Confederates was Garibaldi's apparent belief that unless the North fought to free the slaves, the war was merely a localized civil war with no international or ideological implications. Such a position made it clear that to the renowned hero of nationalism, the centrality of slavery to the Confederacy meant that the Confederacy's bid for nationhood had no similarities to the nationalist struggles for freedom that Garibaldi himself supported and represented. Indeed, since Confederates had long been coopting the language of nationalism to express their commitment to proslavery power, Garibaldi's answer struck right at the heart of Confederates' international, and national, self-image. As Confederates confronted the issues that Garibaldi's support for the United States raised for their international comparisons, however, they held fast to their self-identification as a nation, much like Italy, seeking admittance to the family of nations. Instead of abandoning their comparisons with Italy and aspiring nations in Europe, Confederates developed strategies for dealing with Garibaldi's implicit rejection of these comparisons that would allow them to continue using an international perspective in order to legitimize their new nation.

The first step in this process was simple denial. As rumors that Garibaldi might fight for the United States broke in the spring of 1861, white southerners initially argued that Garibaldi would never accept an invitation from the United States, and therefore the invitation was of little consequence. In particular, these first southern reports on the invitation stated that Garibaldi was so preoccupied in Italy that he could not come to the aid of the United States, thereby dismissing any possibility that Garibaldi would accept the invitation. Because Garibaldi's response had yet to be published, these early reports could ignore the issue of slavery. The *New Orleans Picayune,* for example, declared, "It is not on the eve of a second war between Austria and Italy, that the Nizzan hero will desert his beloved country," further stating, "We are inclined, on the contrary, to believe that Garibaldi was never more than now engaged in preparing an attack on the Austrians."[11]

Moving beyond simple denial, other southerners mocked what they characterized as merely a rumor of the Union's invitation to Garibaldi. The *Columbus Enquirer,* for example, dismissed the news as not only unsubstantiated but also an "amusing rumor."[12] By late summer this strategy was gaining momentum, with the *Richmond Daily Dispatch* calling the *New York Tribune's* report of the invitation "one of the *Tribune's* latest and best jokes upon the gullibility of its readers," and further commenting the next day that "there is no authenticated statement in regard to Garibaldi's offer of his services to the Federal Government. It is probably a canard."[13]

John Mitchel's aggressive reaction to the Garibaldi rumors provided another variation on this strategy of denial, adding dramatic statements of southern superiority to the dismissal of the possibility that Garibaldi would actually join the United States. As he responded to the rumors, Mitchel not only scoffed at them, stating the "announcement . . . merits confirmation," but also cast suspicion on the utility of such an arrangement between Garibaldi and the United States. As Mitchel imagined, "It is hard to see how [Garibaldi] could employ his special talents in the great Republican rail-splitting cause," a position that he followed with his vision of Garibaldi as jailed and whipped by South Carolinians should he accept the Union's offer.[14] To Mitchel at least, even if the rumors were true, they were of little concern if Garibaldi would be unable to effectively defeat the Confederate war effort. In a similar approach, another article in the *Charleston Mercury,* potentially penned anonymously by Mitchel, essentially warned Garibaldi and the world that if Garibaldi would be foolish enough to fight for the United States, the South would easily and resoundingly defeat him. Calling on the memory of southern heroes of the American Revolution, this article proclaimed that the South has "not lost the guerilla breed; and the sons of Sumter, and Marion, and Pickens . . . are ready to teach him the Swamp Fox and Game Cock lessons, such as he never could learn at the hands of Neopolitans and Austrians."[15] By claiming southern superiority over Garibaldi, these reports sought to minimize Garibaldi's stature and therefore the power of his potential support for the United States; if Garibaldi did not have the strength to defeat the South, then his potential support for the United States was of little consequence.

Even as simple dismissiveness was the predominant response in reports from the spring and summer of 1861, southern responses that preceded confirmation of the rumors did at times engage the issue of the potential connection between Garibaldi's cause and that of the North more deeply. Alongside claims that Garibaldi would never come to the aid of the United States and threats to Garibaldi's safety should he do so, elite southerners also argued that the very reason Garibaldi would never fight for the North was that the Union's values were contrary to Garibaldi's own. Adopting this strategy, the *New Orleans Picayune* reassured its readers that Garibaldi could never "espouse a cause" such as the northern one "for which he can entertain no degree of sympathy."[16] A reporter for the *Macon Telegraph* mocked the idea of Garibaldi fighting for the United States, exclaiming, "As if [Garibaldi] would come here to overthrow what he was seeking to establish in his own land."[17] The *Richmond Daily Dispatch* asserted that should Garibaldi fight for the United States, he "degenerates from a patriot to an adventurer" by undertaking "a crusade which can only end in loss of reputation and grievous personal discomfiture."[18] A widely reprinted news item pointed out that the United States, not Garibaldi, had made the offer, allowing for the possibility that Garibaldi would join white southerners in scoffing at a misguided attempt to pull Garibaldi away from his own values.[19] If Garibaldi's cause was not that of the United States, it stood to reason, it must be more closely related to that of the Confederacy, and therefore Confederates' international comparisons would be secure.

As elite white southerners developed explanations for why Garibaldi's cause was not that of the North, they did not limit their criticism to Garibaldi and his potential effectiveness and virtue, or lack thereof. Southern commentators also belittled the United States itself for making such an invitation, further seeking to disprove any ideological affinity between the two parties. Ignoring Garibaldi's antislavery beliefs and focusing instead on the relatively less-threatening proposed military relationship between Garibaldi and the United States, these Confederates claimed that the invitation had more to do with northern desperation and weakness than with any compatibility between Garibaldi's ideology and nationalism and that of the United States. For example, the *Richmond Daily Dispatch* wrote that this proposal was "mortifying" to northern officers, "who cannot fail to see in such stuff an imputation upon their own intelligence and efficiency," adding that "if the world can show a more disgusting want of chivalry and courage, we know not where it can be found."[20] Mississippian H. C. Clarke wrote in his published diary that "the Federal government despairs of finding able Generals and officers at home, to engage in its unholy war against the South," and that the North instead "makes overtures to all the broken down Generals and officers of European nations to come and assist them," emphasizing the theme of northern weakness.[21] Reports indicating that Europeans similarly ridiculed northerners' supposed dependence on outside aid seemed to support Confederates' claims that the invitation was about lack of northern strength rather than similarity between the Union's ideals and Garibaldi's own.[22]

Southern commentators took their denials of ideological compatibility between the North and Garibaldi a step further by claiming that if Garibaldi would never fight for the United States because of the incompatibility of the Italian and northern causes, and the North's invitation revealed desperation rather than natural affinity, then any northern soldiers fighting in Garibaldi's name would also be in violation of, rather than adherence to, Garibaldi's principles. Southern analysis of the Garibaldi Guard, or 39th New York Volunteers, reveals that Confederates criticized northern soldiers fighting in Garibaldi's name as an additional way of disproving any ideological connection between Garibaldi and the United States. Southern writers latched on to any evidence that the Garibaldi Guard was failing, attributing this failure to the supposed mismatch between the ideals of the unit's namesake and the cause for which it fought. For example, a former Italian citizen who was naturalized as a citizen of the Confederacy wrote, "Should the intention of forming such a legion be true, no Italian may enlist under its banner." Explaining his reasoning, this Italian American declared, "The Italians of this time are naturally bound to respect, and everywhere to sustain, the principle which Italy has assumed in fighting the battles of her independence . . . the principle that every nation has a natural right of choosing her own government," adding, "Is not the principle on which Italy has struggled entirely the same as that which the South has adopted in America?"[23] This writer was not alone in his estimation that the Garibaldi Guard failed to live up to its namesake's cause; southern journalists referred to the members of the Garibaldi Guard, as well as other immigrants enlisted in the U.S. Army, as "desperate adventurers" rather than committed and principled nationalists.[24] Resignations from the Garibaldi Guard, and especially desertions *from* the Garibaldi Guard *to* the Confederate Army, further proved to Confederates that Garibaldi's cause was that of the South, not the North. As the *Richmond Daily Dispatch* reported, six deserters who fled the Garibaldi Guard to instead join the Confederate Army would now be "fighting to uphold liberty, and not to put it down."[25]

When Garibaldi's reply to the United States, declaring his support for the northern cause and for abolition, was published in southern and international newspapers in the early fall of 1861, southerners could no longer pretend that there was no truth to the rumors of Garibaldi's sympathy for the United States. Even as they were forced to deal with the reality of the invitation, however, Confederates maintained their international comparisons. Confederates began manipulating the symbol of Garibaldi as they continued to convince themselves that the Confederacy did follow the model of Italy. Southern commentators calculated that if they could prove Garibaldi did not deserve his status as an international symbol of nationalism, then his support for the United States, and his belief that emancipation was integral to liberal nationalism, would be less problematic for their vision of the Confederacy as equal to Italy. Reversing the earlier southern stance of attributing Italian victory to Garibaldi and his virtues, southerners now claimed that Garibaldi had never actually deserved this praise, and that Garibaldi was not in fact a representative of nationalism after all.

As news spread of Garibaldi's favorable response to the United States, the *Richmond Daily Dispatch* was particularly vocal in remaking the symbol of Garibaldi. Writers for the *Dispatch* asserted that Garibaldi himself had nothing to do with his own victories and argued that circumstances outside of Garibaldi's control, rather than his inherent possession of the positive values of nationalism, had led to his success in Italy. Critically, as the *Dispatch* sought to detach Garibaldi from the ideals of nationalism with which he was associated, it still attempted to connect the South to those same ideals. For example, the *Dispatch* had already claimed that Garibaldi had succeeded in Italy not due to any particular virtue but because he was the "right man in the right place" to lead his soldiers in fighting for "a cause which, in many respects, resembled that of the South—the deliverance of a Southern clime and a gallant people from Northern oppressors and invaders. The Italian volunteers who composed his legion resembled in many respects our Southern volunteers." Were Garibaldi to lead less gallant men, such as those in the North, however, he would be "a very ordinary person."[26] Now, after confirmation of the rumor, the *Dispatch* repeated this claim that the only reason for the success of Garibaldi's armies was that his soldiers had resembled those who would later fight for the Confederacy, using this interpretation to praise southern soldiers by claiming that "ninety-nine out of every hundred men in the Southern army is a Garibaldi in all heroic qualities, and superior to him in all that constitutes a man."[27] Committed to this strategy of discrediting Garibaldi, the *Dispatch* wrote a few months later that "the triumphs of Garibaldi were the result, not so much of his personal valor, as of the cause which he represented, and which bore him upward and onward as the ocean wave bears the foam which glitters upon its crest. It was because he led a people struggling precisely as the Southern people are struggling for deliverance from foreign domination, that he achieved victories which could never have been gained by ten thousand Garibaldi's in opposition to that cause."[28] According to the *Dispatch*, Garibaldi's connection to the cause of nationalism was incidental; while the Italian cause for which Garibaldi fought had indeed been noble, Garibaldi himself contributed nothing of particular value to this cause, especially compared to the volunteer soldiers, similar to those of the South, who were supposedly the true inspiration for Italian nationalism. By separating Garibaldi from the cause that had made him famous, and therefore undermining his appeal as a representative of the strengths of nationalism, these Richmond writers sought to claim that the South, not Garibaldi, held a true appreciation for the values of nationalism.

An additional strategy for separating Garibaldi from the virtues of nationalism, and therefore claiming that Garibaldi's support for the North did not discredit southerners' self-comparisons with Italy, criticized Garibaldi by directly calling him a hypocrite. In this view, only a hypocrite could fight *for* nationalism in Italy and then consider fighting *against* nationalism in America. In yet another attempt to discredit Garibaldi, the *Richmond Daily Dispatch* argued that if Garibaldi fought for the North, he would be "in opposition to the very principles for which he contended in Italy."[29] George N. Sanders, a former U.S. diplomat and political radical who was working abroad to further the cause of the Confederacy, wrote in a letter to Hungarian patriot Lajos Kossuth that if Garibaldi aided the United States, such aid "would be a burning and devouring lie to all of his eventful and hitherto glorious career."[30] The *Richmond Examiner* outright described northern appeals to Garibaldi and foreign soldiers as "inexpressible meanness and hypocrisy."[31] If Garibaldi was a hypocrite, he could no longer be considered a symbol of nationalistic virtue, leaving the nation he had rejected—the Confederacy—as the new exemplar of these values. With their portrayals of an insignificant and hypocritical Garibaldi, Confederates remade the symbol of Garibaldi, allowing them to preserve their claims to represent the ideals they celebrated in Italian nationalism.

Southern responses to the United States' offer to Garibaldi became less frequent in the opening months of 1862, as Confederate writers felt secure in their manipulation of Garibaldi's image and as more current events attracted southern attention. Confederates did not completely abandon their efforts to remake the image of Garibaldi, however. In August 1862, Garibaldi amassed an army and marched toward Rome with the intention of claiming it for the new nation of Italy. Not yet ready to commit to removing the pope from his temporal power over Rome, the new Italian government responded by sending its own army to stop Garibaldi. Garibaldi was quickly defeated in a brief skirmish at Aspromonte during which Garibaldi was wounded and arrested. Confederate publications seized the opportunity of Garibaldi's humiliating defeat to continue bolstering their negative image of Garibaldi as a failed nationalist. The *New Orleans Picayune* reported, for example, that Garibaldi was nothing more than a "rebel against his own Government" and an "invader, without national authority," and the *New Orleans Delta* agreed that Garibaldi acted merely as an "agitator."[32] The *Alexandria Gazette* declared Garibaldi's defeat to be unsurprising, considering the "rash and ill advised" nature of his actions.[33] Emphasizing Garibaldi's supposed lack of patriotic virtue, the *New Orleans Delta* wrote that Garibaldi's description of his plans for Rome amounted to "the words of a madman or traitor." While the *Delta* professed grief that Garibaldi's career would come to such an end, and was therefore willing to excuse him from the punishments for treason, the author nonetheless asserted that "he should be treated rather as an over-excited enthusiast," still declaring Garibaldi's actions to be inconsistent with the principles of nationalism.[34] Such claims recast Garibaldi as a private citizen acting in an ill-advised, insane, or even criminal manner, rather than as a glorious nationalist leading a rightful revolution. In white southerners' analysis, Garibaldi's failed attempt to unite Rome to the Italian nation was only proper, as Garibaldi himself was now, according to southerners, a failed nationalist himself.

The supposed hypocrisy of Garibaldi's support for the United States continued to play a central role in southerners' image of Garibaldi as a failed nationalist, leading the *Macon Telegraph* to directly connect Garibaldi's failure at Aspromonte to the failure of the plan for Garibaldi to join the United States in its fight against the Confederacy. Garibaldi, the journalist for the *Telegraph* wrote, "will find few sympathizers except in the kindred North, which at one time was eager to have him at the head of a Federal army." In contrast, "the South has seen enough of European revolutionists to understand that they are as selfish and heartless as the despots whom they seek to overthrow. . . . We trust we have heard the last of Garibaldi."[35] While a few southern journalists expressed sympathy for Garibaldi's plight, in reverence to his contributions to the Italian nation, they nonetheless remained committed to the idea that Aspromonte made Garibaldi a joke or embarrassment.[36] Overall, southern opinion-makers took the opportunity of Aspromonte to continue to enhance their image of Garibaldi as defeated and irrelevant, no longer a symbol of nationalism.

Even as southern reporters criticized Garibaldi's failure, Confederates once again turned their attention to the issue of Garibaldi's support for the United States when the invitation for Garibaldi to fight for the North appeared to be renewed in the fall of 1862. After Garibaldi was defeated and arrested at Aspromonte, Heinrich Theodore Canisius, the American consul in Vienna, took it on himself to reopen negotiations with the Italian general. This time Garibaldi was willing, but the U.S. government, unable to endorse public praise of a jailed rebel, was no longer interested. Because Canisius forwarded their correspondence to the press, however, Garibaldi's interest in fighting for the United States was well-known.[37]

White southerners utilized all the strategies they had developed in order to respond to the first invitation to deal with this second show of support by Garibaldi for the United States. Confederate reporters transitioned easily from criticizing Garibaldi's military failure, which after all they attributed in no small part to his failed nationalism, to once again discrediting him for wanting to fight for the North. As southerners had after the first invitation, the *Richmond Daily Dispatch* mocked the North's desperation and denigrated Garibaldi's success, claiming that "the Federalists must be hard run for military leaders when they have to apply to that defeated, wounded, captured, played-out European brigand."[38] Going even further, the *New Orleans Delta* wrote that Garibaldi was "a poor and disloyal citizen of his own country" and "detrimental to the cause of constitutional liberty" in Italy; in this view, Garibaldi not only had failed to accomplish the goals of Italian nationalism but also had harmed the pursuit of those goals, and therefore was certainly not a worthy representative of the ideals of Italian nationalism.[39]

As in the first southern attempts to remake the image of Garibaldi, southern commentators disassociated Garibaldi from his own cause and made it clear that any action by Garibaldi to aid the United States would be hypocritical or, at the minimum, in violation of the ideals of nationalism. The *Columbus Enquirer*, for example, reported that if Garibaldi should come to the United States, he would do so as a mere "land pirate" rather than a representative of the cause of nationalism.[40] The perceived support of some members of the foreign press bolstered Confederates' case; as the *Augusta Daily Constitutionalist* informed its readers, the English papers "have already commenced to sneer at the idea of Garibaldi taking service under the United States government. The writers assert that he should go to the South, where nine millions of people are fighting for the right to govern themselves."[41] While the reaction to the supposed second invitation utilized the same strategies created in response to the first, it was relatively less widespread. For the most part, southerners let news of Garibaldi's renewed interest in fighting for the United States pass with little original commentary.[42] Confederates, busy with the business of waging war, were secure in their negative portrayal of Garibaldi; a simple reminder to fellow southerners of the previously developed reasons why Garibaldi's support for the North did not disprove Confederate comparisons with Italy was sufficient by late 1862.

In addition to renewing his interest in fighting for the United States, however, Garibaldi continued to make his stance on the Civil War and on slavery clear in other ways throughout the war. In late 1862, southerners read about an address that Garibaldi had issued to the people of England in which he asked the British to aid the struggle against "traffickers in human flesh."[43] In response to Garibaldi's British address, the *Columbus Enquirer* sarcastically referred to Garibaldi as "the hero of everybody else's business, except his own."[44] Garibaldi's antislavery sentiments were further conveyed by a letter sent on Garibaldi's behalf by one of his officers, responding to a Colorado man's pleas for international aid in the Civil War. In a statement widely republished throughout the South, Garibaldi's officer "pledge[d] [Garibaldi] strongly in favor of the North, as an opponent of slavery."[45] Despite clarifying the depth of Garibaldi's antislavery beliefs, however, southern periodicals seemed content to rely on the general reports and let this letter pass largely without challenge or commentary, as they had with Garibaldi's antislavery address and the second negotiation between Garibaldi and the United States. Even when providing analysis, for example, the *Alexandria Gazette* went so far as to claim that, practically speaking,

Garibaldi's abolition address was "point no point."[46] Confederates clearly felt secure in the work they had already done of rendering Garibaldi's abolitionism unproblematic for the South, allowing them to largely rely on their now long-standing negative views of Garibaldi.

Although Garibaldi's late 1862 antislavery proclamations were able to pass largely unnoticed, not all expressions of abolitionism by Garibaldi were as easily ignored. The final major event in the ongoing challenge that Garibaldi's support for the United States presented for Confederate comparisons with Italy came with a widely published August 1863 letter from Garibaldi to Lincoln. Responding to the Emancipation Proclamation, Garibaldi praised Lincoln as the "heir of the aspirations of Christ and of John Brown" and enthused that "an entire race of men" is "restored by you to the dignity of man, to civilization, and to love."[47] Since Confederates frequently equated Lincoln with the terrible despots who had fought against Garibaldi and Italian nationalists, this exchange highlighted the reality that, despite the comparisons Confederates had created between their cause and that of Garibaldi and other foreign nationalists, they were not, in fact, fighting the same fight. Further, such a widely publicized exchange between two famous national leaders attracted more attention, and therefore created a bigger threat for Confederate comparisons, than had the late 1862 events, forcing Confederates to respond once again.

As with the rumors of a second invitation for Garibaldi to fight for the United States, responses to this letter followed the initial pattern. The *Richmond Enquirer* mocked Garibaldi as "the biggest fool in the world" for writing the letter to Lincoln, the "next biggest" fool.[48] Southern reporters variously referred to the letter as "blasphemous" and "monstrous."[49] *Southern Punch,* a short-lived Confederate humor weekly established by John Wilford Overall in Richmond in 1863, adopted the strategy of attempting to discredit Garibaldi's contributions to his own success, claiming that Garibaldi's celebrity was due to raw courage rather than to any particular virtue or adherence to principles of nationalism.[50] Even with this more widely reported exchange between Garibaldi and Lincoln, however, more involved analyses were not necessary. The symbol of Garibaldi had already been remade within the Confederacy. Southern manipulation of Garibaldi as a nationalist hero had already discredited him in southern minds, and comparisons between the Confederacy and Italy were secure, at least from threats from Garibaldi.

Faced with Garibaldi's support for the United States and the threat that this support posed to their international contextualization of their own nationalist movement, Confederates created a uniquely southern vision of Garibaldi in which Garibaldi no longer represented the positive values of nationalism. Such an action bolstered southern nationalists' larger strategy of manipulating the definition of liberal nationalism in order to claim liberal nationalist movements as a precedent for their own attempt at nation-building. This remaking of the meaning of Garibaldi also protected Confederates' ability to continue translating their desire to create a proslavery form of nationhood into the international language of nationalism, despite the ideological mismatch between slavery and the liberal nationalism Garibaldi represented. As they attempted to limit the association of Garibaldi with the desired ideals of nationalism, elite white southerners strove to alter the domestic and international discourses about nationalism and its symbols in order to reconcile southern slavery with liberal nationalism. Through their responses to this contradiction, Confederates recommitted themselves to their own, limited definition of nationalism and to the idea that this southern nationalism represented a legitimate attempt at nation-building.

Garibaldi's support for the United States presented an early but lasting symbolic challenge to Confederates' self-equation with Italy. Garibaldi was not the only foreigner to point out the contradictions between slavery and liberal nationalism, however, and his support for the United States was not the only challenge to Confederate self-comparisons with aspiring nations in Europe. Confederates' international comparisons faced very pragmatic challenges as well. In particular, the much-hoped-for official diplomatic recognition that Confederate officials had sought from the beginning of the war failed to materialize, casting serious doubts on Confederates' vision of the Confederacy as an equal member of the community of nations. Southern opinion-makers who shaped domestic discourse about the place of the Confederacy in the world were aware of Confederate diplomatic efforts and failures, and throughout the war used their analysis of the Confederacy's supposed claims to diplomatic recognition to bolster their efforts to legitimize and defend the southern nation through international contextualization.

Through 1861 and early 1862, Confederates who analyzed foreign opinion remained convinced, as they had been in the months immediately following secession, that their official diplomatic recognition would be forthcoming, especially due to their claims of similarity with Italy, a new nation that had been recognized by major powers including Great Britain, France, and the United States in the late spring of 1861.[51] As the *Charleston Mercury* exclaimed, "Upon every principle of the laws of nations, [the Confederate States] have a right to be recognized as one of the nations of the world," just as with Italy.[52] The

Confederacy had done its duty in proving that it met the requirements for nationhood according to Confederates; as the Clarksville, Texas, *Standard* declared, "We have placed the Governments of Europe in possession of the proofs of our independent organization as a nation, and of our ability to maintain our Government. We have brought the case of our Republic fully within the rule of a *de facto* Government, a rule which has been invariably recognized and acted upon by all the powers of the civilized world."[53] Despite this Confederate confidence in the new southern nation's claim to legitimate nationhood, however, a combination of poor Confederate diplomatic strategy, European preoccupation with their own affairs and related desire to avoid an American war, and growing European sympathy for the United States, particularly after the announcement of the Emancipation Proclamation, meant that the Confederacy never received official recognition from the nations of Europe.[54]

Confederate conviction that the Confederacy, like Italy, deserved recognition required Confederates to explain why recognition was being withheld from the Confederacy but not Italy. As with Garibaldi's alliance with the United States, southerners using the liberal international perspective to legitimize the Confederacy initially opted to defend rather than discard their comparisons with Italy. Confederates developed various explanations as to why European powers would not recognize the Confederacy, despite the supposed similarity between the Confederacy and recognized nations in Europe. These explanations reveal less about the actual reasons for the lack of recognition than they do about the importance of the international perspective from which Confederates viewed their nation, as well as these Confederates' commitment to their international comparisons.

One of the first southern responses to lack of recognition was to claim that European powers were always slow to recognize new nations, and therefore the lack of recognition had nothing to do with any Confederate failings. This argument began as early as the spring of 1861 before Great Britain and France had extended recognition to Italy. Reporters and analysts pointed out that although France and Great Britain had not yet recognized the Confederacy, they also had yet to recognize Italy, and therefore the Confederacy should not be concerned. For a brief time at least, the fact that Italy had yet to be recognized seemed to excuse the fact that the Confederacy was also unrecognized.[55]

While this initial strategy allowed Confederates to ignore slavery and its incompatibility with liberal nationalism, domestic discussions of the lack of recognition did frequently engage the issue of slavery. In particular, southern commentators argued that Europeans were incorrect in seeing slavery as inconsistent with the standards of nationalism that Confederates sought to claim, and that this ignorance, rather than any true ideological issues, prevented European recognition of the Confederacy. John Mitchel, for example, explained that the northern blockade of southern harbors allowed the North a monopoly over the news being sent to Europe; in his estimation, "the Southern harbors being closed up, and the Southern mails for Europe being stopped, our Yankee brethren have the ear of the world; [European audiences] are at their mercy in the matter of our supply of news from that continent; and they present to [European audiences] the conduct and progress of their great war just in the light which suits themselves."[56] Mitchel's statement implied of course that this northern perspective was inaccurate, and if white southerners could get pro-southern news to Europe, Europeans would have a more accurate view of the war, slavery, and the Confederacy.

This idea of European ignorance served as a call to arms for fellow southerners, with Confederate writers urging their readers to do their part in reeducating Europe. As one journalist for the *Charleston Courier* declared in an article reprinted in other southern periodicals, "Our country and its institutions have been so persistently misrepresented to the world by the press of the Northern States, that in many parts of enlightened Europe we are regarded as a semibarbarous people." This writer suggested that the World's Fair of 1862 in London provided an opportunity for reeducation, and that "each State in the Confederacy ought to take this matter in hand, and provide for the expenses of transportation" of southerners and southern products to London.[57]

While the idea that Europeans were simply misinformed about slavery and the Confederacy had its roots in the early days of the Confederacy, it gained further publicity when Edward Pollard, an ardent secessionist and influential journalist, advocated for this belief in his analyses of the Confederacy and the war. Pollard had been one of the more outspoken advocates of secession and would go on to play a critical role in the formation of the Lost Cause. During the war, he used his considerable platform as editor of the *Richmond Examiner,* along with his authorship of several pamphlets, to spread his views. Moving beyond early war declarations that Europeans simply did not know enough about the South to fairly evaluate slavery, the South, and the war, Pollard asserted that over time, the increased exposure to the Confederacy that Europe had gained during the early years of the Civil War would actually reverse Europeans' opinion of slavery. In particular, he claimed that the wartime abuses committed by northern abolitionists had caused European sympathy for those abolitionists to wane, and that "the war had also given occasion to intelligent persons in all parts of the world for a more thorough, a more interested and a more practical study of slavery in the South," one that caused stories of "fiendish masters" to become "objects of skepticism or derision in Europe."[58] Because Europeans now understood that the North actually had no love for slaves, and that southern slavery was not as harmful and immoral as Europeans had believed, Pollard claimed, they could now realize that slavery was not incompatible with the principles of nationalism and would thus soon support the Confederacy.[59]

Rejecting the incompatibility of slavery and ideas of liberty and equality, Pollard and fellow Confederates remained committed to a southern vision of liberal nationalism, continuing to assert that slavery was compatible with the principles of nationalism exhibited by aspiring nations abroad. Still hopeful of foreign aid, these southern commentators argued that Europeans would support the South when they realized that the issues of slavery and abolition were more complicated than Europeans believed, that the Civil War was about nationality as well as slavery, and thus that slavery did not preclude a legitimate claim to nationhood. Ignorance, these southerners argued, not ideology prevented Europeans from recognizing the South.

Despite the predictions of Pollard and his fellow elite southerners, Europeans' greater exposure to the southern institution of slavery did not cause them to support the Confederacy. On the contrary, Lincoln's issuance of the Emancipation Proclamation turned European sentiment against the southern nation. By the midpoint of the war in 1863, with official diplomatic recognition seeming ever less likely, southern nationalists once again found it necessary to remake their international comparisons. In order to explain why the Confederacy still failed to receive recognition, white southerners rejected the successful Italy as a point of comparison for Confederate recognition, dropped the idea of educating Europeans about slavery, and instead compared themselves to aspiring nations in Europe that had not received the recognition that Confederates believed they deserved.

Finally recognizing that most aspiring European nations had not been successful, Confederates using a liberal international perspective now cast the Confederacy as just one of many hopeful nations to be unjustly excluded from the family of nations. The *Richmond Examiner* pointed out, for example, that European powers had not cared about the suffering of Hungary, Poland, and Ireland any more than they did about that of the Confederacy.[60] *Southern Punch* likewise declared, "Europe stood by and was *particeps crimines* in the murder of Polish nationality," lamenting, "and yet we look to one or two of the Five Powers for succor in this desperate struggle of ours, against a despotism equal in power and diabolism to that of Russia. If the shriek of Poland whom they do not dislike, cannot arouse their armed sympathy, of what avail are the appeals of the South whom they do dislike on false philanthropic and political principles?"[61]

Reverend Stephen Elliot, the presiding bishop of the Episcopal Church of the Confederacy, similarly argued that "revolution, and European cabinets will consider our movement to be revolution, has had no friends among the crowned heads of Europe since the convulsions which have swept over their dominions again and again since 1789." After extolling the virtues of nations such as Greece that the great powers of Europe supposedly failed to support, Elliot turned his attention away from the possibility of recognition to focus instead on the changing Confederate public opinion regarding hopes for that recognition, asking, "Should we, in the face of such examples, lean upon any such hope as foreign intervention? It was well, perhaps, ere we had become conscious of our internal resources, that the public mind should have been flattered with such a delusion. Possibly it encouraged some who might otherwise have fainted in the hour of our weakness, but now, when we have aroused ourselves like a strong man from sleep, and such a reliance is no longer of any consequence to us, it is well to say that we should never have looked for it."[62] To Elliot, history taught that recognition would not be forthcoming, but the supposed strength of the Confederacy meant that lack of recognition was not a problem. If European powers failed to recognize the Confederacy, southern nationalists argued, they had equally failed to recognize supposedly legitimate and suffering nations in Europe. The Confederacy was not alone in its lack of recognition and therefore could still be portrayed as a legitimate nation.

Of course, comparisons with defeated nations could only be so satisfying to an aspiring nation still defending its independence and aware that although most aspiring European nations had failed, a few had indeed achieved the recognition the Confederacy sought. Accordingly, southern commentators during the middle and late periods of the war expanded the accusations of hypocrisy that they had leveled against Garibaldi to now accuse European nations of the same hypocrisy for refusing to recognize the Confederacy. In particular, Confederates argued that the Confederacy—which had now successfully sustained itself and waged war for years—was stronger than other nations that had been recognized, and they questioned why, in light of this national strength, recognition of the Confederacy continued to be withheld. The *Southern Illustrated News,* a Confederate-era weekly out of Richmond, declared (contrary to the ample evidence of the many failed aspiring nations in Europe) that "the Confederate States are the only new power [Great Britain] has refused to recognise, and yet they have manifested a degree of strength greater than all those we have enumerated put together. We have, under these circumstances, we think, some right to be indignant."[63] The lack of recognition of the Confederacy, southern nationalists argued, was due to the hypocrisy of foreign powers rather than a failure of Confederate nationalism.

The lack of official diplomatic recognition, while primarily an issue for Confederate diplomats in Europe, resonated with domestic commentators and opinion-makers. Confederates at home had to either confront the reality that the lack of recognition, while largely due to issues unrelated to the Confederacy's similarities or lack thereof to aspiring European nations, nonetheless suggested that their international comparisons were incorrect, or alternatively find a way to claim that, even in the face of failure in the international court of opinion, the Confederacy was a legitimate aspiring nation. Through claiming that slavery was only a problem due to European ignorance, that lack of recognition was a European pattern rather than a response to the Confederacy, and that European powers were hypocrites for recognizing other aspiring nations but not the Confederacy, Confederates defended their vision of the Confederacy as part of a larger trend of nationalist movements seeking independence for aspiring nations.

Although lack of diplomatic recognition and official aid was the greatest failure of Confederate diplomatic efforts abroad, the failure to win more widespread and enduring support among the general populations in Europe also contributed to Confederate difficulties abroad. While many British and other Europeans did support the Confederacy, Confederates were aware that this support and sympathy was not as widespread or enthusiastic as the support and sympathy given to various nationalist movements in Europe. Elite white southerners had watched carefully as Europeans and Americans alike exploded in sympathy for nationalist movements from the Greek independence movement to the revolutions of 1848 to the Italian Risorgimento. Now that white southerners were undertaking their own experiment in nation-building—one they claimed followed the precedent of those earlier and much-celebrated movements—they wondered where their support and praise was. Extending their claims of hypocrisy due to lack of recognition, southern nationalists embracing a liberal international perspective argued that the lack of support given to the Confederacy in general, not just the lack of official diplomatic recognition, was hypocritical when contrasted with the outpouring of sympathy shown for other nationalist movements.

Early accusations of hypocrisy targeted Europeans who fought for the U.S. Army. Even though many foreign-born Union soldiers saw their service to the United States as advancing the causes of their nations in Europe, to many Confederates these foreign-born soldiers fought against the principles for which their nations in Europe stood. For example, the *Richmond Daily Dispatch* withdrew any sympathy the South had given to foreign nationalists on the basis that "the Europeans whom we have been sympathizing with so universally compose the vast bulk of the army which is invading our country," adding that "the great motive urged upon them for enlistment is, that if this 'rebellion' is not put down, the cause of freedom Abroad will suffer! So that freedom in America must perish in order that freedom in Europe may be established."[64] John Mitchel praised Irishmen fighting for the South and mocked the idea of Irish soldiers in the North taking up arms against the southern rebellion, scoffing, "as if the very idea of rebels and rebellion were the thought most abhorrent in Irish nature."[65] Similarly, the *Augusta Daily Constitutionalist* wondered how Thomas Francis Meagher, a leading Irish nationalist who joined the U.S. Army and recruited his fellow Irishmen to fight for the North, could exhibit "such inconsistency" to aid in the subjugation of the South, when the South was the true hope for the principles Irishmen held dear.[66] The Confederacy, its proponents argued, fought for the same cause as did Ireland and other aspiring nations in Europe, and therefore immigrants claiming to fight for the same principle in the North as they had in Europe were hypocrites.

By 1862 and 1863, driven by the growing enmity toward the North that wartime sufferings engendered, Confederates expanded their accusations of hypocrisy from foreign-born soldiers fighting for the United States to criticize the United States itself. Paradoxically, Confederates expressed disbelief that northerners refused to acknowledge the connection between the ideals of the nationalist movements they had supported in Europe and the ideals of the Confederacy. The *Richmond Daily Dispatch* was again one of the main supporters of this argument, crying that "whether it was . . . Irish rebels against England, Greeks against Turkey, Frenchmen and Germans against their kings, or Italy against the Austrians, the North boiled over with enthusiasm in their cause," only "attach[ing] any opprobrium to the name of rebel; a name which has always heretofore been with them a synonym for all that is praise worthy and glorious" when the South itself "threw off the chains of vassalage and determined to be free."[67]

This belief that northerners acted as hypocrites in denying self-determination in the South while supporting it in Europe was common among southern intellectuals and power-brokers. Robert Barnwell Rhett, fire-eating secessionist and Confederate congressman, concurred with this conclusion, informing a convention of the state of South Carolina that the North demonstrated a disregard for freedom of which "history has no such record," as the North declared "with a hypocrisy only possible with an unparalleled depravity" that they "are contending for the liberties of the earth" while truly setting back the cause of "free government" for "centuries."[68] Similarly, in a clear condemnation of the North, pamphleteer T. W. MacMahon wrote that northerners, "accustomed to weep over the fate of Greece, Poland, and Hungary—accustomed to espouse the cause of Lombardy and Venetia against Austria, the cause of the Papal States against the Pope—they have voted thousands, reckoned by hundreds, of men, and millions of money, to support a despotism, compared with which, those of King Bomba and Francis Joseph were balm."[69] John O'Sullivan, sympathizing with the Confederacy and already disillusioned with the North for waging war instead of letting the South secede peacefully, likewise accused the North of replicating Russia's oppression of Poland by perpetuating war against the southern states and therefore betraying the American Revolution.[70] As the reality of war pervaded the South, elite southerners and their supporters explained southern suffering to their fellow countrymen by claiming that the hypocritical North actively fought to limit in the South the same principles that it had praised abroad.

Despite the fact that the United States fought a war against southern nationalism, Confederates still managed to be offended that northerners did not celebrate the South's claim to nationhood in the ways that they had those of other aspiring nations, proving the importance of this comparison to southern nationalists' perception of the South as an independent nation. Confederates' liberal international perspective claimed that the Confederacy, like Poland, Italy, and other aspiring nations of Europe, fought for liberty and against tyranny. Any nation that supported these causes in Europe, then, must support them in America too or else be a hypocrite. Certainly these arguments ignored the real hypocrisy of claiming to support slavery and the ideals of liberalism at the same time. Confederates had proven willing, however, to manipulate ideals and symbols in order to preserve their own sense of their nation as part of a century of nationalism. By pointing out what they perceived to be an inconsistency in the United States' reaction to new nations, Confederates sought to maintain their own position as a legitimate new nation, similar to those in Europe.

Of course, the ultimate challenge facing white southerners' attempt to build a new nation went beyond a lack of sympathy and support and encompassed the actual failure to win independence on the battlefield. As such, the harshest wartime reality that southern nationalists had to respond to was their inability to defend their new nation. Southern nationalists' commitment to the vision of the Confederacy as one of many legitimate nations seeking membership in the international family of nations proved so strong that, even as military defeat loomed in the closing months of the war, Confederates turned once again to their international perspective. Now they utilized comparisons with aspiring nations in Europe to help them contemplate the possibility of defeat, just as they had once used these international comparisons to process the possibilities of secession and independent nationhood. Again acknowledging that so many of the aspiring nations they admired had not succeeded in establishing independent nationhood, southern nationalists facing defeat drew comparisons between the plight of these unfortunate nations and the situation that they believed white southerners would face if the North were victorious.

This international contextualization of the doom of defeat returned to the comparisons of tyranny and oppression that white southerners had originated during the crisis over territorial slavery in 1850. As the *Augusta Chronicle and Sentinel* warned as early as 1863, nations are responsible for their own fate, and the Confederacy, "the newest born of the nations, having before it so marked a warning," should "heed the warnings of history" lest it suffer the same fate as Poland, "blotted from the map."[71] This type of rhetoric increased in 1864 and 1865 as military success seemed less likely. No less an authority than the Confederate Congress warned its citizens that "the fate of Ireland at the period of its conquest, and of Poland, distinctly foreshadows what would await us" if the Confederacy fell to the United States.[72] Similarly, the *Richmond Whig* expounded at length on the similarities between Ireland's oppression by England and the subjugation that the South could expect upon reentering the United States. The journalist for the *Whig* declared, "Prior to our present struggle, in our general sympathy with the Irish . . . we had about as much of the 'Irish question' here as on the other side of the Atlantic. We were then in the position toward them simply of amateurs. But the South now regards the condition of Ireland with a deeper interest, as affording a most instructive lesson and warning of what she might expect could either subjugation or reconstruction be the result of our contest," going on to detail the similarities between Ireland and the South in order to highlight the lack of representation and political power Ireland had within Great Britain and that a defeated South could thus expect from the North.[73] Similarly, Confederate senator Benjamin Hill asserted that if the South gave in to Lincoln, it would become the Hungary, Poland, and Ireland of America and make those oppressed nations feel like a "paradise."[74] International comparisons provided southern nationalists with a way to understand what was at stake as defeat loomed, as well as with a way to continue encouraging their fellow southerners to help stave off that defeat.

Despite Confederates' assertions that their nation deserved legitimacy, and that foreign recognition and independence would quickly be forthcoming, the Confederacy failed to secure national independence. The liberal international perspective that resonated so widely throughout the Confederacy was built on false premises, as a slaveholding nation could never live up to the standards of nationalism that prevailed in the climate of mid-nineteenth-century liberal nationalism. The international community rejected the Confederacy from the family of nations, most pointedly by refusing diplomatic recognition. Giuseppe Garibaldi, international symbol of nationalism, revealed some of the reasons behind this lack of support and recognition when he repeatedly expressed his sympathy for the United States and its war against slavery. If the Confederates' comparisons had resonated more widely internationally, these dual rejections likely would not have occurred.

Even as international events highlighted the differences between the Confederacy and aspiring nations in Europe, however, many Confederates remained committed to their vision of their nation as one of many aspiring nations legitimately seeking independence. Instead of switching strategies, Confederates spent their energies developing ways to defend their comparisons. These Confederates claimed that the lack of diplomatic recognition was due to European policy rather than Confederate failings. They called foreigners and foreign powers hypocrites for supporting other nationalist revolutions but not the Confederacy, and they sought to remake the symbol of Garibaldi, detaching him from the principles of nationalism with which he was so closely associated in order to mitigate the harm that his support for the United States did to Confederate comparisons with Italy. When defeat seemed unavoidable, Confederates then turned to these comparisons once again to help them make sense out of their failure. Throughout the war, evidence continually mounted that disproved and rejected Confederates' comparisons with aspiring nations abroad. Confederate responses to this failure of their liberal international perspective reveals just how committed southern nationalists were to proving that the Confederacy was one of many new nations aspiring to membership in the international community of nations in the middle of the nineteenth century. These responses also reveal the extent to which Confederates were willing and able to ignore the ideological problems that plagued these comparisons, rejecting the reality that slavery opposed the same liberal ideals that southern nationalists tried to claim through international comparisons.

8

We Stand Alone

THE EVOLUTION OF THE CONSERVATIVE
AND UNIONIST INTERNATIONAL PERSPECTIVES

In May 1864, even as the Civil War raged, the *Richmond Examiner* turned its attention to international relations, reflecting on Europeans' perception and treatment of white southerners. The writer for the *Examiner* was not overly positive in his assessment; on the contrary, he listed the myriad ways that Europeans supposedly rejected white southerners and their institution of slavery, concluding, "We stood alone-all alone. We stand alone, even now; for we have no faith in our European admirers." With this statement, the writer echoed the thoughts of many Confederates in the later years of the Civil War who wondered why, despite their glorious self-image of the Confederacy as one of many legitimate aspiring nations, the southern nation had failed to garner support from nations abroad. By 1864, the optimism of the opening months of the Confederacy had waned, and Confederates were increasingly forced to grapple with the reality that they were not being welcomed as a new member of the international family of nations. Indeed, the writer for the *Examiner* stated bluntly that "we shall continue to stand alone after the contest is over," recognizing that, regardless of the outcome of the Civil War, Europe would not widely embrace southern slaveholders.

To the *Examiner,* however, while this international isolation "is a bleak position," it was "not an unhealthy one." The writer adapted the conservative international perspective's claim that the southern nation was the best exemplar of the values of nationhood, arguing that it was the Confederacy's very superiority—supposedly rooted in slavery—that led to its international isolation. As he explained, white southerners were "content to keep aloof from the 'spirit of progress' which is making all over the world such a sad hotch-potch of the elements of true civilization." Indeed, he declared, "it is to this isolation, which once seemed so cruel to so many cultivated minds and sensitive hearts at the South, that we owe all that is distinctively noble in our nationality. Slavery has discouraged immigration. Slavery has driven off many restless, hyper-energetic factors of our society. Slavery has discouraged manufactures. Slavery has prevented the accumulation of such colossal fortunes as we find in the free states." Such a celebration of slavery as a positive force reflects ideology far more than reality; nonetheless, this statement reveals that even in the face of international isolation, white southerners valued slavery so highly that they were willing to give up international support in order to retain the institution they believed was the purifying element of southern society. To win international support, according to the *Examiner*, would require giving up slavery in favor of the "spirit of progress," a trade that would result only in the destruction of civilization. Better, the writer declared, to remain superior but isolated.[1]

As the *Examiner*'s analysis reveals, wartime realities threatened Confederates' conservative international perspective, just as they had the liberal international perspective. The Confederates who used liberal comparisons to describe the Confederacy as a nation equal to aspiring nations abroad, even in the face of lack of support from foreign powers, were not alone in having to reassess their strategies for deploying an international perspective as secession and the early days of the Civil War gave way to a long war and ultimately the defeat of the Confederacy. Other groups of white southerners, including Confederates adopting a more conservative international perspective, as well as Unionist southerners, also found it necessary to respond to wartime realities.

Indeed, more conservative Confederates such as the writer for the *Examiner* faced a similar challenge to their more liberal counterparts in having to reconcile the Confederacy's lack of success, both on the battlefield and in the realm of international diplomacy and opinion, with their claims of legitimacy and greatness. For Confederates using the conservative international perspective, this challenge was intensified by their argument that they represented a superior form of nationalism. If the Confederacy really did exhibit the best form of nationhood the world had ever seen, then it should have already received support from admiring nations abroad, leading the Confederacy to a victorious independence that had yet to materialize. When official diplomatic recognition was not forthcoming, these Confederates first declared their international isolation to be proof of their uniqueness and therefore superiority, as in the article in the *Examiner*. The lack of affinity with liberal nations, however, additionally opened up the possibility of a different kind of alliance, with conservative Confederates debating the idea of turning to the conservative powers of Europe in a desperate attempt to receive recognition on the basis of shared conservative, rather than liberal, ideals, even if doing so meant allying with powers previously denounced as despotic. With both strategies, these Confederates remained committed to the conservative international perspective that defined and legitimized the Confederacy as a nation elevated by its uniquely conservative form of nationalism.

Meanwhile, for Unionist southerners, the inability of the United States to fully stop the Confederate rebellion and reunite the nation only affirmed their conviction that Confederates and their sympathizers were the true despots of the South, creating oppression like that seen in Europe. Further, to southern Unionists, even impending victory by the United States did not erase the European-style despotism that Confederates had established in the South. Accordingly, southern Unionists expanded and embellished their vision of Confederates as tyrants, with the hardships of war leading southern Unionists to lash out against Confederates' European-style despotism, even on the brink of Union victory. As with Confederates endorsing the more liberal international perspective, both Confederates utilizing the more conservative international perspective and southern Unionists remained committed to their international perspectives throughout the Civil War, despite any challenges and threats that wartime events and even Confederate defeat posed.

As the Confederacy fought for its independence on the battlefield, southern nationalists using the conservative international perspective continued their attempts to legitimize the southern nation through international analysis. In particular, as the possibilities of secession gave way to the reality of war, these Confederates advanced their self-comparison with failed European nations, renewing their assertions that the southern nation's conservatism set it apart from the rest of the international family of nations and thus constituted a purer and more positive form of nationhood and nation-building than that exhibited by European nationalist movements. For example, in 1863, George Fitzhugh blamed John Locke's liberal principles of human equality for destroying government and stability in Europe, leading to the revolutions that had swept the continent for the past several decades. He contrasted the "Southern Revolution of 1861" with the earlier Lockean revolutions, describing the southern revolution as "reactionary and conservative . . . a solemn protest against the doctrines of natural liberty, human equality and the social contract."[2] This vision of the Confederacy as purifying revolution with its conservatism resonated throughout the war; in 1864, Reverend William A. Hall celebrated, for example, that "this Revolution has a profound significance in that *it is a great historic protest, the only one of the sort in history, against philosophic infidelity and disorganizing wrong. We are combatting a fanaticism*" that characterized European revolutions. In contrast with the harmful philosophies of Europeans, Hall declared, "this Revolution has an intense significance, in that *it marks the beginning of what certainly seems to be the last period of human history.* . . . It seems proper to describe the present period as the Period of Conservatism."[3] To southern conservatives, the creation of the southern nation continued to stand as an exemplar of conservatism in action, as well as a rebuke to the supposedly harmful liberalism that had driven nationalist revolutions in Europe.

Although some wartime Confederates spoke generally of revolutions, most advocates of the conservative international perspective retained their emphasis on racial inequality throughout the war. Southerners adopting the conservative international perspective thus remained clear throughout the war that slavery was the key to the conservatism that elevated the Confederacy above European revolutions. Ignoring the actual harms of slavery—to society, government, and individuals—conservative Confederate analysts continued to argue that slavery allowed for the creation of a superior society and purified white nationalism. For example, the *Augusta Daily Constitutionalist,* a leading proponent of the conservative international perspective during the war years, declared that slavery would not only strengthen the Confederacy and preserve republicanism but also that, without slavery, white southerners would become "the Spain and Italy, the hybrid of America, the lazaroni of the world," dismissing these nations and their people as unfit for the international favor that was granted to them but withheld from the Confederacy.[4] The *Index,* Confederate propagandist Henry Hotze's London newspaper, wrote that the North was similar to oppressive Russia while the South resembled patriotic, freedom-loving Poland, which had recently lost a struggle against Russian control. Hotze made a critical exception to this comparison, however, in claiming that racial slavery in the South ensured that the Confederacy would be successful where Poland failed.[5] While much of the rest of the Atlantic world understood that slavery set the Confederacy apart from other aspiring nations in a negative way, according to conservative southerners the South's unique institution of slavery merely meant that the Confederacy was superior to nations based on more liberal principles.

Wartime Confederates, as with secessionists before them, likewise remained convinced that one of the benefits of this distinctly conservative nation was that the Confederacy created a nation uniquely free of the chaos and violence they believed resulted from excess equality and had therefore accompanied aspiring European nations. For example, in his 1862 inaugural address, Governor Zebulon Baird Vance of North Carolina celebrated that "mob violence, that dangerous offspring of revolution, has been equally repressed by the conservatism of our people."[6] The idea that the Confederacy was unique in its avoidance of violence paradoxically persisted even throughout many long, violent years of war, with the Confederate Congress still asserting in 1864 that the Confederacy "is a child of law instead of sedition, of right instead of violence, of deliberation instead of insurrection. Its early life was attended by no anarchy, no rebellion, no suspension of authority, no social disorders, no lawless disturbances. . . . The utmost conservatism marked every proceeding and public act," in contrast to the European revolutions that had not shown such conservatism and restraint.[7] Such formulations obviously ignored the extreme violence of the Civil War, as well as the domestic discord within the Confederacy and the violence that was inherent to the maintenance of slavery; ignorance was necessary to claim instead that the Confederacy's conservatism created order and peace. Confederates using the conservative international perspective proved equally willing as their more liberal counterparts, however, to manipulate reality in order to defend their vision of a pure, ideal conservative southern nation. Even throughout a brutal war, the supposedly conservative nature of the southern revolution furnished proof for southern conservatives that the southern nation, unlike aspiring nations in Europe, upheld the principles of conservatism rather than giving in to the excesses of liberalism.

Although Confederates remained committed to the conservative international perspective throughout the war, wartime circumstances forced them to respond to the lack of success of this perspective, just as Confederates using the liberal international perspective had been forced to do. In particular, lack of international support and diplomatic recognition proved equally damning to Confederates using both perspectives. Confederate hope for international aid and recognition that had swelled through 1861 waned as the war wore on with no offers of foreign aid. In the later years of the war, as foreign support continued to be withheld and as battlefield defeats mounted, conservative analyses of the South's place within the international community shifted their usage of their international perspective from defending the southern revolution to explaining why the South's international isolation was not a problem and did not disprove the supposed glories of the Confederacy. Here, the conservative comparisons, unlike the liberal ones, provided Confederates with an unexpected strategy for explaining not only why the Confederacy failed to achieve international support, but also why that lack of support was not a problem.

As Confederates expanded their conservative international perspective to address the lack of international sympathy and diplomatic recognition, they used their belief in the Confederacy's uniqueness and even supremacy to claim that the Confederacy was so superior to liberal nations in Europe that lack of compassion from these liberal powers was only to be expected. After all, if the Confederacy truly held different national values and followed a different model of nationalism than did Europeans, it perhaps made sense that Europeans rejected this new model. For example, in an exuberantly punctuated statement, the *Augusta Daily Constitutionalist* lamented that "our social organization and our labor system are such as the world, in this enlightened (!) day, puts under the ban of its reprobation," recognizing that "we stand almost alone as to our peculiar institutions." To the writer in the *Constitutionalist,* however, standing alone was a positive for the Confederacy, as the institution of slavery created greater harmony and peace in the South than was found in other nations.[8] The *Richmond Examiner*'s declaration of the positive merits of retaining slavery, even at the cost of international support, likewise advanced the idea that the Confederacy's slavery set it apart from other nations but that such a position was preferable to the alternatives.[9]

These white southerners recognized that slavery distinguished the Confederacy from many of the other nations of the Atlantic world. They purposefully failed, however, to deal with the reasons why slavery was dwindling internationally, thereby leaving the Confederacy standing alone in the international community. Instead, they continued to assert that the slave-based southern nation would create a purer, more stable form of nationalism, founded on the basis of white supremacy, now expanding on those claims to assert that the Confederacy's isolation was only natural given its uniqueness and superiority.[10] The Confederacy may have been exceptional among nations of the world, even to the point of lacking sympathy and aid from foreign powers, but to some Confederates, that was acceptable, as what they perceived to be the benefits of slavery simply ensured that the South stood alone at the top.

Taking their international perspective to the logical next step, conservative Confederates began arguing that while the conservatism of the Confederacy failed to win sympathy or official recognition from the traditional liberal powers of Europe, such a situation still left conservative empires—the enemies of aspiring liberal nations—as potential allies. Accordingly, conservative Confederate writers and journalists began advocating for a new diplomatic strategy that targeted more monarchical and aristocratic, and therefore more conservative, powers in Europe. In this strategy, diplomats should focus on nations such as the Papal States and Austria rather than the more liberal nations such as Great Britain that formed the basis of Confederate diplomacy throughout the war. If liberal nations naturally rejected the conservative South, these Confederates argued, then conservative powers would recognize the superiority of the conservative southern model of nationhood and would provide the assistance that the Confederacy so desperately needed. Seeking aid from such powers required Confederates to ignore their previous negative characterizations of rulers like the pope as despotic, but, enchanted by the purifying possibilities of their own conservatism, Confederates endorsing the conservative international perspective proved willing to shift their opinions on European empires if doing so would aid the Confederacy.[11]

As Confederates looked for a conservative ally abroad, Pope Pius IX provided a particularly appealing option. Although antebellum southerners had described papal temporal control over Rome as tyrannical in the aftermath of the failure of the revolutions of 1848, the pope began evincing support for the Confederacy just as international recognition and support from other European powers seemed increasingly unlikely.[12] The promise of first sympathy and then support from both the pope and, by his influence, other Catholic nations was more than enough for conservative southerners to ignore the pope's previous rights violations, leading these southerners to craft international comparisons that focused on the conservative, rather than liberal, affinity between the Confederacy and Catholic powers in Europe, beginning with the pope himself.[13]

Southern discourse turned its attention to the pope in the summer of 1863, when the southern press reported on papal sympathy for the Confederacy in response to a widely publicized letter from Pius IX to Archbishop John Hughes of New York. In this letter of October 1862, Pius IX urged American Catholics to make peace with the Confederacy. Southern journalists eagerly seized on this message as evidence that, with the pope urging peace, northern Catholics would reject the United States' war effort, thereby hindering the United States' military chances and ultimately aiding the Confederacy. As the *Richmond Whig* explained, "A failure on the part of the Yankee Government to yield to a request of the [Catholic leaders] in behalf of peace, would inevitably enlist the sympathies of the Catholics of the United States on the side of the South. . . . The estrangement of Catholic aid and sympathy in the North . . . would reduce Northern resources in the matter of fighting material to a standard scarcely consistent with the possibility of a much longer continuance of the war."[14] Confederates were particularly convinced that Irish Catholic immigrants in the North, who constituted about 6 percent of United States troops, would heed the pope's directive to make peace, thereby depriving the United States of a critical portion of its manpower.[15] William F. Samford, for example, so strongly believed in the pope's ability to influence the Irish that he claimed papal support for peace between the United States and Confederacy would be definitive in winning the war for the Confederacy. To Samford, even claims such as "Vicksburg has fallen" and "Charleston will fall" were of little account, as he replied, "Yes—and what of it?" Instead, he urged his readers to notice "Lincoln's dependence! Pope Pius tells the Archbishop Hughes to promote peace. There is an end of Irish recruits."[16] The letter to Archbishop Hughes thus convinced many Confederates that they not only had the sympathy of the pope but also that such sympathy would aid Confederate war efforts, bolstering Confederate claims that a natural conservative affinity between the Confederacy and the pope would ultimately lead to Confederate victory.

Excited by the possibility of sympathy from the pope and thus from Catholics more broadly, conservative Confederates turned their attention to the potential creation of a new Catholic government on their own border, enthusiastically supporting France's attempt to establish a French-controlled Mexican Empire. In particular, conservative Confederates hoped that a Catholic Mexico, governed by a conservative emperor, would join the pope in sympathizing with the Confederacy. Indeed, events in Mexico seemed to create new possibilities for governance in the Americas, even as the United States was engaged in civil war. As the United States and the Confederacy fought for control north of the border, France opened war against the republican Mexican government led by Benito Juárez, succeeding in toppling Juárez and paving the way for Napoleon III to establish Maximilian as emperor of Mexico in 1864. Although Maximilian's reign ended quickly with the reestablishment of republican rule and the execution of the emperor in 1867, and despite U.S. opposition to European intervention in Mexico, the overthrow of the republican government of Mexico constituted yet another mid-nineteenth-century contest between conservative and liberal forms of governance.[17]

As they considered the new possibilities in Mexico, conservative Confederates viewed Maximilian's brief rule as a potential opportunity for the Confederacy. The *Richmond Whig* wrote approvingly, for example, of the Catholic desire to establish a strong Catholic kingdom in the Americas in order to solidify the church's control over the large Catholic populations in South America. The *Whig* saw such a development as positive for the Confederacy; anticipating the appointment of Maximilian as emperor of Mexico, the author argued that "it will not be surprising if one of his earliest official acts be the recognition of the Confederate states." Convinced as southern journalists were in response to the pope's letter to Hughes that Catholics would act in unison, the writer for the *Whig* added that such recognition by a new Mexican emperor "will follow, as we may reasonably anticipate, recognition by his brother, the Emperor of Austria, and no doubt by Spain. Catholic influence everywhere will be vigorously exercised to conciliate the favor of the Southern Confederacy."[18]

Explaining one possibility for the seemingly natural alliance between imperial Mexico and the Confederacy, the *New Orleans Picayune* wrote that the pope was influenced by the French invasion of Mexico when he wrote his letter to Hughes, and that presumably the pope urged peace in order to solidify southern independence and pave the way for a Confederate-Mexican alliance. Such an alliance would provide a friendly neighbor to the Confederacy and grant the pope a stable Catholic state in America. Critically, to the *Picayune,* this was not just an alliance of convenience; as the author explained, the "Church needed some conservative basis on this continent . . . where the instability of civil governments had rendered its rights of property so insecure."[19] With property rights, particularly the right to property in the form of slavery, so central to the conservative Confederate nation, an alliance between imperial Mexico and the Confederacy made sense to some white southerners, not just out of mutual defense but due to shared values.

Building off of visions of a Catholic Mexico allying with the Confederacy, conservative Confederates increasingly believed that papal sympathy toward the Confederacy would ultimately result in actual aid and recognition from first the pope and then his Catholic allies throughout Europe. Southerners were particularly excited when news spread of a December 1863 letter from the pope to Jefferson Davis in which the pope addressed Davis as the president of the Confederate States of America. The letter did not have an official standing, nor was it intended to, and some of the initial southern reports on the letter, published in January 1864, made no mention of any implications for diplomatic recognition or intervention.[20] Convinced of the affinity between the Confederacy and conservative Catholic nations, however, it took little time for Confederates to seize on the idea that this letter could be more meaningful. Very quickly, southern journalists began celebrating this letter as proof that, in addressing Davis as the president of the Confederacy, the pope had granted official diplomatic recognition to the Confederacy. For example, singing the pope's praises, the *Richmond Whig* exclaimed in February that "there is no courteous acknowledgement which a great people and government can tender, that is not due to His Holiness Pope Pius the IXth, for the dignified and manly tone of his letter to President Davis. It is the first courteous acknowledgement of virtual independence yet hazarded by the narrow-minded potentates of Europe; and coming from so distinguished a source, we may well prize it," both for its sentiment and for its ability to diminish support for the North.[21] Similarly, the *New Orleans Picayune* reported in March that, according to the New York papers, "the letter of His Holiness the Pope to Jefferson Davis was intended to be one of 'recognition,'" with L. Q. C. Lamar concurring that the pope had "pronounced us a *nation.*"[22] The belief that the letter was intended to grant recognition to the Confederacy became increasingly widespread even among the wire reports; in January, the *Alexandria Gazette,* for example, had published without challenge that "it is said that the recent correspondence between the Pope and President Davis does not compromise the Pope's neutrality," but by April the same paper was printing reports that stated instead that "the pope has declared our nationality an established fact."[23] Primed by their belief in papal sympathy toward the Confederacy, southern journalists chose to interpret a sympathetic letter as a sign of official recognition. Such an interpretation aided conservative Confederates in making the case that, despite the failure of desired liberal alliances, conservative alliances would still save the Confederacy.

The supposed recognition of the Confederacy by the pope did not only cement an alliance between the Papal States and the Confederacy in the minds of conservative white southerners, however; given the vast influence that Confederates believed the pope wielded, they anticipated that papal recognition would also usher in a new stage of widespread official diplomatic recognition of, rather than just sympathy toward, the Confederacy by other Catholic nations of Europe. The *Augusta Daily Constitutionalist* printed an article from the *Petersburg Express,* for example, that evinced surprise and disappointment that although the pope "recognizes the Confederacy in broad and clear terms . . . France, Austria, Portugal, Piedmont, all Catholic States, move not a finger towards the promotion of his benignant and honorable counsels in the matter, but treat them with silent contempt."[24] Hope was resilient, however, and even in January 1865, a writer by the initials H. L. B. declared, "Having, therefore, truth and justice on our side recognized by the representatives from the Northern branch of the church—as I feel confident would be the case—it would not be long before His Highness, the Pope, would obtain the recognition of our independence by the Catholic powers of Europe, and America."[25]

In fact, as late as February 1865, some Confederates were so convinced of the impending recognition of the Confederacy by conservative powers that rumors and reports abounded of a secret pro-Confederate Catholic conspiracy. In this southern conspiracy theory, the Catholic powers of Europe had secretly agreed to recognize the Confederacy after the second inauguration of Lincoln in March, on the basis that the Confederate states would not have participated in the American presidential election of 1864 and were therefore no longer a part of the United States. Even the vehemently Unionist *Brownlow's Knoxville Whig* reported on an article from the *New York Tribune* that declared "a secret league in the Roman Catholic powers of France, Spain and Austria, under guidance of the Pope, has been formed and pledged to recognize the Confederacy after the 4th of next March, on the ground that it will not participate in the Presidential election."[26] Other southern periodicals, more sympathetic to the rumors than the *Knoxville Whig,* also saw this report as worthy of republication.[27] Despite the obviously unlikely nature of a secret conspiracy meeting to recognize an aspiring nation on the brink of utter defeat, some white southern opinion-makers nonetheless held out hope that the affinity between the pope and the Confederacy could create a last-minute miracle.

Such faith was premised in part on the belief that a shared conservatism had predisposed these European empires to support the Confederacy, even without papal pressure. As Mississippi congressman L. Q. C. Lamar highlighted the pope's sympathy for and recognition of the Confederacy, he also asserted that "Austria and Spain favored our cause, and had declared that our heroism, fortitude, courage and achievements justly entitled us to a position among the nations of the earth."[28] Such a statement ignored the lack of actual support from Austria and Spain and was also a sharp reversal of the almost unanimous loathing that white southerners had used when speaking of Austria as a merciless tyrant. For a white southern population willing to manipulate the ideals of liberal nationalism to claim that a conservative movement based on the defense of slavery fit within the bounds of liberal nationalism as practiced in the middle of the nineteenth century, however, one more instance of ideological manipulation proved entirely possible, especially in the context of rumors of much-needed foreign support and recognition. When presented with a potential ally, conservative Confederates were willing to abandon their earlier positions on Austria, the pope, and European empires in general in order to celebrate a supposed shared conservatism between the Confederacy and conservative European powers, one that would allegedly aid Confederates in securing southern independence.

Lack of success, particularly in the international realm of opinion, severely challenged Confederates' conservative international perspective, threatening the vision of a superior southern nation. Even as their own failure seemed likely, however, Confederates proved as committed to this conservative international perspective as they had to their liberal perspective; rather than recognizing the inaccuracy of their vision of their nation, conservative southerners remained committed to their self-identification as the ideal nation. To continue defending such a national vision in the face of failure, these Confederates argued that rejection by liberal European powers reflected the failure of those nations rather than of the Confederacy and turned instead to conservative powers in Europe, expecting aid from sympathetic conservatives abroad even up until the end of the war. Such commitment to conservative international comparisons reveals the critical importance of this international perspective to Confederates' national self-image.

Just as Confederates who used an international perspective to defend the legitimacy of a southern nation reevaluated and recommitted to their usage of their international perspectives as the war evolved, so too did southern Unionists. During the crisis of secession and commencement of war, southern Unionists, like secessionists, had adopted an international perspective to help them make sense out of the shifting nationality of the South and to defend their position that the South should remain within and return to the United States. While lack of support for their international comparisons led Confederates to redouble their efforts to claim the Confederacy as an ideal nation, for southern Unionists it was the weariness of a lengthening and brutal war that intensified their strategy of using international comparisons to describe the negative consequences of national division and of placing the South under Confederate governance.

Southern Unionists faced serious challenges as the Civil War commenced. A significant number of previously loyal white southerners, including most of the southern Unionist leadership, switched positions and embraced secession and the Confederacy following Lincoln's call for troops after Fort Sumter. The remaining southern Unionists were left to accomplish the much more difficult task of stopping a Confederacy that functioned as a nation rather than simply blocking secession, and to do so without their leadership and while fending off significant pressure from their communities and the Confederate government alike. Nonetheless, a minority of white southerners remained loyal to the United States throughout the war and continued working toward a reunited American nation.[29] As these wartime southern Unionists maintained their stance that the United States should not have been divided, the remaining outspoken Unionist leaders expanded their strategy of using international comparisons to explain the necessity of national reunion by highlighting what they saw as the illegitimacy and despotism of Confederate rule, therefore emphasizing the need to bring the South back under the governance of the United States.

Extending the early war strategy of accusing Confederates of being despots, worse than any that oppressed the peoples of Europe, southern Unionists in the middle stages of the Civil War intensified their accusations against Confederates.

In particular, Tennessee Unionist "Parson" William Brownlow remained one of the most outspoken voices for southern Unionism, particularly by maintaining his Unionist newspaper, *Brownlow's Knoxville Whig,* despite the fact that the Confederate government had forced the closure of the *Whig* early in the war. Brownlow became increasingly outraged throughout the war at what he saw as the escalating militarism and violence of the Confederate government, military, and even supporters. In the early stages of the war, Brownlow had described Confederates as despots for trampling southern Unionists' right to self-government.[30] By the middle of the war, the mounting hardships and sufferings had not endeared the Confederacy to Brownlow at all; instead, such privations stoked a rage in Brownlow against the people he saw as the cause of so much suffering. To Brownlow, not only were Confederate militarism and violence inherently oppressive and tyrannical, but secession and the war should never have happened in the first place, so any suffering inflicted by the war only intensified the despotic and illegitimate nature of the Confederacy.

The despotic nature of Confederate military power and violence thus constituted a central theme of Brownlow's wartime screeds against the Confederate powers, which resumed when Brownlow reopened his newspaper, the *Knoxville Whig,* in late 1863 on the reestablishment of U.S. control in East Tennessee. In a pointedly titled article in February 1864 that asked, "Who Are the Guilty?" Brownlow or one of his editors explained the reasoning behind the equation of Confederates with despots, lamenting that "we still abhor the grinding despotism which has devoured the substance of thousands of loyal men, depopulated the fertile valleys, converted the peaceful neighborhoods . . . into the abodes of worse than lawless banditti," clarifying that Confederates, "the vile leaders of this most infernal crusade, substituted a reign of oppression and terror for the mild government under which, but recently, these sufferers so happily lived."[31] Similarly, of the execution of a southern Unionist who had worked to aid U.S. troops Brownlow wrote, "Now if history can produce any act of tyranny more atrocious and revolting than this, we cannot recall it," adding that a Confederate "imperial tyrant" was responsible for such cruelty.[32] Even the end of Confederate rule in East Tennessee did not end Brownlow's rants against such cruelty by the Confederates, as despite U.S. occupation, the suffering continued. In June 1864, Brownlow wrote that "day by day the rebels become more desperate and cruel," as seen, Brownlow argued, by their increasing outrages against women, including widows who, Brownlow hoped, U.S. troops would leave "no longer at the mercy of the rebel tyrants."[33] The escalating cruelties of the rebels and the ongoing hardships they inflicted in Brownlow's mind made them the worst of tyrants, worse than any history could offer, thereby proving that the South would be better without these Confederate oppressors in control.

Brownlow's concerns were not limited to just despotism, however. Brownlow also worried that the Confederate elite constituted a European-style aristocracy that enhanced the harmful nature of their rule. These ideas are particularly apparent in the *Knoxville Whig*'s editorials on the presidential election of 1864. Once again turning to an international perspective to explain his loathing of despotism, Brownlow or another editor wrote that "all the remnants of the several kinds of defunct *aristocracy*," including "owners of Negroes," "are traitors at heart, and in sympathy with the rebellion" by opposing Lincoln's re-election. In contrast, the *Whig* declared that Lincoln men include "every man not in sympathy with Jeff. Davis and his plundering hordes . . . every friend of peace and . . . restoration of the union . . . and every citizen who realizes that the destruction of our Government would be hailed with joy by the despots of Europe."[34] By 1864, an international perspective that called Confederates aristocratic despots who harmed liberty was central enough to Brownlow's understanding of the issues of the war that it was natural to describe the American presidential election in terms of an international context. As southern Unionists including Brownlow continued to suffer the hardships of war, comparisons that emphasized the illegitimacy of the Confederacy helped them make their case for the reunion of the American nation.

Even as the war finally drew toward its close and U.S. victory seemed assured, Brownlow retained both his anger at the cruelties of the Confederate tyrants as well as his sense that an international lens helped explain the necessity of union. His views were made particularly clear through an early 1865 debate with Confederate sympathizer and Irish nationalist John Mitchel. As the Confederacy faced its defeat, these men's differing views of southern nationhood led them to publicly argue. Using their platforms as journalists, both men lashed out at the other, penning articles attacking their opponent as betraying the best vision of nationhood for the South.

John Mitchel was, like Brownlow, a journalist by profession and had used his journalism to popularize his international vision of the Confederacy. Not only were both Mitchel and Brownlow journalists, however; increasing the similarities between the men, Mitchel had also resided in Brownlow's native East Tennessee in the mid-1850s and had edited his newspaper, the *Southern Citizen,* out of Knoxville in the later years of the decade.[35] Despite sharing an area of residence, a career, and a belief in the utility of an international perspective, however, Brownlow and Mitchel stood on different sides of the debate over the meaning of the Confederacy, the proper form of southern and American nationhood, and the correct application of an international context to these questions. In particular, whereas Brownlow used his international perspective to advocate for union and the end of Confederates' European-style tyranny, Mitchel used an opposing international perspective to legitimize the Confederacy through claims that it fought for the same cause as his native Ireland.[36] Divided by their visions of southern nationhood, these two prominent analysts clashed over their differing visions of the South's national future as the war began grinding to a close in early 1865.

Mitchel, then editing the *Richmond Enquirer,* took the opening shot in the conflict between the two men after Brownlow was elected as the first Reconstruction governor of Tennessee. In an editorial that Brownlow's own paper republished and attributed to Mitchel, the *Enquirer* decried the establishment of U.S. control over former Confederate territories, such as Brownlow's Tennessee. In particular, Mitchel wrote that the election of Brownlow was nothing less than the election of one of the "most serviceable tools of Yankee government, who have always been a scandal and an offense to all moral citizens, a terror to those who do well . . . men who are born mortal enemies of honor and truth." The article went on to attack Brownlow as a "brutal, blaspheming . . . drunken tailor," and an "ignorant, violent, and malignant being" who made the occupation of East Tennessee by U.S. forces "a true reign of terror and a horror" in which Brownlow "has driven from house and home, or slain, or degraded to labor with ball and chain, whatsoever was honest, virtuous, and of good repute." The heart of this attack was Mitchel's belief that U.S. forces, as well as pro-Union governors like Brownlow, would use their newly reclaimed control over the South to create "subjugation and submission."[37]

Brownlow, of course, as a southern Unionist, had made clear his position that it was Confederate, not U.S., rule that created oppression. In response to this attack by Mitchel, Brownlow initially shrugged, taking such vicious criticism from the man he called the "Irish traitor" as a "compliment." Brownlow, like Mitchel, was well aware that the two men fell on opposite sides of the debate about nationality and the force of government. As such, for Mitchel to accuse Brownlow of horrible acts of illegitimate power must, to Brownlow's mind, mean that he was doing things right.[38]

While Brownlow initially received Mitchel's attack with equanimity, however, his calm did not last long, and the Irish nationalist and Confederate sympathizer quickly became a favorite target of Brownlow's rage at the treason and cruelties of the tyrannical Confederates. A week after publishing Mitchel's article, Brownlow returned the attack. After recounting what Brownlow considered to be Mitchel's treason against England, Brownlow colorfully described Mitchel as "the concentrated embodyment of all that is arrogant, vile, mean, and rebellious—of all that is treason and fiendish by nature—the Irish brute—this depraved tool of a rotten but dying despotism . . . this representative of hell in the garb of a man . . . this spunger upon traitors for a living—this defunct patriot—this sensorious incarnation of all that is damnable."[39] With such enthusiastic defamations, Brownlow made clear that his main problem with Mitchel was that in first fighting to overthrow British rule, and then in supporting Confederate attempts to overthrow the United States, Mitchel was a traitor—or, in other words, was known for violating proper national values and loyalties.

Mitchel's status as both an Irish nationalist and a Confederate nationalist was the key to Brownlow's vision of Mitchel. To Brownlow, Mitchel was a career traitor, seeking to overthrow legitimate government both in Europe and America. Mitchel himself personally embodied the liberal international perspective by implicitly and explicitly blending Irish and Confederate nationalisms. Thus, as Brownlow rejected Mitchel, he likewise rejected the liberal international perspective that Mitchel represented, instead furthering his own Unionist international perspective by characterizing pro-Confederate Mitchel as a despot, following from Brownlow's conviction that Confederates were the worst despots in history.

Interestingly, Brownlow remained relatively unconcerned by the fact that Mitchel had denigrated him personally, still concluding that Mitchel "is not able, at home or abroad, to damage any man by his tongue or pen!" In Brownlow's mind, the conflict between him and Mitchel was ideological rather than personal, with the real issue being their disagreement over the proper form of government for the South, as well as the identity of the despot oppressing the South and, ultimately, the place of the South within the international conversation about nationhood and governance.[40] To Mitchel, who believed the Confederacy fought for the same cause as his cherished Ireland, Unionist Brownlow acted as an agent of northern despotism; to Brownlow, instead, pro-Confederate Mitchel was a traitor against both Great Britain and the United States in seeking to support despotism by overthrowing legitimate governments.

Both men wanted many of the same things for the South. In particular, they shared a loathing of despotism and a desire for free government. They disagreed sharply, however, on the best means of achieving those goals. The passion revealed by their exchange proves just how important these questions of despotism, government, and nationhood were to southerners throughout the Civil War, both Unionist and Confederate alike. This passion also helps explain why, as wartime demands and developments disproved and threatened the comparisons that Confederates like Mitchel drew between the Confederacy and aspiring nations like Ireland, Confederates intensified rather than rejected the international comparisons that helped them define and legitimize the southern nation. Further, Brownlow's vehemence in attacking Mitchel helps illustrate the growing anger that characterized the international perspective of southern Unionists in the middle and late stages of the war, as, outraged by the ongoing nature of their suffering, southern Unionists intensified their usage of international comparisons to attack the aristocratic and despotic nature of the Confederacy. Even on the brink of victory, southern Unionists felt the sting of war and used their international perspective to dramatize why, despite impending national reunion, the existence of the Confederacy created deep problems for the South and for the American nation.

The questions debated throughout the South during the Civil War mattered deeply. Any strategy that helped Confederates or southern Unionists to advance their preferred forms of southern nationhood, including that of applying an international perspective, was worth preserving, even if it required ideological manipulation or growing extremism. Elite white southerners did not idly play with the idea of the South as part of the larger mid-nineteenth-century conversation on nationhood; to white southerners across the political spectrum, this international contextualization of southern nationhood was critical to their ability to understand and advocate for their desired visions of southern nationhood. An international perspective proved so central to white southerners' understanding of their nationhood that, despite the challenges of war and, in some cases, of ideological inaccuracy, they continued to defend their international visions of the South's nationhood. To white southerners during the Civil War, their own nationality could not be understood apart from the larger international discourse on nationalism.

Conclusion

In the late spring of 1865, the Confederate States of America officially ended in defeat, with white southern nationalists relinquishing their dream of an independent southern nation. The international perspectives that these white southern nationalists had used to make their case for why the South deserved national independence, however, had been failing for months, if not years. The lack of support from within and without the South proved that the international community rejected the image of the Confederacy as the latest in a long line of aspiring nations, much less the idea that the Confederacy represented a purified and superior version of nationhood. Such a lack of support more closely reflected reality, as a slavery-based nation did not indeed reflect or purify the values of liberal nationalist movements.

Although Confederate responses to the failure of their international comparisons most often denied the contradiction between slavery and liberal nationalism, a few Confederates showed glimmers of understanding that the Confederacy did not fully follow the precedent of aspiring nations abroad. As the end of the war drew near, the *Richmond Whig,* in an article republished in other southern journals, had the clearest statement of understanding of the problems that threatened Confederates' self-comparisons with aspiring nations in Europe. The editor of the *Whig* admitted that if the international audience only believed white southerners' claims that the Confederacy was motivated by the spirit of European nationalists, then southern victory would be assured—and yet, victory seemed to be slipping away. As the *Whig* explained, "We have been in the habit of flattering ourselves that we have already developed a high degree of those qualities which excite the sympathy of the world on behalf of struggling nationality; that we have already equaled the heroism of the Greeks . . . the fortitude of the American colonists." Despite such flattery, the author admitted that "we are yet very far from having equaled, or even approached, that high standard." Instead, despite the Confederate heroism of the last four years of war, were the Confederacy to admit defeat, "we should be known in history simply as a very foolish people who undertook what they had not the nerve to carry through." Even victory, however, would not bring the Confederacy the acclaim granted to other nations, the author declared, arguing that even with success, "we could claim nothing more than a decent place among people who have risen to nationality by force of their virtue and endurance."

To explain why even a victorious Confederacy would be limited to a "decent place" won by "endurance" rather than ideology, the author admitted that "we cannot rival the height of Grecian glory until we realize the depth of Grecian adversity. It is precisely for this reason that the historical examples so often quoted as bearing upon our situation are felt to be inapplicable." The "historical examples" of Italy, Ireland, Poland, and Hungary had become almost a litany throughout sectional tension, secession, and the Civil War, with southerners parroting the idea that the South stood at the end of that list as yet another oppressed but aspiring nation. As the writer for the *Whig* recognized, however, the lack of oppression faced by white southerners meant that these comparisons could not be accurate—the "historical examples" were "inapplicable." As proof of this inaccuracy, the author went on to list the many ways in which the Confederacy had not faced the adversity of other aspiring nations.

Despite years of international comparisons claiming equivalency between the suffering experienced by white southerners and nationalists abroad, the writer for the *Whig* recognized that elite white southerners had indeed not faced the oppression and tyranny that justified liberal nationalist movements in Europe. Accordingly, the Confederacy could not emulate the admirable qualities of these movements abroad, and therefore did not deserve equal glory or legitimacy.[1] For at least this one Confederate, impending defeat brought with it recognition that the liberal international comparisons with which Confederates had sought to legitimize their nation throughout secession and war were, in fact, rhetorical inventions. The Confederacy was not like new and aspiring nations in Europe and did not have similar legitimacy on the basis of shared liberal nationalist principles.

Elite white southerners such as the writer for the *Whig* who debated the national future of the South joined an already-active international conversation. Residents of the nineteenth-century Atlantic world, citizens of nations both aspiring and established, fiercely debated questions of nationhood. Ideas of democracy, citizenship, abolition and slavery, independence or empire, aristocracy and monarchy, shaped both political discourse and reality.

To elite white southerners seeking to understand, debate, and shape their own nationality and national future, the conversation about their nationhood could not, and should not, take place apart from this larger international conversation. Whether Unionist, liberal Confederate, or conservative Confederate, southerners made their case for their vision of southern nationhood through the international language of nationalism. In an era of aspiring and defeated nations, the would-be nation crafted by the white slaveholding elite did indeed appear to represent either one more of many varied attempts at either legitimate nation-building or, conversely, illegitimate rebellion, depending on one's perspective. In a political climate defined by claims of liberty and tyranny, the legitimacy of an independent southern nation, or, to the contrary, of the United States' efforts to block such an independent southern nation, depended on perception of who was on the right side of these values. Critically, at a time when republicanism seemed on the retreat throughout the world, such a determination could decide nothing less than the future of republicanism. Similarly, amid a fierce and changing debate on citizenship and slavery, the success or failure of a slaveholding nation would help determine the future of slavery. The choices that white southerners made regarding their national values and nationhood resonated not just with white southerners but with the larger international community.

The international perspectives that white southerners developed to help them process and develop their own nationality reveal the complicated, contested nature of white southerners' nationhood. Southern nationalism did not emerge in a vacuum, either chronologically or geographically. Antebellum white southerners' observations of nationalist movements abroad began preparing them to consider their own nationhood long before the creation of the Confederacy. Southern analysis of the European revolutions of 1830 and 1848 helped them develop a vision of the proper enactment of nationalism, thereby clarifying their own national values. Through the sectional tension of the 1850s, southern reaction to issues ranging from territorial slavery to filibustering to exiled European revolutionaries helped white southerners build a new sense that the South differed from the North on issues of nationhood, preparing them to consider the possibility that the South could be an individual nation worthy of discussion within the international conversation on nationhood.

As ideas of secession increasingly resonated through the South, white southerners elaborated on this vision of their region as part of the international debate on nationhood, developing competing international perspectives to help them advocate for their desired form of southern nationhood. Useful in navigating the secession crisis, Confederates and Unionists alike found these perspectives critical to their national self-definitions during the war and remained committed to these perspectives through the long, hard years of war, even manipulating ideals and symbols or becoming increasingly extreme in order to continue defending their ideas of the South. White southerners did not agree on the particular form of international perspective that was most accurate, but they did agree on the utility of the international contextualization of the South, and they did prove remarkably flexible in and committed to their usage of these perspectives. Internationalizing southerners' discourse on nationhood thus highlights the reality that the evolution of white southerners' views of nationhood in the middle of the nineteenth century was a lengthy, complicated, and contentious process.

The defeat of the Confederacy provided definitive answers and conclusions to some of the issues and questions that white southerners, in conversation with the international community, had been debating. The South would not become an independent nation. Slavery would be ended within the United States. The seceded southern states would rejoin the nation of the United States of America. On these points, the verdict of the war was clear—even if the execution of these points was far less clear and would be subject to much debate throughout the coming period of Reconstruction.

The answers provided by the war also vindicated or disproved the three international perspectives that white southerners had developed in different ways. For southern Unionists, who had used an international perspective to defend the necessity of a united American nation and to criticize the actions of Confederates, the verdict of the war provided vindication. And yet, the hardships of a long brutal war and a contested national reunion ensured that southern Unionists, like their Confederate counterpoints, would continue to deal with the aftermath of Confederates' attempts to create an independent southern nation.

For Confederates, however, the dream of international acceptance that fueled both the liberal and conservative secessionist-Confederate perspectives was ended. Former Confederates now faced the failure of their international self-perception, along with the defeat of their attempts at nation-building. More liberal southern nationalists who had claimed that the Confederacy followed in the footsteps of aspiring nations in Europe by seeking to overthrow a tyranny and create an independent, self-governing nation would no longer have any claim to being one of many aspiring new nations. No longer could they wrap their proslavery sentiment in the guise of liberal nationalism, nor could they hope to levy that pretense into proslavery nationhood. At best, they had to resign themselves instead to being one of many defeated nations. Southern nationalists who had claimed that the slavery of the Confederacy purified liberal nationalism of the excesses that had doomed it abroad faced even deeper defeat. With the end of slavery, the cornerstone national institution on which they had built their vision of a nation was ended, and their claim that slavery was necessary for a strong nation was disproven. In Reconstruction, former Confederates would shift their international perspectives from defending southern nationalism to making sense of both their lost Confederate nationhood, as well as their renewed American nationhood.

NOTES

Introduction

1. For examples of white southerners' desire to emulate the nationalistic virtues of Garibaldi, see "Ben McCullough," *Richmond Daily Dispatch,* May 21, 1861; and "Editorial Miscellany," *DeBow's Review,* April 1861, 502.

2. Gay, "Lincoln's Offer of Command to Garibaldi," 69; Doyle, *Cause of All Nations,* 15–26.

3. For an overview of the revolutions of 1848, see Sperber, *European Revolutions.* For analysis of the causes and goals of nineteenth-century nationalist movements, see Kramer, *Nationalism in Europe and America.*

4. Sperber, *European Revolutions.*

5. Doyle, *Cause of All Nations;* Doyle, *American Civil Wars;* Doyle and Pamplona, *Nationalism in New World;* Quigley, *Shifting Grounds;* Fleche, *Revolution of 1861.* David T. Gleeson and Simon Lewis have also situated the American Civil War within a broader global context in *Civil War as Global Conflict.* Timothy Roberts and Paola Gemme have analyzed American reactions to nineteenth-century nationalist movements. Roberts, *Distant Revolutions;* Gemme, *Domesticating Foreign Struggles.* Such work builds on the hints of an international perspective within southern nationalism that scholars including Drew Gilpin Faust and Elizabeth Fox-Genovese and Eugene D. Genovese identified in earlier works. Faust, *Creation of Confederate Nationalism,* 8–10; Fox-Genovese and Genovese, *Mind of the Master Class,* 41–68. Civil War scholars are not alone in internationalizing southern and American history. Among other scholars emphasizing transnational history, Thomas Bender has analyzed connections between U.S. and world history, and Caitlin Fitz has identified the importance of American analysis of Latin American revolutions on the development of the second party system and ideas of white U.S. exceptionalism, while Matthew Karp has revealed that southern slaveholders saw themselves as a critical part of international politics and economics. Bender, *Nation among Nations;* Fitz, *Our Sister Republics;* Karp, *This Vast Southern Empire.* Additionally, comparative historians including Enrico Dal Lago and Peter Kolchin have identified connections between the nineteenth-century South and nations abroad. Dal Lago, *Agrarian Elites;* Kolchin, *Unfree Labor;* Kolchin, *Sphinx on the American Land.*

6. Famously, Benedict Anderson identifies the critical importance of print culture to the creation of nationalism in his influential *Imagined Communities.*

7. Between 1850 and 1860, for example, the number of periodicals in the South grew from 503 to 847. Although this still represented only one-eighth of the nation's periodicals, these southern periodicals had enormous influence on the South and dominated the news industry in the region. Reynolds, *Editors Make War*, 3–11.

8. For analysis of the second party system and slavery, see Ashworth, *Republic in Crisis*, 37–49, 128–31; and Cooper, *Liberty and Slavery*, 195–267.

9. For example, see Hobsbawm, *Nations and Nationalism since 1780*.

10. For analysis of the theories and historiography of nationalism, see Lawrence, *Nationalism: History and Theory*. For analysis of the evolution of nationalism within European culture, see Leerssen, *National Thought in Europe*. For analysis of Enlightenment-inspired ideas, including ideas of government and their influence on the age of revolutions, see Israel, *Revolution of the Mind*.

11. For analysis of romanticism in southern nationalism, see Quigley, *Shifting Grounds*; and Osterweis, *Romanticism and Nationalism in the Old South*.

12. For analysis of conservatism and liberalism as expressed in the evolving ideas of nationalism in the nineteenth-century Atlantic world, see Kramer, *Nationalism in Europe and America*, esp. 1–56; and Hobsbawm, *Age of Revolution*. For analysis of these ideologies in the American political tradition, see Bailyn, *Ideological Origins of the American Revolution*; and Wood, *Radicalism of the American Revolution*.

13. For analysis of antebellum southern political values and beliefs, see Cooper, *Liberty and Slavery*; Tate, *Conservatism and Southern Intellectuals*; O'Brien, *Conjectures of Order*; Genovese, *Southern Tradition*; and Genovese, *Slaveholders' Dilemma*. Historians are increasingly recognizing the ways in which antebellum white southerners saw themselves as a forward-looking part of the modern world. See Barnes, Schoen, and Towers, *Old South's Modern Worlds*.

14. Historiography of southern nationalism initially focused on debating whether such nationalism was strong or weak. For examples of each school of thought, see Beringer et al., *Why the South Lost the Civil War*; and Gallagher, *Confederate War*. Additionally, scholars have analyzed southern nationalism to understand its contents and construction. Most notably, Drew Gilpin Faust identifies slavery and religion as primary sources of southern nationalism. Faust, *Creation of Confederate Nationalism*. More recent influential works on southern nationalism include Rubin, *Shattered Nation*; Quigley, *Shifting Grounds*; Binnington, *Confederate Visions*; and Bernath, *Confederate Minds*.

15. "A Declaration of the Immediate Causes Which Induce and Justify the Secession of South Carolina from the Federal Union," Avalon Project of Yale Law School, http://avalon.law.yale.edu/19th_century/csa_scarsec.asp. For analysis of southern justifications for secession, see Doyle, *Cause of All Nations*, 27–37; Faust, *Creation of Confederate Nationalism*, 14; Fleche, *Revolution of 1861*, 132–50; Quigley, *Shifting Grounds*, 77–83, 145–57; and Rable, *Confederate Republic*, 44–49.

16. For analysis of the evolution of the goals of Mazzini and his fellow liberals, see Riall, *Italian Risorgimento*, 66–70.

17. Looking primarily at northerners, Timothy Roberts and Paola Gemme both argue that Americans initially reacted with pride that the United States had inspired the European revolutions, while the failure of these revolutions intensified Americans' sense of exceptionalism. Roberts, *Distant Revolutions;* Gemme, *Domesticating Foreign Struggles.*

1. The Revolution of '76 Extending Itself across the Seas

1. G. W. K. [George W. Kendall], "European Correspondence," *New Orleans Picayune,* September 6, 1849.

2. For analysis of the international celebrity of Garibaldi, see Riall, *Garibaldi.*

3. See Fleche, *Revolution of 1861,* 18–19; and Wiltse, "A Critical Southerner." In *Distant Revolutions,* Timothy Roberts provides in-depth analysis of general American reactions to the revolutions of 1848. This chapter expands our understanding of the southern reaction to European revolutions by revealing which factors drove this response; by explaining how this southern response, like the broader American response, evolved in reaction to changing events and shifting ideas; and by showing how white southerners used this response to fuel their developing sense of nationalism and of the South as part of an international conversation on nationhood.

4. Roberts argues in *Distant Revolutions* that the overall American response was initial enthusiasm followed by dismay at the failure of the revolutions.

5. Fox-Genovese and Genovese, *Mind of the Master Class,* 41–44.

6. For analysis of American enthusiasm for Greek independence, see Pappas, *United States and the Greek War for Independence;* Brewer, *Greek War of Independence;* and Winterer, *Culture of Classicism.*

7. "Greece," *Natchez Gazette,* December 13, 1823. See also "Turkey and Greece," *Fincastle Mirror,* August 22, 1823; and *Charleston Courier,* December 25, 1823.

8. Pappas, *United States and the Greek War for Independence,* 32.

9. "Greek Cause," *Richmond Enquirer,* January 31, 1824; "Eloquent Appeal," *Southern Recorder,* May 4, 1824. For more examples of southern support, see also "State of Europe," *Charleston Courier,* August 20, 1822; Rev. Jack Lumpkin, "A Discourse," *Augusta Chronicle,* August 6, 1823; "Greece," *Ariel,* December 5, 1825; *Charleston Courier,* May 11, 1826; "A Meeting of the Friends of the Greeks," *Georgian,* April 25, 1828; "Civil and Religious Liberty," *Georgian,* October 11, 1828; and "Eleventh Annual Report of the Young Men's Bible Society of Alexandria," *Alexandria Phenix Gazette,* April 25, 1832. As part of his larger discussion of American aid, Paul Pappas provides examples of support and aid in South Carolina, Louisiana, Mississippi, and Virginia. Pappas, *United States and the Greek War for Independence,* 37–38.

10. For examples of southern support for Ireland, see *Louisiana Courier,* July 28, 1823; and *Alexandria Phenix Gazette,* July 7, 1825. For support of the Italian states, see *Genius of Liberty,* September 19, 1820; "God Speed the Good Cause," *Richmond Enquirer,*

May 8, 1821; and "Sardinia," *Alexandria Gazette,* May 11, 1821. For support of France, see *Charleston Courier,* September 13, 1830; "The French Revolution," *Augusta Chronicle,* September 15, 1830; *Richmond Enquirer,* September 24, 1830; "Volunteer Toasts," *Charleston Courier,* September 25, 1830; "Celebration of the Liberty of France," *Georgian,* October 12, 1830; "The Late Revolutions," *Natchez Gazette,* December 1, 1830; and *New Orleans Bee,* March 28, 1831. For support of Poland, see *Alexandria Phenix Gazette,* March 9, 1831; and "Poland," *Southern Clarion,* June 10, 1831. For support of Belgium, see "The Revolution in the Netherlands," *City Gazette,* November 1, 1830; and *City Gazette,* January 15, 1831.

11. "Friends of Ireland," *City Gazette,* January 20, 1829; "Anniversary of the Hibernian Society," *Charleston Courier,* March 20, 1826; *City Gazette,* July 7, 1828; "Address," *Alexandria Gazette,* March 26, 1835; "St. Patrick's Benevolent Society of Columbia," *South Carolina State Gazette,* March 22, 1828; "St. Patrick's Day," *Georgian,* March 18, 1826; "St. Patrick's Day," *Georgian,* March 19, 1827; "St. Patrick's Day," *Georgian,* March 18, 1829; "St. Patrick's Day," *Charleston Courier,* March 19, 1829; "St. Patrick's Day," *Georgian,* March 19, 1830; "Festival of St. Patrick," *Georgian,* March 20, 1832; "St. Patrick's Day," *Charleston Courier,* March 20, 1833; "St. Patrick's Day," *National Banner and Nashville Whig,* March 23, 1836.

12. *Genius of Liberty,* September 19, 1820. See also "Naples-Piedmont," *Richmond Enquirer,* May 18, 1821; *Augusta Chronicle,* May 24, 1821; and *Louisiana Courier,* June 6, 1821.

13. *New Orleans Bee,* March 28, 1831; *Charleston Courier,* September 13, 1830; "Great French Celebration," *City Gazette,* September 25, 1830; "Celebration of the Liberty of France," *Georgian,* October 12, 1830; "Celebrations in Honor of the French," *Richmond Enquirer,* October 18, 1830; "Celebration," *Georgian,* October 25, 1830; *Natchez Gazette,* November 17, 1830.

14. "Poland," *Alexandria Phenix Gazette,* August 2, 1831. See also "Poland Still Bleeds!" *Southern Clarion,* October 21, 1831; "Melancholy Situation of Poland," *Richmond Enquirer,* June 14, 1831; and "Fall of Warsaw—Confirmed," *Georgian,* November 9, 1831.

15. *City Gazette,* January 15, 1831. See also George Tucker, "A Discourse on the Progress of Philosophy," *Southern Literary Messenger,* April 1835, 406.

16. "St. Patrick's Day," *Georgian,* March 19, 1822; "Communicated," *Alexandria Herald,* July 12, 1822; *Augusta Chronicle,* July 9, 1823; "Fourth of July: St. Andrew's Parish Celebration," *City Gazette,* July 7, 1824; "4th of July in Twiggs County," *Georgia Journal,* July 27, 1824; "American Friendly Association," *Charleston Courier,* February 24, 1825; *Pensacola Gazette,* September 17, 1825; "Communicated," *Winyaw Intelligencer,* July 11, 1827; "Celebrations in Honor of the French," *Richmond Enquirer,* October 18, 1830.

17. "Volunteer Toasts," *Charleston Courier,* September 25, 1830. See also "Gen. La Fayette," *Richmond Enquirer,* November 12, 1824; and "Volunteer Toasts," *Charleston Courier,* September 25, 1830. Although speaking of Latin American revolutions, Caitlin

Fitz has identified toasts as a significant way for antebellum Americans to signal their support for revolutions abroad. Fitz, *Our Sister Republics.*

18. For analysis of the importance of republicanism to antebellum southern politics, see Ford, *Origins of Southern Radicalism;* Holt, *Political Crisis of the 1850s;* Thornton, *Politics and Power in a Slave Society;* Greenberg, *Masters and Statesmen;* and Shalhope, *Roots of Democracy.*

19. George Tucker, "A Discourse on the Progress of Philosophy," *Southern Literary Messenger,* April 1835, 406.

20. "Cause of the Greeks," *City Gazette,* January 9, 1824.

21. *Genius of Liberty,* September 19, 1820.

22. "Greece," *Louisiana Courier,* May 27, 1822.

23. "Greece," *Alexandria Herald,* December 27, 1822.

24. *New Orleans Bee,* March 28, 1831. See also Stephen Edward Rice, "Address of Stephen Edward Rice, Esq," *Augusta Chronicle,* March 25, 1828; A Native of Augusta, "For the Chronicle: The Cause of the Greeks," *Augusta Chronicle,* March 17, 1824; "Oration," *Carolina Sentinel,* July 19, 1823; "Greece," *Ariel,* December 5, 1825; and *Georgian,* May 6, 1831.

25. "Oration," *Carolina Sentinel,* July 19, 1823. See also "Gen. La Fayette," *Richmond Enquirer,* November 12, 1824; and *City Gazette,* March 18, 1825.

26. "Cause of the Greeks," *City Gazette,* January 9, 1824.

27. "Celebration of the Fourth of July in the Parish of Terrebonne," *Louisiana Courier,* July 28, 1823. See also "An Oration, Delivered at the Court-House in Little Rock," *Arkansas Gazette,* July 12, 1825; "St. Patrick's Day," *Georgian,* March 18, 1826; *Charleston Courier,* May 11, 1826; and "Oration," *Alexandria Phenix Gazette,* February 26, 1827.

28. "At a Meeting: Oration," *Alexandria Gazette,* July 10, 1823.

29. "Oration, Pronounced by William A. McRea, Esq," *Alexandria Gazette,* February 28, 1824. For more examples of southern analysis of the strengths and superiority of the United States, see "Address," *Charleston Courier,* January 9, 1827; Henry Freeman, "An Oration," *Augusta Chronicle,* July 25, 1827; William P. Hort, "An Oration," *Pensacola Gazette,* July 27, 1827; and "Mr. Curtiss' Oration," *Georgia Journal,* July 14, 1828.

30. For overview and analysis of the revolutions of 1848, see Sperber, *European Revolutions;* and Dowe et al., *Europe in 1848.*

31. Historians who study American reactions to the revolutions of 1848 have generally agreed that Americans compared these revolutions to their own American Revolution. See Gemme, *Domesticating Foreign Struggles;* and Roberts, *Distant Revolutions,* although these historians are not primarily considering the influence of this analysis on the development of southerners' nationalism. Elizabeth Fox-Genovese and Eugene D. Genovese briefly identified southern reactions to foreign revolutions as characterized by both enthusiasm and trepidation. Fox-Genovese and Genovese, *Mind of the Master Class,* 41–68. While focusing primarily on the years of the Civil War itself, Andre M.

Fleche notes white southerners' rejection of radical labor activism and embrace of self-determination. Fleche, *Revolution of 1861.*

32. See Roberts, *Distant Revolutions,* for analysis of the American response to 1848.

33. *New Orleans Picayune,* May 3, 1848. See also Sylvias, "From Washington," *Macon Telegraph,* April 11, 1848; J. F. G. Mittag, "Semper Ego Auditor Taritum?" *Charleston Courier,* March 21, 1849; and "Hungary," *Floridian and Journal,* June 16, 1849.

34. "Germanic Confederation," *Augusta Chronicle and Sentinel,* May 18, 1848. See also "American Progress," *New Orleans Picayune,* April 20, 1849. For a scholarly analysis of the international influence of the American Declaration of Independence, see Armitage, *Declaration of Independence.*

35. "Hungary," *Southern Literary Messenger,* August 1851, 506.

36. J. F. G. Mittag, "Semper Ego Auditor Taritum?" *Charleston Courier,* March 21, 1849. See also "European Affairs," *Richmond Whig,* May 16, 1848; and "Address of the Irish Confederation," *Standard,* May 6, 1848.

37. Maximilian Schele de Vere, "Glimpses at Europe in 1848, Part III: The Lombardo-Veneto Kingdom," *Southern Literary Messenger,* April 1849, 194; "The French Republic," *Southern Quarterly Review,* July 1848, 207; Truth-Teller, "Washington Correspondence," *New Orleans Picayune,* April 16, 1848; "Italy," *Southern Patriot,* February 7, 1848; "Austria and Sardinia," *New Orleans Picayune,* April 19, 1849; "Two Unquiet Regions," *New Orleans Picayune,* April 27, 1849; "More of Southern Italy," *New Orleans Picayune,* August 30, 1851; G. W. K., "European Correspondence," *New Orleans Picayune,* September 26, 1849; "Kossuth and the English," *New Orleans Picayune,* December 4, 1851; "A Series of Casualties," *Savannah Daily Republican,* May 26, 1849; "Hungary," *Floridian and Journal,* June 16, 1849; "Fate of Hungary!" *Floridian and Journal,* September 15, 1849; R., "New York Correspondence," *New Orleans Picayune,* September 17, 1849.

38. "Hungary," *Floridian and Journal,* June 16, 1849. See also "The Fourth of July," *Charleston Courier,* July 4, 1848.

39. Excelsior, "From New York," *Macon Telegraph,* May 1, 1849. See also G. W. K., "European Correspondence," *New Orleans Picayune,* April 30, 1849.

40. For analysis of the importance of conservatism to antebellum southern thought, see McCurry, *Confederate Reckoning;* Sinha, *Counterrevolution of Slavery;* and Tate, *Conservatism and Southern Intellectuals.*

41. Charles M. Wiltse identified this strain of thought in Calhoun's writings in his article "A Critical Southerner." For more examples of southerners' concerns about Europeans' ability to implement republican regimes, or the insufficient republicanism of Europeans, see Kamfur, "Foreign Correspondence of the Journal," *Alabama Journal,* October 24, 1851; and "From New York," *Macon Telegraph,* May 1, 1849.

42. G. W. K., "European Correspondence," *New Orleans Picayune,* May 4, 1848.

43. G. W. K., "European Correspondence," *New Orleans Picayune,* November 30, 1848. See also G. W. K., "European Correspondence," *New Orleans Picayune,* December 6, 1848; G. W. K., "European Correspondence," *New Orleans Picayune,* July 19, 1849; and G. W. K., "European Correspondence," *New Orleans Picayune,* September 6, 1849.

44. "Mr. Kendall's Letters Again," *New Orleans Picayune,* August 6, 1848.

45. G. W. K., "European Correspondence," *New Orleans Picayune,* July 6, 1848.

46. P. C. G., "Paris in a State of Siege," *Richmond Enquirer,* July 21, 1848. See also "Affairs in France," *Alexandria Gazette,* June 2, 1848; G. W. K., "European Correspondence," *New Orleans Picayune,* November 14, 1848; and "Letters from a New Contributor," *Southern Literary Messenger,* November 1848, 657–63.

47. G. W. K., "European Correspondence," *New Orleans Picayune,* March 24, 1850.

48. G. W. K., "European Correspondence," *New Orleans Picayune,* November 14, 1848. See also W. R. Taber Jr., "To the Public: The Essentials of a Republic," *Charleston Courier,* December 31, 1853; G. W. K., "European Correspondence," *New Orleans Picayune,* February 11, 1849; and Maximilian Schele de Vere, "Glimpses at Europe in 1848, Part II: The German Parliament," *Southern Literary Messenger,* March 1849, 129–40.

49. William W. Mann, "Paris Correspondence," *Southern Literary Messenger,* May 1849, 271. See also Sylvias, "From Washington," *Macon Telegraph,* April 11, 1848.

50. "The Fourth of July," *Charleston Courier,* July 4, 1849. For analysis of the importance of social order to southern values, see Bonner, *Mastering America,* 286–89; Genovese, *Slaveholders' Dilemma,* 10–12; and Tate, *Conservatism and Southern Intellectuals,* 30–76, 136–51.

51. "Revolutions: Progress and Effects of Republican Opinions," *New Orleans Picayune,* March 28, 1848. See also "Hungarian Republic," *Augusta Chronicle and Sentinel,* July 17, 1849.

52. G. W. K., "European Correspondence," *New Orleans Picayune,* July 6, 1848; G. W. K., "European Correspondence," *New Orleans Picayune,* November 14, 1848; G. W. K., "European Correspondence," *New Orleans Picayune,* November 19, 1848.

53. "Mr. Kendall's Letters Again," *New Orleans Picayune,* August 6, 1848. See also "The Fourth of July," *Charleston Courier,* July 4, 1848.

54. This dismay at the failure of the revolutions to live up to the standard of the United States was typical of the American response to 1848. Roberts, *Distant Revolutions.* In their disappointment, white southerners were not so much forging new ideas on governance as using the opportunity and debate to refine and clarify their particular interpretations of national values and nationalism.

55. "Hungarian Republic," *Augusta Chronicle and Sentinel,* July 17, 1849. See also "France and Austria," *New Orleans Picayune,* October 11, 1849.

56. G. W. K., "European Correspondence," *New Orleans Picayune,* April 30, 1849.

57. "France," *Charleston Courier,* October 24, 1848.

58. "France," *New Orleans Picayune,* October 28, 1848.

59. "Revolutions," *New Orleans Picayune,* March 28, 1848. See also "The French Republic," *Alexandria Gazette,* April 1, 1848; "From New-York," *Macon Telegraph,* April 18, 1848; and "Foreign News," *Augusta Chronicle and Sentinel,* April 3, 1848.

60. William W. Mann, "Paris Correspondence," *Southern Literary Messenger,* May 1849, 267–72. See also G. W. K., "European Correspondence," *New Orleans Picayune,*

December 6, 1848; G. W. K., "European Correspondence," *New Orleans Picayune,* July 6, 1848; and "Affairs of Europe," *Richmond Whig,* June 4, 1850.

61. "French Intervention at Rome," *New Orleans Picayune,* May 15, 1849; "More of Southern Italy," *New Orleans Picayune,* August 30, 1851. See also G. W. K., "Editorial Correspondence," *New Orleans Picayune,* February 4, 1852; *Savannah Daily Republican,* September 15, 1851; and "Rome and Her Besiegers," *New Orleans Picayune,* July 17, 1849.

62. "European Affairs," *New Orleans Picayune,* August 18, 1849; "The French in Italy," *New Orleans Picayune,* June 6, 1849; "Affairs of Europe," *Columbus Enquirer,* June 12, 1849.

63. "Revolutions: Progress and Effects of Republican Opinions," *New Orleans Picayune,* March 28, 1848.

64. "Mr. Kendall's Letters Again," *New Orleans Picayune,* August 6, 1848.

65. G. W. K., "European Correspondence," *New Orleans Picayune,* September 6, 1849.

66. "Important Foreign News," *Texian Advocate,* November 9, 1848. See also "Address of the Irish Confederation," *Standard,* May 6, 1848; "A Series of Casualties," *Savannah Daily Republican,* May 26, 1849; and "The Fall of Venice," *New Orleans Picayune,* September 14, 1849.

67. "French Revolution," *Augusta Chronicle and Sentinel,* March 23, 1848. See also "French News," *Columbus Enquirer,* March 28, 1848; and "France and Austria," *New Orleans Picayune,* October 11, 1849.

68. *New Orleans Picayune,* May 3, 1848; "Italy," *New Orleans Picayune,* February 10, 1848; "American Progress," *New Orleans Picayune,* April 20, 1849; "Hungary," *Floridian and Journal,* June 16, 1849; *Augusta Chronicle and Sentinel,* May 1, 1848.

69. "Democratic Mass Meeting," *Standard,* July 29, 1848. See also "Hungary," *Floridian and Journal,* June 16, 1849; and "France and Poland," *Standard,* May 27, 1848.

70. Lucy Riall argues that Garibaldi's exploits in South America and then in the short-lived Roman Republic won him international acclaim and popularity, making him one of the first figures to achieve worldwide fame. This fame was in part intentional, as Garibaldi's image as a nationalist hero was carefully crafted, even during his active career, to achieve political purposes such as strengthening national unity within Italy. Garibaldi's popularity continued to grow, culminating in international acclaim and celebration of Garibaldi, his virtues, and his place in the Italian nation after his successful campaign in Sicily in 1860. Riall, *Garibaldi.*

71. For a sampling of southern reports on Garibaldi, see "Garibaldi in Retirement," *Richmond Daily Dispatch,* December 8, 1860; "Garibaldi at Home," *Richmond Daily Dispatch,* February 8, 1861; "Garibaldi," *Augusta Chronicle and Sentinel,* June 15, 1849; *Charleston Mercury,* July 1, 1859; "Arrival of Garibaldi," *Alabama Journal,* August 7, 1850; "Garibaldi to Victor Emmanuel," *New Orleans Delta,* June 6, 1860; "An Italian Patriot's Wife," *Standard,* August 13, 1859; and "Garibaldi," *New Orleans Picayune,* August 17, 1849.

72. "Garibaldi," *Charleston Courier,* July 30, 1850; "Garibaldi," *Alabama Journal,* August 5, 1850.

73. B., "En Avant!" *Southern Literary Messenger,* March 1850, 142. See also Phi Ro, "Washington Correspondence," *New Orleans Picayune,* August 13, 1849.

2. Let the South Take Warning

1. "Nashville Convention Meeting on Saturday Night," *Richmond Enquirer,* April 23, 1850.

2. Historians who have identified the critical importance of territorial slavery, including the debate over the Compromise of 1850, to creating the political conflict of the 1850s include Holt, *Political Crisis of the 1850s,* esp. 84–92; Potter, *Impending Crisis;* and Walther, *Shattering of the Union.* For an overview of the filibuster movement, including southern involvement, see May, *Manifest Destiny's Underworld.*

3. Historians have established that white southerners' defense of slavery and political development was tied to their fears of losing self-government to a growing northern population. See Sinha, *Counterrevolution of Slavery,* 33–62; Bonner, *Mastering America,* 41–78, 149–83; Holt, *Political Crisis of the 1850s,* 52–56; Karp, *This Vast Southern Empire;* and Ford, *Deliver Us from Evil.* At the same time that slaveholders feared what they saw as a consolidating abolitionist threat to slavery, northerners feared what they saw as the growth of southern slaveholders' power. Davis, *Slave Power Conspiracy.*

4. Sylvias, "From Washington," *Macon Telegraph,* February 6, 1849.

5. "Congress," *Richmond Whig,* April 2, 1850. For more international comparisons casting the South as an oppressed European nation, see "Admission of California," *Alexandria Gazette,* February 23, 1850; "Speech of Mr. Clay," *Macon Telegraph,* February 19, 1850; "Speech of the Hon. A. G. Brown, of Mississippi," *Mississippi Free Trader,* March 6, 1850; "Speech of Mr. Hunter of Virginia, on the Territorial Question," *Richmond Enquirer,* April 5, 1850; and Citizen of Claiborne, "Home Correspondence," *Mississippi Free Trader,* July 3, 1850. For analysis of the evolution of slaveholders' desire for expansion, see Bonner, *Mastering America,* 3–40.

6. "Gen. Felix Huston's Speech," *Mississippi Free Trader,* September 25, 1850.

7. "Nashville Convention Meeting on Saturday Night," *Richmond Enquirer,* April 23, 1850.

8. Felix Huston, "To the Members of the Nashville Convention," *Mississippi Free Trader,* June 5, 1850.

9. "Thirty-First Congress—1st Session," *New Orleans Picayune,* February 1, 1850. See also "Speech of Mr. Clingman, of North Carolina, on the Territorial Question," *Richmond Whig,* February 5, 1850.

10. "Speech of Mr. Hilliard of Ala.," *Alabama Journal,* March 2, 1850.

11. "Messrs. Bailey and Harman," *Macon Telegraph*, September 23, 1851. See also "Virginia Resolutions Respecting Slavery," *Alexandria Gazette*, February 7, 1849.

12. "Watchman, What of the Night?" *Macon Telegraph*, October 29, 1850. See also *Macon Telegraph*, February 11, 1851; and "A Manifesto," *Macon Telegraph*, March 11, 1851.

13. "Great and Enthusiastic Meeting—Reception of Hon. A. G. Brown at Jackson," *Mississippi Free Trader*, October 23, 1850. See also "Speech of Hon. A. G. Brown," *Mississippi Free Trader*, December 11, 1850.

14. "Central Southern Rights Association," *Richmond Enquirer*, January 21, 1851.

15. "Address of the Whig Members of the Legislature and Convention," *Alexandria Gazette*, April 30, 1851.

16. P., "The People," *Southern Quarterly Review*, January 1854, 33.

17. F. A. Ross, "Letter from the Rev. Dr. Ross, of Huntsville, Ala., to the Rev. Dr. A. Barnes, of Philadelphia," *Charleston Mercury*, February 21, 1857. See also "The Fugitive Slave Law and the Union," *Mississippi Free Trader*, September 10, 1851; and "Substance of the Remarks of the Hon. Judge Rice," *Charleston Courier*, July 30, 1851.

18. For analysis of the southern fire-eaters, especially their influence on the secession movement, see Walther, *Fire-Eaters*.

19. "Speech of the Hon. A. G. Brown, of Mississippi," *Mississippi Free Trader*, March 6, 1850.

20. "Another Sign," *Richmond Enquirer*, October 15, 1850. See also "Facts to Be Remembered," *Mississippi Free Trader*, December 18, 1850.

21. "General Felix Huston's Speech at Lexington, Miss.," *Mississippi Free Trader*, December 18, 1850; also republished as "The Prospect before Us—Slavery—The Union," *Macon Telegraph*, January 7, 1851. See also Felix Huston, "To the Members of the Nashville Convention," *Mississippi Free Trader*, June 5, 1850.

22. "Speech of the Hon. A. G. Brown, of Mississippi," *Mississippi Free Trader*, March 6, 1850.

23. "Consequences of Secession," *Macon Telegraph*, May 27, 1851. See also "Remarks of Hon. Wm. F. Colcock," *Charleston Courier*, July 1, 1851.

24. Houston, *Speech of Hon. Sam Houston*, 8–9.

25. "Great States Becoming Small Ones," *Texian Advocate*, August 14, 1851.

26. Boyd, *Speech of Hon. Samuel S. Boyd*, 3. See also the republishing of an 1851 speech by Edward Everett on similar themes in "The Fearful Reckoning," *Fayetteville Observer*, March 4, 1861.

27. Barnard, *No Just Cause for a Dissolution*, 6–7.

28. Americanus, "The Dissolution of the Union," *Arkansas Gazette*, April 5, 1850.

29. Curtius [William John Grayson], "The Wrongs of the South, Greater Than Those of Hungary or Poland," *Charleston Courier*, July 25, 1851.

30. Curtius, "The Wrongs of the South, Greater Than Those of Hungary or Poland," *Charleston Courier*, July 25, 1851.

31. For analysis of the filibuster expeditions, see May, *Manifest Destiny's Underworld*.

32. On filibustering and the South, Robert E. May argues that filibustering became seen as southern rather than American during the course of the 1850s. May, *Southern Dream;* May, *Manifest Destiny's Underworld,* 249–80. For analysis of proslavery imperialism, see Karp, *This Vast Southern Empire;* and Johnson, *River of Dark Dreams.*

33. "The Cloven Foot," *Richmond Enquirer,* September 18, 1849.

34. "The Whig Party," *Alabama Journal,* August 9, 1852. See also A Virginian, "To the People of Virginia," *Richmond Whig,* October 29, 1852.

35. "American Lust of Dominion," *New Orleans Picayune,* July 21, 1850.

36. "Cuba," *New Orleans Picayune,* August 7, 1851.

37. "Cuba Revolution," *Florida Republican,* August 14, 1851.

38. "England and Nicaragua," *New Orleans Picayune,* May 19, 1856. See also "The Recognition of Nicaragua," *New Orleans Picayune,* May 23, 1856.

39. "The Nicaraguan Minister," *Columbus Enquirer,* May 20, 1856.

40. "The Cuban Trials," *Mississippi Free Trader,* March 26, 1851.

41. "Hungarian Fund," *Arkansas Gazette,* April 9, 1852. See also "American Sympathy with Cuba," *Arkansas Gazette,* August 22, 1851; and "Letter from New York," *Alexandria Gazette,* September 4, 1851.

42. "Garibaldi and Walker," *Columbus Enquirer,* July 7, 1860. See also "English Fillibustering," *Richmond Whig,* September 15, 1857.

43. Chat, "Correspondence to the Free Trader: Letter IX," *Mississippi Free Trader,* January 7, 1852. See also "The President and the South," *Mississippi Free Trader,* January 14, 1852; and "Fillmore and Cuba—Lopez and Kossuth," *Mississippi Free Trader,* December 17, 1851.

44. *Arkansas Gazette,* September 19, 1851. See also Samuel R. Walker, "Cuba and the South," *DeBow's Review,* November 1854, 522; and "American Lust of Dominion," *New Orleans Picayune,* July 21, 1850.

45. "Letter from New York," *Alexandria Gazette,* September 4, 1851.

46. "National Morals," *Star,* July 10, 1850.

47. "Letter from New York," *Alexandria Gazette,* September 4, 1851.

48. "National Morals," *Star,* July 10, 1850.

49. For information on the federal response to filibustering, see May, *Manifest Destiny's Underworld,* 117–68; and May, *Southern Dream,* 22–76. For analysis of the southern response to anti-filibustering within the federal government, see May, *Southern Dream,* 22–45, 111–89.

50. "The Cuban Trials," *Mississippi Free Trader,* March 26, 1851.

51. "The President and the South," *Mississippi Free Trader,* January 14, 1852.

52. "Hungarian Fund," *Arkansas Gazette,* April 9, 1852. See also "American Sympathy with Cuba," *Arkansas Gazette,* August 22, 1851; "Fillmore and Cuba—Lopez and Kossuth," *Mississippi Free Trader,* December 17, 1851; and "The Difference," *Mississippi Free Trader,* March 24, 1852.

53. "Senator Houston's Speech," *Alexandria Gazette,* March 24, 1853. See also "The Whig Party," *Alabama Journal,* August 9, 1852.

54. This concern fit with broader white antebellum southern fears of abolitionism stoking race rebellion, in the United States as well as in the Caribbean, from which, slaveholders feared, rebellion would spread to the South. Racial nationalism was not as prominent within white southerners' discussions of the European revolutions but did otherwise constitute an important strand of southern thought. See Rugemer, *Problem of Emancipation;* Guterl, *American Mediterranean;* and Clavin, *Toussaint L'Ouverture and the American Civil War.*

55. "The President and the South," *Mississippi Free Trader,* January 14, 1852.

56. "The Difference," *Mississippi Free Trader,* March 24, 1852. See also Samuel R. Walker, "Cuba and the South," *DeBow's Review,* November 1854, 519–24. An article from the *Richmond Enquirer,* republished in Carlile, *Cincinnati Platform,* 12–13, espoused the opposing view, claiming that an international perspective revealed southern conservatives should, according to southern values, oppose intervention in the form of filibustering.

57. The American government did not officially intervene in the case of Hungary, although Congress debated intervention when Lajos Kossuth toured the United States to raise funds and support for Hungarian independence.

3. A Tool Wherewith to Promote Agitation

1. As reported in "Mr. Mitchel's Position on the Slavery Question," *Baton Rouge Advocate,* January 27, 1854. For analysis of Mitchel and slavery, see McGovern, *John Mitchel,* 119–54.

2. For discussions of Americans' welcome of and enthusiasm for foreign revolutionaries, see McGovern, *John Mitchel,* 94–117; Riall, *Garibaldi,* 106–14; Spencer, *Louis Kossuth and Young America,* 1–11; and Fleche, *Revolution of 1861,* 19–23.

3. Spencer, *Louis Kossuth and Young America,* 66–72.

4. Levine, *Spirit of 1848,* esp. 150–58; McGovern, *John Mitchel,* 119–54.

5. For an overview of American reactions to Kossuth and the ultimate result of Kossuth's tour, see Spencer, *Louis Kossuth and Young America,* esp. chaps. 5–7, 10–13.

6. Chat, "Letter X," *Mississippi Free Trader,* January 14, 1852.

7. "Kossuth and His Mission," *New Orleans Picayune,* December 17, 1851. See also "Letters from New York," *New Orleans Picayune,* December 13, 1851; "Our Country and Kossuth," *Alexandria Gazette,* December 13, 1851; and "Kossuth and the English," *New Orleans Picayune,* December 4, 1851.

8. Donald S. Spencer reveals that although Americans initially embraced Kossuth as a representative of the Hungarian cause, as soon as they realized that Kossuth was urging official intervention, Americans rejected both Kossuth and his pleas, in large part due to the precedent of Washington's Farewell Address. Spencer, *Louis Kossuth and Young America,* 49–64, 136–44, 151.

9. "Kossuth," *Macon Telegraph,* January 6, 1852.

10. Pacificus, *Alexandria Gazette,* December 16, 1851.

11. Clemens, *Speech of Mr. Clemens . . . Dec. 10, 1851,* 4–6. The idea that Kossuth's request for intervention violated American nonintervention was widespread in southern periodicals throughout Kossuth's tour in the United States and even after. See also Antelope, "New York Correspondence," *New Orleans Picayune,* December 19, 1851; "More about Kossuth and His Policy," *Savannah Daily Republican,* December 31, 1851; Le Diable Boiteux, "Washington Correspondence," *New Orleans Picayune,* January 9, 1852; A. A. D., "Kossuth," *Alabama Journal,* January 9, 1852; "The American Policy," *New Orleans Picayune,* January 15, 1852; "John C. Calhoun, the Younger, of South Carolina, Now of Florida, on Kossuth and Intervention," *Charleston Courier,* January 19, 1852; "Kossuth," *Alabama Journal,* April 16, 1852; and "Kossuth and Intervention," *Southern Quarterly Review,* July 1852, 221–34.

12. "Kossuth and Lopez," *Macon Telegraph,* February 10, 1852.

13. Chat, "Letter X," *Mississippi Free Trader,* January 14, 1852. See also "The Kossuth Failure," *New Orleans Picayune,* May 2, 1852; and "The Wildfire," *Alexandria Gazette,* January 7, 1852.

14. "Washington Correspondence," *New Orleans Picayune,* January 22, 1852.

15. "Kossuth," *Alabama Journal,* April 16, 1852.

16. "Kossuth's Speech," *New Orleans Picayune,* April 1, 1852.

17. "Kossuth in Georgia and South Carolina," *Macon Telegraph,* April 20, 1852.

18. "Hon. W. R. Smith and Sargent's Speaker," *Alabama Journal,* May 6, 1852. For more southern analyses of the differing sectional reactions to Kossuth, see "The Kossuth Failure," *New Orleans Picayune,* May 2, 1852; Le Diable Boiteux, "Washington Correspondence," *New Orleans Picayune,* April 23, 1852; "Communicated," *Galveston Weekly Journal,* May 21, 1852; and "Kossuth," *Alabama Journal,* April 16, 1852.

19. "The Wildfire," *Alexandria Gazette,* January 7, 1852.

20. "The Kossuth Failure," *New Orleans Picayune,* May 2, 1852.

21. Il Segretario [Edward William Johnston], "Editorial Correspondence," *Richmond Whig,* February 3, 1852.

22. "Kossuth and Lopez," *Macon Telegraph,* February 10, 1852.

23. A. A. D., "Kossuth," *Alabama Journal,* January 9, 1852. See also "Signs at Washington," *Alabama Planter,* December 29, 1851.

24. Chat, "Correspondence to the Free Trader: Letter IX," *Mississippi Free Trader,* January 7, 1852. For additional expressions of belief in the similar positions of Hungary and Cuba, see "Letter from New York," *Alexandria Gazette,* September 4, 1851; *Arkansas Gazette,* September 19, 1851; and "Fillmore and Cuba—Lopez and Kossuth," *Mississippi Free Trader,* December 17, 1851. Robert E. May reveals that throughout the late antebellum period, southerners did increasingly support filibustering at a higher rate than northerners. May, *Southern Dream.*

25. "Kossuth and Lopez," *Macon Telegraph,* February 10, 1852.

26. "The President and the South," *Mississippi Free Trader,* January 14, 1852. For other accusations that northerners' lack of support for Cuba, despite their support for Kossuth, was due to antisouthern or antislavery sentiment, see "The Difference,"

Mississippi Free Trader, March 24, 1852; and "Hungarian Fund," *Arkansas Gazette,* April 9, 1852.

27. "Kossuth and Kinkel," *Richmond Whig,* February 3, 1852.

28. "More about Kossuth and His Policy," *Savannah Daily Republican,* December 31, 1851. See also "The Whig Party," *Alabama Journal,* August 9, 1852.

29. Spencer, *Louis Kossuth and Young America,* 65–72, 76–81, 95–106.

30. "The Kossuth Excitement and the Slavery Question," *Savannah Daily Republican,* December 29, 1851. See also Penna. Avenue, "Letter from Washington," *Alexandria Gazette,* December 29, 1851.

31. Le Diable Boiteux, "Washington Correspondence," *New Orleans Picayune,* January 9, 1852.

32. "The Designs upon Kossuth," *New Orleans Picayune,* December 15, 1851.

33. "Kossuth in a Slave State," *Mississippi Free Trader,* March 24, 1852.

34. "Signs at Washington," *Alabama Planter,* December 29, 1851.

35. *Arkansas Gazette,* September 19, 1851; "John Mitchel," *Woodville Republican,* December 27, 1853; "The Southern Citizen," *Southern Sentinel,* February 3, 1858.

36. "Dinner to John Mitchel by the Citizens of Richmond," *Richmond Whig,* May 30, 1854; "Remarks of Mr. F. H. Hatch," *Baton Rouge Advocate,* February 25, 1854.

37. "Mr. Mitchel's Position on the Slavery Question," *Baton Rouge Advocate,* January 27, 1854. For further analysis of this issue, see McGovern, *John Mitchel,* 119–54.

38. Gleeson, *Green and the Gray,* 10–27, 69; Fleche, *Revolution of 1861,* 28–30; Bruce, *Harp and the Eagle,* 136–40.

39. Mahin, *Blessed Place of Freedom,* 21–28; Bruce, *Harp and the Eagle,* 136–40.

40. Gleeson, *Green and the Gray,* 10–50.

41. *Alexandria Gazette,* April 25, 1854; "Dinner to John Mitchel by the Citizens of Richmond," *Richmond Whig,* May 30, 1854; "John Mitchel's Paper, the 'Southern Citizen,'" *New Orleans Daily True Delta,* January 29, 1858; "John Mitchel," *Charleston Courier,* September 24, 1857.

42. "Letter from Hon. L. M. Keitt," *Baton Rouge Advocate,* September 6, 1855.

43. "John Mitchel's Southern Tour," *New Orleans Delta,* May 16, 1858.

44. "Remarks of Mr. F. H. Hatch," *Baton Rouge Advocate,* February 25, 1854.

45. "Political Sophistry—A Stupid Fallacy Exposed," *Baton Rouge Advocate,* August 17, 1855.

46. Bay State, "Boston Correspondence," *Charleston Courier,* February 2, 1854.

47. "John Mitchell [*sic*] and Abolitionism," *Richmond Whig,* March 17, 1854.

48. "Speech of Roger A. Pryor, Esq.," *Richmond Whig,* May 28, 1858; "Prattville, July 24, 1859," *Daily Confederation,* July 28, 1859.

49. For general southern reaction to, and praise of, the unification of Italy, see "United Italy," *New Orleans Picayune,* October 5, 1860; "Letter from Italy," *New Orleans Picayune,* April 28, 1861; and "The Kingdom of Italy," *Richmond Enquirer,* November 27, 1860.

50. Phi Ro, "Washington Correspondence," *New Orleans Picayune*, August 13, 1849. See also G. W. K., "European Correspondence," *New Orleans Picayune*, September 19, 1849; "Garibaldi," *Augusta Chronicle and Sentinel*, June 15, 1849; and "Garibaldi," *Alabama Journal*, August 5, 1850.

51. *New Orleans Picayune*, December 6, 1859.

52. "Garibaldi and His Proclamation," *New Orleans Daily True Delta*, June 23, 1859. For other examples of Garibaldi as the symbol of Italian nationalism and of the virtues of Italian nationalism, see George William Bagby, "Editor's Table: Death of Count Cavour," *Southern Literary Messenger*, July 1861, 72–80; and "Gen. Garibaldi," *Macon Telegraph*, June 28, 1859.

53. "Garibaldi and Italy," *New Orleans Picayune*, September 23, 1860. See also "Entry of Garibaldi into Naples—Exciting Scene," *Augusta Chronicle and Sentinel*, October 4, 1860; and "Garibaldi and His Proclamation," *New Orleans Daily True Delta*, June 23, 1859.

54. "United Italy," *New Orleans Picayune*, October 5, 1860. See also "Entre of Garibaldi into Naples—Exciting Scenes," *Houston Telegraph*, October 11, 1860.

55. "Garibaldi," *Richmond Daily Dispatch*, September 16, 1861. For more accounts of Garibaldi fighting despotism, see also "Garibaldi and Walker," *Columbus Enquirer*, July 7, 1860; and "Garibaldi," *San Antonio Ledger and Texan*, September 29, 1860. For additional praise of Garibaldi's virtues, including republicanism, see "Strange Bedfellows," *New Orleans Daily True Delta*, June 10, 1859; and "Victor Emanuel," *Richmond Daily Dispatch*, December 20, 1860.

56. "Gen. Garibaldi," *Macon Telegraph*, June 28, 1859.

57. "The Revolt in Lombardy," *New Orleans Picayune*, June 11, 1859. See also "Garibaldi and His Proclamation," *New Orleans Daily True Delta*, June 23, 1859.

58. "The Red Shirt," *Richmond Daily Dispatch*, December 1, 1860.

59. Advertisement, *Daily Confederation*, July 21, 1859; "Fashion Letter," *Charleston Mercury*, December 31, 1859; "The Fashions," *Charleston Mercury*, January 15, 1861; "Notes of the War," *Charleston Mercury*, June 26, 1861; Advertisements, *Daily Confederation*, November 11, 1859; "How Garibaldi Dresses," *Richmond Whig*, July 24, 1860.

60. Nero, "For the Confederation: A Question for Junius," *Daily Confederation*, July 2, 1859.

61. "Wanted Immediately," *New Orleans Daily True Delta*, December 6, 1860.

62. Dufour, *Gentle Tiger*, 61–69, 36–60, 82–87, 111–15.

63. K., "Letter from London," *New Orleans Picayune*, October 28, 1860.

64. "Tribute of Respect," *Richmond Daily Dispatch*, January 24, 1863. See also "Killed and Wounded Louisianians in the Virginia Campaigns," *New Orleans Picayune*, July 29, 1862; "Wheat's Battalion," *Richmond Daily Dispatch*, June 5, 1862; and "Dead on the Field of Honor," *Richmond Enquirer*, July 1, 1862.

65. "A Military Celebrity," *New Orleans Daily True Delta*, September 23, 1864.

66. "Arrival," *Charleston Courier*, June 24, 1861.

67. "Garibaldi's Movements," *Augusta Chronicle and Sentinel,* August 24, 1860; "Americans in Garibaldi's Army," *New Orleans Picayune,* November 22, 1860. See also *Alexandria Gazette,* January 21, 1861; and "The Americans in Garibaldi's Army," *New Orleans Daily True Delta,* November 18, 1860.

4. Equal among the Other Nations

1. "The Fourth of March," *Richmond Daily Dispatch,* March 4, 1861.

2. "The Spirit of Nationality," *Richmond Daily Dispatch,* May 7, 1861.

3. Among other sources of southern nationalism and justifications for secession, historians have identified religion and slavery (Faust, *Creation of Confederate Nationalism*), constitutional and rights-based arguments (for an overview, see Doyle, *Cause of All Nations,* 27–37), history and personal experiences (Quigley, *Shifting Grounds*), and romanticism and cultural elements (Osterweis, *Romanticism and Nationalism in the Old South;* Bernath, *Confederate Minds;* Taylor, *Cavalier and Yankee*). For additional analysis of southern nationalism, see Rubin, *Shattered Nation;* and Binnington, *Confederate Visions.*

4. See Faust, *Creation of Confederate Nationalism,* 14; Fleche, *Revolution of 1861,* 132–50; Quigley, *Shifting Grounds,* 77–83, 145–57; and Rable, *Confederate Republic,* 44–49.

5. For analysis of white southern concerns about the restriction of slavery as harming liberty, particularly fears of the Republican Party, see Cooper, *Liberty and Slavery,* esp. 248–81.

6. C. C. Clay Jr., "Letter from Hon. C. C. Clay, Jr.," *Charleston Mercury,* June 1, 1860.

7. Power, *Proceedings of the Mississippi State Convention,* 77.

8. Rutledge, *Mr. Douglas and the Doctrine of Coercion,* 3–4.

9. "Mr. Douglas and Coercion," *Charleston Mercury,* October 23, 1860. For similar ideas, see also "To the People of the South," *Charleston Mercury,* November 5, 1860.

10. "Words of Prophecy," *Nashville Union and American,* November 18, 1860. See also "Insult Added to Injury," *Nashville Union and American,* November 29, 1860.

11. A National Democrat, "The Crisis—Letters from the People," *Baton Rouge Advocate,* December 9, 1860. For more examples of calls to action via comparisons with European despotisms, see A. Roane, "The South, In the Union or Out of It," *DeBow's Review,* October 1860, 448–65; and "The Fourth of March," *Richmond Daily Dispatch,* March 4, 1861.

12. Python [John Tyler Jr.], "The Secession of the South," *DeBow's Review,* April 1860, 386.

13. A. Roane, "The South, In the Union or Out of It," *DeBow's Review,* October 1860, 457–58. See also J. M. Mason, "The Proposed State Convention," *Richmond Daily Dispatch,* December 1, 1860; and James L. Bowen, "Communication: To the Citizens of Virginia of Northern Origin," *Alexandria Gazette,* May 17, 1861.

14. "National Danger," *Macon Telegraph,* June 28, 1861. For more examples of accusations of northern harm to southern self-government, see "United Action of Virginia," *Richmond Daily Dispatch,* May 30, 1861; and "The 'Combinations' Spreading," *New Orleans Picayune,* April 28, 1861.

15. "How Will They Dare?" *New Orleans Picayune,* January 29, 1861.

16. "Secession Is Freedom," *Charleston Mercury,* December 10, 1860.

17. Davis, "Remarks on the Special Message," 129. See also Hunter, "Speech . . . on the Resolution Proposing to Retrocede the Forts," 282; "Out of Their Own Mouths," *New Orleans Picayune,* January 30, 1861; and "Concession, or Not?" *New Orleans Picayune,* January 10, 1861.

18. For a discussion of types of nationalism, see Kramer, *Nationalism in Europe and America.* Although focused primarily on a domestic context, historians have long recognized the importance of southern claims to distinctiveness, the most important of which was the myth that southerners were descended from cavaliers and northerners from Puritans. See Taylor, *Cavalier and Yankee.* Michael T. Bernath has more recently emphasized cultural distinctiveness as central to southern nationalism. Bernath, *Confederate Minds.* Paul Quigley does internationalize these claims to distinctiveness, revealing the influence that European ethnic nationalism had on the development of southern nationalism. Quigley, *Shifting Grounds,* esp. 30–41. Historians have also long debated whether or not the antebellum South was in fact distinct; for historians who accept the South as a unique region, see Cash, *Mind of the South;* and Cobb, *Away Down South.* For historians who interpret the South as American, and therefore not distinct, see Pessen, "How Different from Each Other"; Potter, *Impending Crisis;* Degler, *Place over Time;* and Stampp, *Imperiled Union.*

19. Edward McCrady, "To the Electors of St. Philip and St. Michael," *Charleston Mercury,* September 21, 1860.

20. "Address of Mr. Townsend on the Measures of Remedy for the South," *Charleston Mercury,* June 14, 1860; "Meeting in St. John's Colleton," *Charleston Mercury,* June 13, 1860.

21. "The Spirit of Nationality," *Richmond Daily Dispatch,* May 7, 1861.

22. "Virginia State Convention—Able Letter from Senator Mason," *Augusta Chronicle and Sentinel,* December 5, 1860. See also Gilmer, *Letter Addressed to Hon. Wm. C. Rives,* 10; and R. L. Gibson, "Our Federal Union," *DeBow's Review,* July 1860, 36–37.

23. A. Roane, "The South, In the Union or Out of It," *DeBow's Review,* October 1860, 448, 457–58. See also "Concession, or Not?" *New Orleans Picayune,* January 10, 1861.

24. "Secession Is Freedom," *Charleston Mercury,* December 10, 1860.

25. "Cotton for the Government," *Macon Telegraph,* June 8, 1861.

26. "The Military Despotism," *Charleston Mercury,* May 25, 1861.

27. Rutledge, *Mr. Douglas and the Doctrine of Coercion,* 4–5.

28. "Brethren Agree," *New Orleans Picayune,* June 19, 1861.

29. "National Danger," *Macon Telegraph*, June 28, 1861.

30. J. M. [John Mitchel], "Paris Correspondence," *Charleston Mercury*, June 8, 1861.

31. J. M., "Affairs in Europe: Our Paris Correspondence," *Charleston Mercury*, August 24, 1861.

32. Mack Smith, *Making of Italy*; Riall, *Italian Risorgimento*.

33. "New Line of Sectionalism," *New Orleans Picayune*, December 8, 1860.

34. "Progress of the Revolution in South Carolina: Action of the Legislature," *Richmond Whig*, November 13, 1860. See also "Legislative Proceedings," *Charleston Courier*, November 10, 1860. For assessments of Italy as having been created through unification, see "The Union of Italy," *Richmond Daily Dispatch*, December 1, 1860; and "Italy United," *Richmond Daily Dispatch*, November 28, 1860.

35. "French Recognition of a Southern Government," *Augusta Daily Constitutionalist*, February 13, 1861.

36. "Correspondence of the Courier," *Charleston Courier*, March 13, 1861. See also "Virginia State Convention," *Alexandria Gazette*, March 18, 1861.

37. "Secession in Ireland," *Charleston Mercury*, January 31, 1861. Such a report shows that, although Italy was the most successful and therefore frequent model of "secession" to southern secessionists, it was not the only aspiring European nation that southerners characterized as seeking secession from an empire.

38. "Extract of a Speech of Lieut. Governor Reynolds," *Charleston Mercury*, February 11, 1861.

39. Hubbard, *Burden of Confederate Diplomacy*; Owsley, *King Cotton Diplomacy*; Mattson, "Pariah Diplomacy," 9–21.

40. Confederate secretary of state R. M. T. Hunter did authorize Mason to inform the British government of the Confederacy's supposed similarities to Italy, emphasizing the positive actions Britain had taken toward Italy. However, diplomatic strategies predominantly focused on the economic importance of cotton. Hubbard, *Burden of Confederate Diplomacy*, 21–27, 59.

41. J. M., "Our Paris Correspondence," *Charleston Mercury*, December 20, 1860.

42. "American Affairs in France," *Richmond Daily Dispatch*, July 11, 1861.

43. "Italian and Southern Independence," *Richmond Daily Dispatch*, July 13, 1861. See also "French Recognition of the Confederate States of America," *Richmond Daily Dispatch*, July 3, 1861.

44. Gamma, "Letter from Paris," *New Orleans Picayune*, July 13, 1861. The southern press also eagerly reported instances of Europeans' equating the Confederacy's claims to recognition with those of Italy; see also "Our Foreign Policy," *Charleston Mercury*, October 29, 1861; "French Recognition of a Southern Government," *Augusta Daily Constitutionalist*, February 13, 1861; and "France and the South," *Charleston Mercury*, May 10, 1861.

45. Pro-Confederate sentiment in Europe and in the United States developed particularly among conservative elements who feared democracy or, in the case of some European conservatives, desired the downfall of American republicanism. For analysis

of European opinion on the Civil War, see Hubbard, *Burden of Confederate Diplomacy*, 20, 36; Mahin, *Blessed Place of Freedom*, 170; Blackburn, *French Newspaper Opinion*, x–xi; Jones, *Blue and Gray Diplomacy*, 1; Campbell, *English Public Opinion*, 163–93; and Blackett, *Divided Hearts*, 7, 61–75. Copperhead or Peace Democrats were the most notable group of northerners who opposed the war. Copperheads attracted more politically conservative supporters and were united in their desire for personal liberties; as such, they, like Confederates, feared Lincoln's consolidation of federal power. See Weber, *Copperheads*; and Neely, *Fate of Liberty*.

46. "The Despots of Europe," *Staunton Spectator*, June 4, 1861.

47. "The True Issue in the Presidential Election," *Charleston Mercury*, October 12, 1860.

48. Anglo-Californian, *The National Crisis*, 14–15.

49. Bassett, *A Northern Plea for the Right of Secession*, 7.

50. William Smith O'Brien, "Smith O'Brien on the American War," *Charleston Courier*, August 6, 1862.

51. "The Germans in Carolina," *Charleston Courier*, June 24, 1861. See also Anglo-Californian, *The National Crisis*, 16. For analysis of antiwar northerners and northern criticism of Lincoln, see Weber, *Copperheads*; and Neely, *Fate of Liberty*.

52. "English Opinion of American Affairs," *Richmond Daily Dispatch*, September 7, 1861. See also "Comments of the *London Times* on American Affairs," *Richmond Whig*, July 22, 1862; "Garibaldi and the English Press," *Augusta Daily Constitutionalist*, October 14, 1862; "Tone of the French Press on the Southern Movement," *Charleston Mercury*, February 14, 1861; "A German Professor on the American Quarrel," *Index* (London), October 29, 1863; and "Extracts from Mr. Long's Speech," *Staunton Spectator*, May 3, 1864.

53. O. A. Lochrane, "To the Irish People," *Augusta Daily Constitutionalist*, May 16, 1861.

54. "An Important Document—Eloquent Appeal from Major Tochman," *New Orleans Daily True Delta*, June 2, 1861.

55. "French Recognition of the Confederate States of America," *Richmond Daily Dispatch*, July 3, 1861. See also "The American Question in France," *New Orleans Daily True Delta*, September 29, 1861; and "Later from Europe," *Fayetteville Observer*, July 8, 1861.

56. "France and the Southern Confederacy," *Richmond Daily Dispatch*, May 6, 1861; "France and the South," *Charleston Mercury*, May 10, 1861. In general, French conservatives favored the Confederacy because they believed a failure of American democracy would vindicate authoritarian regimes in France; however, overall French opinion was divided, and official recognition of the Confederacy was never granted. Blackburn, *French Newspaper Opinion*; Doyle, *Cause of All Nations*, 98–99, 242–43.

57. "England and the Southern Confederacy," *Charleston Mercury*, May 19, 1861; "England and the Southern Confederacy," *Augusta Daily Constitutionalist*, May 19, 1861; "English Press on Recognition," *Macon Telegraph*, May 24, 1861.

58. "American Affairs in Europe: Recognition of the Southern Confederacy," *Richmond Examiner,* February 7, 1862.

59. "Southern Independence Association of London," *Weekly Register,* March 5, 1864; Smith, *A Letter to a Whig Member,* 35. See also "European Opinion," *Charleston Mercury,* April 1, 1864.

60. Doyle, *Cause of All Nations,* 142–45.

61. Spence, *On the Recognition,* 2, 5–6, 7–8.

62. Spence, *On the Recognition,* 24. See also Spence, *The American Union,* 143.

5. Without a Parallel and Without a Rival

1. Spratt, *The Philosophy of Secession,* 5, 8. See also L. W. Spratt, "Slave Trade in the Southern Congress," *Charleston Mercury,* February 13, 1861.

2. For analysis of the ideological bases of the European revolutions, see Israel, *Revolution of the Mind,* esp. 37–91; and Hobsbawm, *Age of Revolution.* For analysis of contemporary nineteenth-century understandings of nationalism and nationalist movements, see Doyle, *Cause of All Nations,* 87–93; Fleche, *Revolution of 1861;* and McDaniel, *Problem of Democracy.*

3. Although the revolutions of 1848 were themselves not entirely liberal, they were largely premised on extending, not restricting, rights. For a survey of the social and political background of the revolutions of 1848, see Sperber, *European Revolutions,* 5–104.

4. For analysis of antebellum white southerners' political values, see Genovese, *Southern Tradition,* 28–32; 42–49; Sinha, *Counterrevolution of Slavery;* and Tate, *Conservatism and Southern Intellectuals.*

5. Robert E. Bonner argues that southern slaveholders saw their efforts to protect slavery as part of a legitimate debate over the form and nature of the American nation, and that as part of this debate, slaveholders argued that through slavery, they were upholding the original values of the Revolution. Bonner, *Mastering America,* 41–78, 149–83. See also Tate, *Conservatism and Southern Intellectuals,* 30–76, 189–245; Sinha, *Counterrevolution of Slavery;* McCurry, *Confederate Reckoning;* Genovese, *Slaveholders' Dilemma;* and Guterl, *American Mediterranean,* 47–78.

6. For examples of southerners claiming that slavery created the best nation, see L. W. Spratt, "Slave Trade in the Southern Congress," *Charleston Mercury,* February 13, 1861; and "The Address of the People of South Carolina, Assembled in Convention, to the People of the Slaveholding States of the United States," *Macon Telegraph,* January 8, 1861.

7. For examples of southern analysts blending liberal and conservative values, see "The Union: Its Benefits and Dangers," *Southern Literary Messenger,* January 1861, 1–4; and J. S. L., "The Pro-Slavery Confederacy," *Augusta Daily Constitutionalist,* January 29, 1861.

8. For examples of southerners blending liberal and conservative values and interpretations of European nations as they contextualized the South internationally, see Joseph

E. Brown, "Governor's Message," *Macon Telegraph*, November 12, 1861; and Hall, *Historic Significance of the Southern Revolution*, 5–17.

9. For examples of the liberal international perspective in the *Richmond Examiner*, see *Richmond Examiner*, July 29, 1862; and "The Insurrection of Poland," *Richmond Examiner*, June 26, 1863. For examples of the conservative international perspective, see *Richmond Examiner*, September 5, 1861; and *Richmond Examiner*, November 25, 1861.

10. Congress of the Confederate States of America, *Address of Congress to the People of the Confederate States*, 4–6; Python, "The Secession of the South," *DeBow's Review*, April 1860, 386–92.

11. For examples of southern nationalist newspapers' international comparisons, see "Secession Is Freedom," *Charleston Mercury*, December 10, 1860; "Our Foreign Policy," *Charleston Mercury*, October 29, 1861; and "The Independence of Nations," *Charleston Mercury*, December 17, 1862. For examples of more cultural journals' international perspectives, see "The Union: Its Benefits and Dangers," *Southern Literary Messenger*, January 1861, 1–4; William H. Holcombe, "The Alternative: A Separate Nationality, or the Africanization of the South," *Southern Literary Messenger*, February 1861, 82–84; George Fitzhugh, "Slavery Aggressions," *DeBow's Review*, August 1860, 132–39; "National Characteristics—The Issues of the Day," *DeBow's Review*, January 1861, 42–53; and A. Featherman, "Our Position and That of Our Enemies," *DeBow's Review*, July 1861, 17–35. Even these publications, however, at times endorsed the other perspective; see "War and Peace," *Charleston Mercury*, February 25, 1863; and Python, "The Secession of the South," *DeBow's Review*, April 1860, 367–92.

12. George Fitzhugh, "Slavery Aggressions," *DeBow's Review*, August 1860, 138–39. See also John Pratt, "Modern Sociological Fiction," *DeBow's Review*, September 1860, 336–39; "National Characteristics—The Issues of the Day," *DeBow's Review*, January 1861, 44–47; and "The Message, the Constitution, and the Times," *DeBow's Review*, February 1861, 163–64.

13. "The South's Power of Self-Protection," *DeBow's Review*, November 1860, 550. See also "The Union: Its Benefits and Dangers," *Southern Literary Messenger*, January 1861, 4; "Foreign News: Gossip of the Correspondents," *Charleston Mercury*, January 3, 1861; and William H. Holcombe, "The Alternative: A Separate Nationality, or the Africanization of the South," *Southern Literary Messenger*, February 1861, 82–84. For analysis of white southerners' fear of racial violence, see also Rugemer, *Problem of Emancipation*; and Clavin, *Toussaint L'Ouverture and the American Civil War*.

14. "The Palmetto Guard—Presentation of Colors," *Charleston Mercury*, May 7, 1861.

15. A. Featherman, "Our Position and That of Our Enemies," *DeBow's Review*, July 1861, 29.

16. "England's Neutrality," *Charleston Mercury*, July 2, 1861. See also Python, "The Issues of 1860," *DeBow's Review*, March 1860, 268.

17. "National Characteristics—The Issues of the Day," *DeBow's Review*, January 1861, 44–47. See also "The Address of the People of South Carolina, Assembled in

Convention, to the People of the Slaveholding States of the United States," *Macon Telegraph,* January 8, 1861; and L. W. Spratt, "Slave Trade in the Southern Congress," *Charleston Mercury,* February 13, 1861.

18. For example, the South Carolina Ordinance of Secession argues that northern anti-slavery actions had violated the Constitution, and therefore South Carolina was released from the compact of states that the Constitution created. See "A Declaration of the Immediate Causes Which Induce and Justify the Secession of South Carolina from the Federal Union." For more discussion of these issues, see Doyle, *Cause of All Nations,* 27–37.

19. Such an argument built on antebellum claims by slaveholding southerners that such southern principles as states' rights constituted valuable contributions to the American experiment. Bonner, *Mastering America,* 41–78.

20. Cleveland, *Alexander H. Stephens,* 717–29.

21. *Richmond Examiner,* August 24, 1861. See also "To What Are We Tending?" *Augusta Daily Constitutionalist,* February 26, 1861; and Palmer, *A Vindication of Secession and the South,* 5, 45–46.

22. "Speech of the Hon. R. B. Rhett, Delivered in the Convention of the State of South Carolina," *Charleston Mercury,* October 29, 1862. See also MacMahon, *Cause and Contrast,* 165–66. For more analysis of these ideas within general southern justifications for secession, see Faust, *Creation of Confederate Nationalism,* 14; Fleche, *Revolution of 1861,* 132–50; Quigley, *Shifting Grounds,* 77–83, 145–57; and Rable, *Confederate Republic,* 44–49.

23. Matthew J. Clavin characterizes secession as a counterrevolution against international liberalism, although his focus is abolition rather than foreign nationalist movements. Clavin, *Toussaint L'Ouverture and the American Civil War.* Manisha Sinha also characterizes secession as a counterrevolution against liberal visions of governance. Sinha, *Counterrevolution of Slavery.*

24. Python, "The Issues of 1860," *DeBow's Review,* March 1860, 268.

25. "European Aid," *Baton Rouge Advocate,* January 2, 1861.

26. Lynchburg Virginian, "Democracy—By a Democrat," *Alexandria Gazette,* April 12, 1858. See also "The Past and Present," *DeBow's Review,* February 1861, 189; and Sidney, "From Abolitionists to Despotism," *Charleston Mercury,* April 20, 1861.

27. R. L. Gibson, "Our Federal Union," *DeBow's Review,* July 1860, 32–34.

28. William H. Holcombe, "The Alternative: A Separate Nationality, or the Africanization of the South," *Southern Literary Messenger,* February 1861, 82.

29. "The Disfederation of the States," *Southern Literary Messenger,* February 1861, 129.

30. Clavin, *Toussaint L'Ouverture and the American Civil War.*

31. "The Union: Its Benefits and Dangers," *Southern Literary Messenger,* January 1861, 4.

32. "The South's Power of Self-Protection," *DeBow's Review,* November 1860, 545–46. See also William H. Holcombe, "The Alternative: A Separate Nationality, or the Africanization of the South," *Southern Literary Messenger,* February 1861, 82–84.

33. John Pratt, "Modern Sociological Fiction," *DeBow's Review,* September 1860, 339.

34. George Fitzhugh, "Slavery Aggressions," *DeBow's Review,* August 1860, 138.

35. A Mississippian, "Our Country—Its Hopes and Fears," *DeBow's Review,* July 1860, 83–85.

36. P. R. G., "The National Crisis," *Richmond Whig,* December 14, 1860.

37. *Richmond Examiner,* September 5, 1861.

38. "The Union: Its Benefits and Dangers," *Southern Literary Messenger,* January 1861, 4.

39. J. H. Van Evrie, "The Black and White Races of Men," *DeBow's Review,* April 1861, 451. See also Bland [J. Randolph Tucker], "The Great Issue: Our Relations to It," *Southern Literary Messenger,* March 1861, 164.

40. Genovese, *Southern Tradition,* 22–24, 31–35; Genovese, *Slaveholders' Dilemma;* Foner, *Politics and Ideology in the Age of the Civil War,* 57–63.

41. "Pecuniary Effects of Secession at the South," *Charleston Mercury,* March 26, 1861.

42. Bland, "The Great Issue: Our Relations to It," *Southern Literary Messenger,* March 1861, 164. See also "The Address of the People of South Carolina, Assembled in Convention, to the People of the Slaveholding States of the United States," *Macon Telegraph,* January 8, 1861; and J. H. Van Evrie, "The Black and White Races of Men," *DeBow's Review,* April 1861, 451.

43. A Mississippian, "Our Country—Its Hopes and Fears," *DeBow's Review,* July 1860, 84. See also L. W. Spratt, "Slave Trade in the Southern Congress," *Charleston Mercury,* February 13, 1861.

44. J. Quitman Moore, "Quo Tendimus?" *DeBow's Review,* October 1860, 442–43. See also "The Slave Institution a Great Military Power," *Richmond Daily Dispatch,* April 6, 1861.

45. J. S. L., "The Pro-Slavery Confederacy," *Augusta Daily Constitutionalist,* January 29, 1861.

46. L. W. Spratt, "Slave Trade in the Southern Congress," *Charleston Mercury,* February 13, 1861.

47. Doyle, *Cause of All Nations,* esp. 7–11, 85–130.

48. For analysis of the rightward turn in Confederate politics, see Doyle, *Cause of All Nations,* 185–209.

49. Stephanie McCurry and Manisha Sinha argue that a desire for limited democracy was a key impetus of southern politics. McCurry, *Confederate Reckoning;* Sinha, *Counterrevolution of Slavery,* 9–62.

50. J. S. L., "The Pro-Slavery Confederacy," *Augusta Daily Constitutionalist,* January 29, 1861.

51. "The Message, the Constitution, and the Times," *DeBow's Review,* February 1861, 163–64. See also Frank H. Alfriend, "A Southern Republic and a Northern Democracy," *Southern Literary Messenger,* May 1863, 285–86.

52. "Monarchy for the South," *Richmond Whig,* February 1, 1861; also published in "Monarchy for the South," *Augusta Chronicle and Sentinel,* January 19, 1861.

53. "The Message, the Constitution, and the Times," *DeBow's Review*, February 1861, 163–64. See also Anglo-Californian, *The National Crisis*, 4–7.

54. "National Characteristics—The Issues of the Day," *DeBow's Review*, January 1861, 47.

55. George Fitzhugh, "The Declaration of Independence and the Republican Party," *DeBow's Review*, August 1860, 179, 186.

56. Right, *Arkansas Gazette*, January 12, 1861.

57. "The Monarchical Governments of America," *Augusta Chronicle and Sentinel*, January 26, 1861.

58. "Monarchy for the South," *Richmond Whig*, February 1, 1861.

59. Georgia, *Augusta Chronicle and Sentinel*, January 31, 1861.

60. "To What Are We Tending?" *Augusta Daily Constitutionalist*, February 26, 1861.

61. "The Message, the Constitution, and the Times," *DeBow's Review*, February 1861, 163–64.

6. Disunion . . . Is Fatal in the End

1. Hinton Rowan Helper's *The Impending Crisis of the South*, which sold over 100,000 copies and helped publicize the Republican critique of the South, was central in inflaming sectional tension in the late 1850s. Helper actually continued to positively self-identify as a southerner despite his antislavery beliefs, and he believed his work would help his native region; however, his concerns with the power of the slaveholding class led him to challenge the southern elite. Brown, *Southern Outcast*, 1–3, 8, 71–72, 82, 89–151.

2. Helper, *Compendium of the Impending Crisis of the South*, 79.

3. Clarke, *Confederate States Almanac*, 158–59. For the text of Wikoff's letter, see Wikoff, *Secession and Its Causes*, 50–51.

4. Rutledge, *Mr. Douglas and the Doctrine of Coercion*, 4, 10–11, 17–18. See also MacDonald, *A Lecture on the American War of Secession*, 13, 18–20.

5. Crofts, *Reluctant Confederates*, xvi–xvii, 104–6, 109–11, 117–27, 130–32, 334–38; Degler, *Other South*, 119–22, 158–63, 184–86; Storey, *Loyalty and Loss*, 6, 20–23.

6. "The Fearful Reckoning," *Fayetteville Observer*, March 4, 1861.

7. "The Madness of Secession: The Lessons of History—What Is the Prospect in Store for Western Virginia?" *Daily Intelligencer*, January 8, 1861. See also "General Assembly of North Carolina," *Fayetteville Observer*, January 21, 1861.

8. "Anti-Secession in North Carolina," *Arkansas Gazette*, January 5, 1861.

9. O. P. Q., "The Voice of Cecil County in the Present Crisis," *Cecil Whig*, May 11, 1861. See also "Speeches at the Electoral Banquet," *Richmond Whig*, December 11, 1860.

10. "From Italy," *Fayetteville Observer*, February 25, 1861.

11. "Speech of Hon. A. H. Stephens of Geo," *Fayetteville Observer*, November 29, 1860; "Hon. A. H. Stephens," *Augusta Chronicle and Sentinel*, November 20, 1860; Stephens, *Assertions of a Secessionist*, 5.

12. Shenandoah, "To the People of Western Virginia," *Daily Intelligencer,* January 15, 1861.

13. "General Assembly of North Carolina," *Fayetteville Observer,* January 21, 1861.

14. Smith, *History and Debates of the Convention,* 82.

15. Bell, *Speech of Hon. James H. Bell,* 16.

16. Union, *Staunton Spectator,* December 18, 1860.

17. "Assembling of Congress," *Staunton Spectator,* December 4, 1860.

18. "Think before You Act," *Staunton Spectator,* January 8, 1861.

19. Crofts, *Reluctant Confederates,* 308–38, 359–60; Storey, *Loyalty and Loss,* 35–39, 56–86.

20. "The Political Crisis," *Fayetteville Observer,* April 8, 1861.

21. Rover, "Letter from Rover," *New Orleans Picayune,* April 11, 1861.

22. Robert J. Walker, "The Position of Leading Men in the Last Campaign and Their Position Now—Robert J. Walker's Speech," *Daily Intelligencer,* April 24, 1861.

23. For a history of Brownlow's public career, see Coulter, *William G. Brownlow.*

24. Brownlow, *Sketches of the Rise,* 235. Brownlow was not alone among wartime southern Unionists in believing that the Confederacy had subverted the will of southerners. Storey, *Loyalty and Loss,* 34; Crofts, *Reluctant Confederates,* 111–16.

25. "Proclamation of Jefferson Davis," *Brownlow's Knoxville Whig,* August 24, 1861.

26. Brownlow, *Sketches of the Rise,* 254.

27. Brownlow, *Sketches of the Rise,* 110.

28. "Afternoon Session," *Daily Intelligencer,* May 14, 1861.

29. Grafton, "A Big Time at Pruntytown," *Daily Intelligencer,* May 18, 1861. For more examples of Unionist accusations that the Confederacy was despotic, see "Henry Clay's Birth-Day," *Fayetteville Observer,* April 18, 1861; "Queer," *Fayetteville Observer,* April 25, 1861; Hamilton, "Address to the People of Texas," 2; and Gantt, "Address in Favor of Reunion in 1863," 206, 222.

30. Carroll, *War Powers of the General Government,* 12.

31. Powell, *Speech of Hon. L. W. Powell,* 13.

32. Brown, "An Address by Col. B Gratz Brown," 4.

33. While secession is the focus of this chapter, it was not the only issue involved with the Civil War that northerners and Europeans debated through an international perspective; abolitionists also saw their mission as international and used international connections to advance their agenda. McDaniel, *Problem of Democracy;* Dal Lago, *William Lloyd Garrison and Giuseppe Mazzini.*

34. Historians of European public opinion on the Civil War have generally concluded that conservatives in Europe leaned toward supporting the Confederacy, while liberals supported the United States as a representative of democracy. Ultimately, the United States won the battle for public opinion abroad, largely after the Emancipation Proclamation made the war about liberal principles, although the Confederacy's claims to self-determination did have some appeal. See Doyle, *Cause of All Nations;* Campbell,

English Public Opinion; Blackett, *Divided Hearts;* and Blackburn, *French Newspaper Opinion.*

35. "British Feeling," *Fayetteville Observer,* February 4, 1861; "Letter from Garibaldi," *Alexandria Gazette,* May 7, 1861.

36. "Speculations in Washington," *Richmond Whig,* May 14, 1861.

37. Peissner, *American Question in Its National Aspect,* 141. See also Train, *Union Speeches Delivered in England,* 46.

38. John E. Wool, "Important Documents: Patriotic Letters from Gen. Wool," *Daily Intelligencer,* January 5, 1861. See also Tuckerman, *The Rebellion,* 40.

39. Beecher, *Freedom and War,* 55, 109.

40. Beecher, *American Rebellion,* 43–44.

41. "The Fearful Reckoning," *Fayetteville Observer,* March 4, 1861.

42. "Why Jeff. Davis Selects Virginia as the Seat of War," *Daily Intelligencer,* April 20, 1861.

43. Hodge, *Disunion and Its Results to the South,* 17.

44. "Secession—A German View," *Charleston Mercury,* April 3, 1861. See also Newman Hall, *American War,* 17–18; and Train, *Union Speeches Delivered in England,* 40–41.

45. Cline, *Secession Unmasked,* 9.

46. Newman Hall, *American War,* 17–18. See also George Brown, "The American War and Slavery," 6; Story, *American Story,* 8–9; and *Letters of John Lothrop Motley and Joseph Holt,* 16–18.

47. Goodwin, *Natural History of Secession,* 217.

48. Reinhart, *August Willich's Gallant Dutchmen,* 16. The equation of southern slaveholders with European aristocrats built on broader concerns with the potential aristocratic nature of slavery. See Doyle, *Cause of All Nations,* 85–86, 99–105; Fleche, *Revolution of 1861,* 117–21; and McDaniel, *Problem of Democracy,* 137–58.

49. Gasparin, *America before Europe,* 55–56. For analysis of Europeans' reasons for denying diplomatic recognition to the Confederacy, see Hubbard, *Burden of Confederate Diplomacy,* 17–32, 41, 55, 123; Campbell, *English Public Opinion,* 11, 18–20; Grant, *American Civil War and the British Press,* 8; and Blackett, *Divided Hearts,* 24–26

50. "The Hon. Charles Sumner on the Result of the Election," *Nashville Union and American,* November 20, 1860.

51. Eddy, *Liberty and Union,* 26. See also James Buchanan, "Message," *Staunton Spectator,* December 4, 1860. This idea of the United States as the best hope of republicanism for the world was common in the North, with even Lincoln believing in this vision. Onuf and Onuf, *Nations, Markets, and War,* esp. 278–307.

52. For statistics on the numbers and percentages of foreign-born soldiers in the U.S. Army, see Lonn, *Foreigners in the Union Army and Navy.* See also Fleche, *Revolution of 1861;* Doyle, *Cause of All Nations;* and Levine, *Spirit of 1848.*

53. Mahin, *Blessed Place of Freedom,* 12.

54. Bruce, *Harp and the Eagle,* 52.

55. Öfele, *True Sons of the Republic,* 70.

56. For more examples and analysis of such comparisons, see Reinhart, *August Willich's Gallant Dutchmen,* 56–67; Engle, "Yankee Dutchmen," 16; and Öfele, *True Sons of the Republic,* 35–36.

57. Mahin, *Blessed Place of Freedom,* 12. See also McPherson, *For Cause and Comrade,* 112–13; and Engle, "Yankee Dutchmen," 16.

58. Bruce, *Harp and Eagle,* 70.

59. Ural, *Civil War Citizens,* 101; McPherson, *For Cause and Comrade,* 113; Öfele, *True Sons of the Republic,* 44–45; Bruce, *Harp and the Eagle,* 2, 55.

7. Of What Avail Are the Appeals of the South

1. For analysis of the American invitation to Garibaldi, see Gay, "Lincoln's Offer of Command to Garibaldi."

2. J. M., "Our Paris Correspondence," *Charleston Mercury,* April 16, 1861.

3. Congress of the Confederate States of America, *Address of Congress to the People of the Confederate States,* 6. For more examples of wartime comparisons of northern and European tyranny, see "Subjugation of the South," *Richmond Daily Dispatch,* February 20, 1862; "Foreign Powers and the United States," *Richmond Daily Dispatch,* February 27, 1862; "All around the Ring," *Augusta Daily Constitutionalist,* October 6, 1863; "Choice of Masters," *Richmond Daily Dispatch,* April 26, 1864; Moore, *God Our Refuge and Strength in This War,* 21; "Northern Despotism," *Richmond Daily Dispatch,* April 24, 1862; MacMahon, *Cause and Contrast,* 165–66; John L. O'Sullivan, "Peace: The Sole Chance Now Left for Reunion," *Charleston Courier,* September 16, 1863; Pollard, *Southern History of the War,* 136; and "The Question of Boundaries," *Augusta Daily Constitutionalist,* December 13, 1861.

4. "Subjugation of the South," *Richmond Daily Dispatch,* February 20, 1862. See also "The Polish Revolution—A Lesson for the South," *Macon Telegraph,* September 9, 1863.

5. John L. O'Sullivan, "Peace: The Sole Chance Now Left for Reunion," *Charleston Courier,* September 16, 1863. O'Sullivan's pro-Confederate efforts abroad were known to and even subsidized by official Confederate propagandists. For analysis of O'Sullivan's contributions to the Confederacy, see Harris, "John L. O'Sullivan Serves the Confederacy."

6. For evidence of southern enthusiasm for Garibaldi, see Phi Ro, "Washington Correspondence," *New Orleans Picayune,* August 13, 1849; "Garibaldi," *Augusta Chronicle and Sentinel,* June 15, 1849; "Garibaldi," *Alabama Journal,* August 5, 1850; *New Orleans Picayune,* December 6, 1859; and George William Bagby, "Editor's Table: Death of Count Cavour," *Southern Literary Messenger,* July 1861, 72–80.

7. "Ben McCullough," *Richmond Daily Dispatch,* May 21, 1861.

8. "Editorial Miscellany," *DeBow's Review,* April 1861, 502.

9. For analysis of abolitionism and democracy in the nineteenth-century Atlantic world, see McDaniel, *Problem of Democracy.*

10. Gay, "Lincoln's Offer of Command to Garibaldi," 69. See also Marraro, "Lincoln's Offer of Command to Garibaldi"; and Doyle, *Cause of All Nations,* 15–26.

11. "The City: The Talk Down Town," *New Orleans Picayune,* April 17, 1861.

12. "Lincoln Calls for Garibaldi," *Columbus Enquirer,* May 31, 1861. This article was republished in other southern journals; for example, see "Lincoln Calls for Garibaldi," *Augusta Chronicle and Sentinel,* May 30, 1861.

13. "A General Wanted," *Richmond Daily Dispatch,* August 14, 1861; *Richmond Daily Dispatch,* August 15, 1861. For more examples of reports that outright dismiss the idea of Garibaldi fighting for the United States, see "Garibaldi," *Richmond Daily Dispatch,* September 7, 1861; "Garibaldi Will Not Come," *Richmond Daily Dispatch,* October 4, 1861; and *Columbus Enquirer,* August 15, 1861. Confederates were not entirely alone in their dismissal; Howard R. Marraro reveals that a month or two after southerners were denying the rumor, northern reports also began doing the same, responding in part to British analysis that having Garibaldi fight for the United States would be harmful to the northern cause. Marraro, "Lincoln's Offer of Command to Garibaldi," 242–44.

14. J. M., "Our Paris Correspondence," *Charleston Mercury,* April 16, 1861.

15. "Garibaldi to the Rescue," *Charleston Mercury,* March 24, 1861.

16. "The City," *New Orleans Picayune,* April 17, 1861.

17. "A Variety of Items," *Macon Telegraph,* August 20, 1861.

18. "Garibaldi," *Richmond Daily Dispatch,* September 16, 1861.

19. "Telegraphic Dispatches," *Columbus Enquirer,* August 15, 1861; "More of the Garibaldi Rumour," *Richmond Examiner,* August 15, 1861.

20. "Garibaldi," *Richmond Daily Dispatch,* September 16, 1861.

21. Clarke, *Diary of the War for Separation,* 71. See also *Richmond Whig,* September 17, 1861; and "A Variety of Items," *Macon Telegraph,* August 20, 1861.

22. *Dallas Herald,* November 13, 1861; "French Views of the American War," *Charleston Mercury,* December 25, 1861; "The European Mails," *Charleston Mercury,* October 17, 1861. Marraro briefly reveals that the British press mocked the North for inviting Garibaldi to fight for the United States. Marraro, "Lincoln's Offer of Command to Garibaldi," 242–43.

23. "To the Italians of America," *Richmond Daily Dispatch,* May 25, 1861.

24. "The Hessians," *Charleston Mercury,* June 7, 1861. See also "A Foreign Corps," *Richmond Daily Dispatch,* June 5, 1861.

25. "The Way It Works," *Richmond Daily Dispatch,* June 18, 1861. See also "Movements and Spirit of the War," *Richmond Examiner,* August 6, 1861; M., "From Fredericksburg," *Richmond Daily Dispatch,* June 18, 1861; and Randolph, "Movements at Norfolk," *Charleston Mercury,* June 22, 1861.

26. "Garibaldi," *Richmond Daily Dispatch,* September 16, 1861.

27. "Garibaldi," *Richmond Daily Dispatch,* November 11, 1861.

28. "Who Is the Started Party," *Richmond Daily Dispatch,* January 17, 1862.

29. "Garibaldi," *Richmond Daily Dispatch,* November 11, 1861.

30. "Letter from George N. Saunders to Louis Kossuth," *Richmond Daily Dispatch,* November 25, 1861.

31. *Richmond Examiner,* October 14, 1861.

32. *New Orleans Picayune,* September 6, 1862; "Garibaldi," *New Orleans Delta,* September 12, 1862.

33. *Alexandria Gazette,* September 9, 1862.

34. "Garibaldi's Fail," *New Orleans Delta,* September 27, 1862.

35. "Garibaldi," *Macon Telegraph,* September 30, 1862.

36. Gamma, "Garibaldi's Wild Goose Chase," *New Orleans Picayune,* September 11, 1862; "Garibaldi," *New Orleans Picayune,* October 5, 1862.

37. Gay, "Lincoln's Offer of Command to Garibaldi," 71–74; Doyle, *Cause of All Nations,* 225–39.

38. "Garibaldi," *Richmond Daily Dispatch,* October 10, 1862.

39. "Garibaldi," *New Orleans Delta,* October 16, 1862.

40. "Garibaldi and His Mercenaries," *Columbus Enquirer,* October 17, 1862.

41. "Garibaldi and the English Press," *Augusta Daily Constitutionalist,* October 14, 1862.

42. "Later from Europe," *Richmond Daily Dispatch,* October 8, 1862; "News by Telegraph," *Mobile Register,* October 8, 1862; "Garibaldi's Army Tendered to the United States," *Charleston Courier,* October 14, 1862.

43. For a full text of Garibaldi's address, see "Garibaldi's Thanks to England," *Public Ledger,* October 21, 1862.

44. "Garibaldi on the South," *Columbus Enquirer,* November 1, 1862.

45. *Charleston Mercury,* December 12, 1862; "Latest from Europe—Still Later," *Augusta Daily Constitutionalist,* December 12, 1862; *Chattanooga Daily Rebel,* December 12, 1862. For a fuller account of this exchange, see "Another Letter from Garibaldi," *New Orleans Delta,* December 19, 1862.

46. *Alexandria Gazette,* October 17, 1862.

47. "From Europe—Letter from Garibaldi to Lincoln," *Richmond Examiner,* September 4, 1863.

48. *Richmond Enquirer,* September 10, 1863.

49. Secessia, "A Blockade Correspondence," *Southern Illustrated News,* November 7, 1863; "Garibaldi's Letter to Lincoln," *Augusta Chronicle and Sentinel,* September 11, 1863; "Beecher and Beauty and the Beast," *Southern Punch,* April 2, 1864.

50. "Garabaldi [sic]," *Southern Punch,* May 7, 1864.

51. Especially in the summer of 1861, Confederate hopes were bolstered by British and French claims of the southern nation's similarity to Italy, which Britain and France had officially recognized; for example, reports claimed that Napoleon III stated that France would soon recognize the Confederacy as it had Italy. See "French Recognition

of the Confederate States of America," *Richmond Daily Dispatch*, July 3, 1861. At times, some English papers also claimed that the Confederacy deserved recognition. See "English Opinion of American Affairs," *Richmond Daily Dispatch*, September 7, 1861; "The American Secession," *Macon Telegraph*, September 16, 1861; and "The Recognition of the Southern Confederacy Not Remote," *Charleston Mercury*, October 31, 1861. In early 1862, the *London Herald* claimed, in an article widely republished throughout the South, that recognitions of new nations such as Italy demanded recognition of the Confederacy. "American Affairs in Europe: Recognition of the Southern Confederacy," *Richmond Examiner*, February 7, 1862; "What Inducements the South Offers to England," *Richmond Daily Dispatch*, February 3, 1862; "Late and Interesting from England," *New Orleans Daily True Delta*, February 11, 1862; "Still Later," *Charleston Courier*, February 3, 1862. For scholarly analyses of foreign sympathy for the South, see Hubbard, *Burden of Confederate Diplomacy*, 20, 36; Mahin, *Blessed Place of Freedom*, 170; Blackburn, *French Newspaper Opinion*, x–xi; Jones, *Blue and Gray Diplomacy*, 1; Campbell, *English Public Opinion*, 163–93; and Blackett, *Divided Hearts*, 7, 61–75.

52. "The Independence of Nations," *Charleston Mercury*, December 17, 1862. See also Spence, *On the Recognition*, 7–8.

53. "Our Foreign Policy," *Standard*, August 17, 1861; Spence, *On the Recognition*, 6.

54. Great Britain came close to recognizing the Confederacy at times from 1861 to 1862 and did, perhaps inadvertently, grant the Confederacy the status of an official belligerent. Hubbard, *Burden of Confederate Diplomacy*, 48, 54, 114; Mahin, *Blessed Place of Freedom*, 167–68. Ultimately, however, the Confederacy was not recognized for a variety of reasons, including weak diplomatic strategy and poor choice of diplomats by the Confederacy, the failure of "king cotton," European hatred of slavery, European desire to avoid war, a lack of Confederate understanding of the realities of international alliances and history, and the fact that Great Britain's interests largely lay in their own affairs. Hubbard, *Burden of Confederate Diplomacy*, 17–32, 41, 55, 123; Campbell, *English Public Opinion*, 11, 18–20; Grant, *American Civil War and the British Press*, 8; Blackett, *Divided Hearts*, 24–26.

55. "The Blockade Question," *Charleston Mercury*, April 6, 1861; "France and the Southern Confederacy," *Richmond Daily Dispatch*, May 6, 1861.

56. J. M., "Our Paris Correspondence," *Charleston Mercury*, August 24, 1861. See also Clingman, "Speech on the State of the Union," 287–88, 296–97.

57. "The World's Fair and the South," *Macon Telegraph*, July 6, 1861. See also "Southern Journals in Europe," *Charleston Courier*, April 28, 1862; "Our Foreign Policy," *Charleston Mercury*, October 29, 1861; and "The English Press and the American Crisis," *New Orleans Daily True Delta*, April 20, 1861. Henry Hotze, an unofficial Confederate propagandist publishing pro-South newspapers in London, was marginally more successful than the official diplomats at increasing sympathy for the Confederacy abroad. Hotze was also more aware of the reality of British sentiment and more willing to be flexible

in his approach than the official diplomats. Hubbard, *Burden of Confederate Diplomacy*, 98–101; Fleche, *Revolution of 1861*, 84–102.

58. Pollard, *Rival Administrations*, 17. See also Pollard, *First Year of the War*, 357–59; and Pollard, *Southern History of the War*, 190.

59. For other examples of this rhetoric, see "Decline of Beecher Stoweism," *Charleston Mercury*, June 21, 1864; "Our Foreign Relations," *Augusta Daily Constitutionalist*, January 30, 1863; and "The Truth from Scotland," *Augusta Daily Constitutionalist*, February 2, 1861. The claim that Europeans would embrace slavery if they knew more about it fit with the larger trend in antebellum southern thought that increasingly embraced slavery as a positive good. O'Brien, *Conjectures of Order*, 2:938–77.

60. *Richmond Examiner*, August 6, 1863.

61. "The Indifference of Europe," *Southern Punch*, February 16, 1864.

62. Elliot, *"Samson's Riddle,"* 11–13.

63. "The Reasons Why We Have Not Yet Been Acknowledged by Great Britain," *Southern Illustrated News*, October 4, 1862. See also "Will There Be Any Foreign Interference?" *Augusta Daily Constitutionalist*, August 1, 1863; "Southern Independence Association of London," *Weekly Register*, March 5, 1864; and "The Confederate States and the Civilized World—Their Relations," *Macon Telegraph*, December 8, 1864.

64. "Garibaldi," *Richmond Daily Dispatch*, November 11, 1861.

65. J. M., "Affairs in Europe: Our Paris Correspondence," *Charleston Mercury*, August 24, 1861.

66. "No Hope for Ireland!" *Augusta Daily Constitutionalist*, September 20, 1861. This idea was occasionally expressed by foreigners as well; for example, see William Smith O'Brien, "Smith O'Brien on the American War," *Charleston Courier*, August 6, 1862.

67. "Northern Despotism," *Richmond Daily Dispatch*, April 24, 1862. See also "Garibaldi," *Richmond Daily Dispatch*, August 18, 1862.

68. "Speech of the Hon. R. B. Rhett, Delivered in the Convention of the State of South Carolina," *Charleston Mercury*, October 29, 1862. This view occasionally was expressed in foreign publications as well; for example, see "Comments of the *London Times* on American Affairs," *Richmond Whig*, July 22, 1862.

69. MacMahon, *Cause and Contrast*, 165–66.

70. John L. O'Sullivan, "Peace: The Sole Chance Now Left for Reunion," *Charleston Courier*, September 16, 1863. See also "The Victims of Presidential Tyranny," *Richmond Daily Dispatch*, August 24, 1861; and "Letter from George N. Saunders to Louis Kossuth," *Richmond Daily Dispatch*, November 25, 1861.

71. "National Retribution," *Augusta Chronicle and Sentinel*, February 1, 1863.

72. "Address of Congress to the People of the Confederate States," *Charleston Mercury*, February 24, 1864.

73. "Reconstruction—A Parallel," *Richmond Whig*, April 5, 1864.

74. "Mr. Hill's Speech," *Macon Telegraph*, February 20, 1865. See also "The New Union," *New Orleans Daily True Delta*, September 25, 1864.

8. We Stand Alone

1. *Richmond Examiner,* May 3, 1864.

2. George Fitzhugh, "The Revolutions of 1776 and 1861 Contrasted," *Southern Literary Messenger,* December 1863, 721–22.

3. Hall, *Historic Significance of the Southern Revolution,* 12–13, 19, 41. For more wartime expressions of the Confederate conservative international perspective, see also Frank H. Alfriend, "A Southern Republic and a Northern Democracy," *Southern Literary Messenger,* May 1863, 285–86; William Henry Trescot, "Letter from Wm. Henry Trescot Esq, of South Carolina, to Hon. J. R. Ingersoll, of Pennsylvania," *Charleston Mercury,* October 17, 1863; and "Speech of Major Gen. Sickles on the Fourth of July," *New Orleans Daily True Delta,* July 7, 1864.

4. "The Future of American Republicanism—Slavery the Basis of Our Safety: No. 2," *Augusta Daily Constitutionalist,* December 10, 1864. See also S., *Augusta Daily Constitutionalist,* March 12, 1865.

5. "A Parallel and a Contrast," *Index* (London), August 6, 1863.

6. "Inaugural Address of Governor Vance, of North Carolina," *Richmond Examiner,* September 11, 1862.

7. Congress of the Confederate States of America, *Address of Congress to the People of the Confederate States,* 2. See also "The Southern Provisional Congress. Its Last Day," *Charleston Mercury,* February 20, 1862.

8. "Cultivate Good Will," *Augusta Daily Constitutionalist,* January 31, 1863.

9. *Richmond Examiner,* May 3, 1864.

10. Historians have identified race as playing a central role in shaping southern nationalism and in encouraging southern nationalists to see the Confederacy as a superior nation. See Rugemer, *Problem of Emancipation;* Guterl, *American Mediterranean,* 60; and Clavin, *Toussaint L'Ouverture and the American Civil War,* 55–76, 144–61.

11. Confederate diplomatic strategy never fully or officially shifted away from the dual powers of Great Britain and France to instead incorporate a strategy of seeking alliances based on conservatism; such ideas were more widespread in popular discourse. However, in the later years of the war, the Confederacy did ultimately increase its diplomatic efforts to other nations. Such efforts included a renewed attempt to gain recognition from Mexico, now under the control of Emperor Maximilian, and to use that alliance to gain a French alliance as well. Confederates also identified Spain as a late possibility to ally with France in recognizing the Confederacy. The Confederacy sent a diplomat to Pope Pius IX, seeking an alliance that would hopefully bring additional alliances with other Catholic powers such as Belgium and France. See Hubbard, *Burden of Confederate Diplomacy,* 46, 160–63; and Owsley, *King Cotton Diplomacy,* 87–133, 446, 495–508.

12. Soon after Pius IX was elected in 1846, many southerners believed his reforms made him an enlightened leader. See *Augusta Chronicle and Sentinel,* October 8, 1847; and "Italy," *Southern Patriot,* February 7, 1848. However, particularly after the creation and

fall of the short-lived Roman Republic and the reassertion of papal authority over Rome, southerners became increasingly convinced that the pope had no right to temporal rule and that his control over the Papal States was thus tyrannical. See W. H. R., "Rome: Papal and Republican," *Southern Literary Messenger*, October 1849, 549; "French Intervention at Rome," *New Orleans Picayune*, May 15, 1849; "Rome and Her Besiegers," *New Orleans Picayune*, July 17, 1849; and "Commendable," *Alabama Journal*, July 10, 1850.

13. Don H. Doyle argues that the Confederacy did indeed feel a sense of ideological kinship with conservative powers, leading them to seek diplomatic alliances with both the pope and Maximilian's Mexican Empire. Doyle, *Cause of All Nations*, 85–130, 185–209, 260–70.

14. "The Pope's Letter to Archbishop Hughes," *Richmond Whig*, August 11, 1863.

15. Estimates show that about 150,000 Irish enlisted in the U.S. Army, out of a total estimate of 2.5 million U.S. (Union) troops. Overall, about 500,000 foreign-born soldiers served in the U.S. Army. When immigrants' sons are included, over 40 percent of U.S. troops were foreign-born or the children of foreign-born. See Doyle, *Cause of All Nations*, 170; and Lonn, *Foreigners in the Union Army and Navy*.

16. William F. Samford, "A Patriotic Letter," *Charleston Mercury*, September 19, 1863. See also Hermes [George William Bagby], "Letter from Richmond," *Charleston Mercury*, September 19, 1863; and "Catholic Influence and the South—Singular Coincidence," *New Orleans Picayune*, September 13, 1863.

17. Sexton, *Monroe Doctrine*, 123–58.

18. "Mexican Recognition," *Richmond Whig*, August 28, 1863.

19. "Catholic Influence and the South—Singular Coincidence," *New Orleans Picayune*, September 13, 1863.

20. See "The Pope and the Confederates," *Augusta Daily Constitutionalist*, January 5, 1864.

21. "A Commissioner to Rome," *Richmond Whig*, February 5, 1864. See also *Alexandria Gazette*, January 18, 1864.

22. "The Pope's Correspondence with Mr. Davis," *New Orleans Picayune*, March 9, 1864; "Speech of Hon. Mr. Lamar on the Confederate Cause in Europe," *Richmond Enquirer*, March 28, 1864. See also "Southern View of European Affairs," *Richmond Whig*, March 29, 1864. For an overview of papal-Confederate relations, see Owsley, *King Cotton Diplomacy*, 495–506.

23. *Alexandria Gazette*, January 19, April 1, 1864.

24. "The Papal Power," *Augusta Daily Constitutionalist*, April 15, 1864.

25. H. L. B., "The True Remedy, No. 2," *Augusta Daily Constitutionalist*, January 19, 1865.

26. "New York, Jan. 30," *Brownlow's Knoxville Whig*, February 1, 1865.

27. "Northern News: Foot in Yankeedom: Wade on the Blair Mission: Recognition Rumors," *Augusta Daily Constitutionalist*, February 4, 1865; "Letter from New York," *New Orleans Picayune*, February 9, 1865.

28. "Speech of Hon. Mr. Lamar on the Confederate Cause in Europe," *Richmond Enquirer,* March 28, 1864.

29. Crofts, *Reluctant Confederates,* 308–60; Storey, *Loyalty and Loss,* 28–39, 56–74.

30. See Brownlow, *Sketches of the Rise,* 110, 235.

31. "Who Are the Guilty?" *Brownlow's Knoxville Whig,* February 6, 1864.

32. "Benjamin's Letter and Rebel Cruelty," *Brownlow's Knoxville Whig,* March 5, 1864. See also "Whistling to Keep Up Their Courage," *Brownlow's Knoxville Whig,* January 23, 1864; and "Address to the President of the United States in Behalf of the People of East Tennessee," *Brownlow's Knoxville Whig,* February 13, 1864.

33. "Rebel Cruelties," *Brownlow's Knoxville Whig,* June 11, 1864. See also "Public Meeting in Blount," *Brownlow's Knoxville Whig,* June 11, 1864.

34. "Who Are for Lincoln and Johnson?" *Brownlow's Knoxville Whig,* September 21, 1864. This view was shared by many northerners, who likewise characterized southern slaveholders as aristocratic. See Doyle, *Cause of All Nations,* 85–86, 99–105; Fleche, *Revolution of 1861,* 117–21; and McDaniel, *Problem of Democracy,* 137–58.

35. McGovern, *John Mitchel.*

36. In particular, Mitchel repeatedly argued that the Irish immigrants fighting for the United States betrayed the Irish cause. For example, see J. M., "Affairs in Europe: Our Paris Correspondence," *Charleston Mercury,* August 24, 1861; and J. M., "Affairs in Europe: Our Paris Correspondence," *Charleston Mercury,* June 8, 1861.

37. "The Richmond Enquirer," *Brownlow's Knoxville Whig,* February 15, 1865.

38. "The Richmond Enquirer," *Brownlow's Knoxville Whig,* February 15, 1865.

39. "A Blackguard on the Rampage," *Brownlow's Knoxville Whig,* February 22, 1865. See also "The Case of John Mitchel," *Brownlow's Knoxville Whig,* July 12, 1865.

40. "A Blackguard on the Rampage," *Brownlow's Knoxville Whig,* February 22, 1865.

Conclusion

1. "The Price of Independence," *Richmond Whig,* December 26, 1864. See also "The Price of Independence," *Augusta Daily Constitutionalist,* December 30, 1864.

BIBLIOGRAPHY

Primary Sources

Newspapers and Periodicals

Alabama Journal (Montgomery)
Alabama Planter (Mobile)
Alexandria (VA) Gazette
Alexandria (VA) Herald
Alexandria (VA) Phenix Gazette
Ariel (Natchez, MS)
Arkansas Gazette (Little Rock)
Augusta (GA) Chronicle
Augusta (GA) Chronicle and Sentinel
Augusta (GA) Daily Constitutionalist
Baton Rouge (LA) Advocate
Brownlow's Knoxville (TN) Whig
Carolina Sentinel (New Bern, NC)
Cecil Whig (Elkton, MD)
Charleston Courier
Charleston Mercury
Chattanooga (TN) Daily Rebel
City Gazette (Charleston, SC)
Cleveland (OH) Plain Dealer
Columbus (GA) Enquirer
Daily Confederation (Montgomery, AL)
Daily Intelligencer (Wheeling, VA)
Dallas Herald
DeBow's Review
Fayetteville (NC) Observer
Fincastle (VA) Mirror
Florida Republican (Jacksonville)
Floridian and Journal (Tallahassee)
Galveston (TX) Weekly Journal
Genius of Liberty (Leesburg, VA)

Georgia Journal (Milledgeville)
Georgian (Savannah)
Houston Telegraph
Index (London)
Louisiana Courier (New Orleans)
Macon (GA) Telegraph
Mississippi Free Trader (Natchez)
Mobile (AL) Register
Nashville Union and American
Natchez (MS) Gazette
National Banner and Nashville Whig
New Orleans Bee
New Orleans Daily True Delta
New Orleans Delta
New Orleans Picayune
Pensacola (FL) Gazette
Public Ledger (Philadelphia, PA)
Richmond (VA) Daily Dispatch
Richmond (VA) Enquirer
Richmond (VA) Examiner
Richmond (VA) Whig
San Antonio Ledger and Texan
Savannah (GA) Daily Republican
South Carolina State Gazette (Columbia)
Southern Clarion (Natchez, MS)
Southern Illustrated News (Richmond, VA)
Southern Literary Messenger
Southern Patriot (Charleston, SC)
Southern Punch (Richmond, VA)
Southern Quarterly Review
Southern Recorder (Milledgeville, GA)
Southern Sentinel (Plaquemine, LA)
Standard (Clarksville, TX)
Star (Raleigh, NC)
Staunton (VA) Spectator
Texian Advocate (Victoria)
Weekly Register (Lynchburg, VA)
Winyaw Intelligencer (Georgetown, SC)
Woodville (MS) Republican

Additional Primary Sources

Anglo-Californian. *The National Crisis.* San Francisco: Towne and Bacon, 1861.

Barnard, Frederick A. P. *No Just Cause for a Dissolution of the Union in Any Thing Which Has Hitherto Happened, but the Union the Only Security for Southern Rights: An Oration.* Tuscaloosa, AL: J. W. and J. F. Warren, 1851.

Bassett, George W. *A Northern Plea for the Right of Secession.* Ottawa, IL: Office of the Free Trader, 1861.

Beecher, Henry Ward. *American Rebellion: Report of the Speeches of the Rev. Henry Ward Beecher.* Manchester, England: Union and Emancipation Society, 1864.

———. *Freedom and War: Discourses on the Topics Suggested by the Times.* Boston: Ticknor and Fields, 1863.

Bell, James H. *Speech of Hon. James H. Bell, of the Texas Supreme Court, Delivered at the Capitol on Saturday, Dec. 1st, 1860.* Austin, TX: Intelligencer Book Office, 1860.

Boyd, Samuel S. *Speech of Hon. Samuel S. Boyd, Delivered at the Great Union Festival, Held at Jackson, Mississippi, on the 10th Day of October, 1851.* Natchez, MS: Office of the Natchez Courier, 1851.

Brown, B. Gratz. "An Address by Col. B Gratz Brown: Slavery in Its National Aspects as Related to Peace and War," presented at the General Emancipation Society, St. Louis, September 17, 1862.

Brown, George. "The American War and Slavery: Speech of the Hon. George Brown, at the Anniversary Meeting of the Anti-Slavery Society of Canada, Held at Toronto, on Wednesday, February 3, 1863," presented at the Anti-Slavery Society of Canada, Toronto, February 3, 1863.

Brownlow, William. *Sketches of the Rise, Progress, and Decline of Secession.* Philadelphia: George W. Childs, Applegate, 1862.

Carlile, John S. *The Cincinnati Platform: Speech of Mr. John S. Carlile, of Virginia, in the House of Representatives, June 21, 1856.* Washington, DC: American Organ, 1856.

Carroll, Anna Ella. *The War Powers of the General Government.* Washington, DC: Henry Polkinhorn, 1861.

Clarke, H. C., ed. *The Confederate States Almanac, and Repository of Useful Knowledge, for 1862.* Vicksburg, MS: H. C. Clarke, 1861.

———. *Diary of the War for Separation: A Daily Chronicle of the Principal Events and History of the Present Revolution, to Which Is Added Notes and Descriptions of All the Great Battles, Including Walker's Narrative of the Battle of Shiloh.* Augusta, GA: Steam Press of Chronicle and Sentinel, 1862.

Clemens, Jeremiah. *Speech of Hon. Jeremiah Clemens, of Ala., on Non-Intervention, Delivered in the Senate of the United States, February 12, 1852.* Washington, DC: Congressional Globe Office, 1852.

————. *Speech of Mr. Clemens, of Alabama, in the Senate of the United States, Dec. 10, 1851, on the Resolution of Mr. Seward Relative to Louis Kossuth.* Washington, DC: Congressional Globe Office, 1851.

Cleveland, Henry. *Alexander H. Stephens, in Public and Private: With Letters and Speeches, Before, During, and Since the War.* Philadelphia: National Publishing, 1866.

Cline, A. J. *Secession Unmasked; or, An Appeal from the Madness of Disunion to the Sobriety of the Constitution and Common Sense.* Washington, DC: Henry Polkin Horn, 1861.

Clingman, Thomas L. "Speech on the State of the Union, Delivered in the Senate of the United States, February 4, 1861." In *Southern Pamphlets on Secession, November 1860–April 1861,* edited by Jon L. Wakelyn, 284–304. Chapel Hill: University of North Carolina Press, 1996.

Congress of the Confederate States of America. *Address of Congress to the People of the Confederate States: Joint Resolution in Relation to the War.* Richmond, VA, 1864.

Davis, Jefferson. "Remarks on the Special Message on Affairs in South Carolina. Jan 10, 1861." In *Southern Pamphlets on Secession, November 1860-April 1861,* edited by Jon L. Wakelyn, 115–42. Chapel Hill: University of North Carolina Press, 1996.

Eddy, Daniel C. *Liberty and Union: Our Country: Its Pride and Peril.* Boston: John M. Hewes, 1861.

Elliot, Stephen. *"Samson's Riddle": A Sermon Preached in Christ Church, Savannah, on Friday, March 27, 1863.* Macon, GA: Burke, Boykin, 1863.

Everett, Edward. *The Questions of the Day: An Address, Delivered in the Academy of Music, in New York, on the Fourth of July, 1861.* New York: George P. Putnam, 1861.

Gantt, Edward W. "Address in Favor of Reunion in 1863." In *Southern Unionist Pamphlets and the Civil War,* edited by Jon L. Wakelyn, 203–44. Columbia: University of Missouri Press, 1999.

Gasparin, Agenor de. *America before Europe: Principles and Interests.* Translated by Mary L. Booth. London: Sampson Low, 1862.

Gilmer, John H. *Letter Addressed to Hon. Wm. C. Rives, by John H. Gilmer, on the Existing Status of the Revolution, &c.* Richmond, VA, 1864.

Goodwin, Thomas Shepard. *The Natural History of Secession; or, Despotism and Democracy at Necessary, Eternal, Exterminating War.* New York: John Bradburn, 1864.

Hall, William A. *The Historic Significance of the Southern Revolution: A Lecture Delivered by Invitation in Petersburg, Va., March 14th and April 29th, 1864, and in Richmond, Va., April 7th and April 21, 1864.* Petersburg, VA: A. F. Crutchfield, 1864.

Hamilton, Andrew Jackson. "Address to the People of Texas." In *Southern Unionist Pamphlets and the Civil War,* edited by Jon L. Wakelyn, 238–54. Columbia: University of Missouri Press, 1999.

Helper, Hinton Rowan. *Compendium of the Impending Crisis of the South.* New York: A. B. Burdick, 1860.

Hodge, William L. *Disunion and Its Results to the South: A Letter from a Resident of Washington to a Friend in South Carolina.* Washington, DC: H. Polkinhorn, 1861.

Houston, Sam. *Speech of Hon. Sam Houston, of Texas, on the Subject of Compromise, in the Senate of the United States.* Washington, DC: Towers, 1850.

Hunter, Robert M. T. "Speech . . . on the Resolution Proposing to Retrocede the Forts . . . Delivered in the Senate of the United States, January 11, 1861." In *Southern Pamphlets on Secession, November 1860–April 1861,* edited Jon L. Wakelyn, 262–83. Chapel Hill: University of North Carolina Press, 1996.

Letters of John Lothrop Motley and Joseph Holt. New York: Henry E. Tudor, 1861.

MacDonald, Dugald. *A Lecture on the American War of Secession, Delivered by Dugald MacDonald, on the 9th of August, 1864.* Montreal: John Lovell, 1865.

MacMahon, T. W. *Cause and Contrast: An Essay on the American Crisis.* Richmond, VA: West and Johnston, 1862.

Moore, T. V. *God Our Refuge and Strength in This War: A Discourse before the Congregations of the First and Second Presbyterian Churches . . . Nov 15, 1861.* Richmond, VA: W. Hargrave White, 1861.

Newman Hall, Christopher. *The American War: A Lecture, Delivered in London, October 20, 1862.* New York: Anson D. F. Randolph, 1862.

Palmer, B. M., ed. *A Vindication of Secession and the South from the Strictures of Rev. R. J. Breckinridge in the Danville Quarterly Review.* Columbia, SC: Southern Guardian Steam-Power Press, 1861.

Peissner, Elias. *The American Question in Its National Aspect: Being Also an Incidental Reply to Mr. H. R. Helper's "Compendium of the Impending Crisis of the South."* New York: H. H. Lloyd, 1861.

Pollard, Edward Alfred. *The First Year of the War.* London: Henry Stevens, 1863.

———. *The Rival Administrations: Richmond and Washington in December, 1863.* Richmond, VA: E. A. Pollard, 1864.

———. *Southern History of the War: The Third Year of the War.* New York: Charles B. Richardson, 1865.

Powell, L. W. *Speech of Hon. L. W. Powell, of Kentucky, on Executive Usurpation, Delivered in the Senate of the United States, July 11, 1861.* Washington, DC: Congressional Globe Office, 1861.

Power, J. L., ed. *Proceedings of the Mississippi State Convention, Held January 7th to 26th, A. D. 1861.* Jackson, MS: Power and Cadwallader, 1861.

Rutledge [William D. Porter]. *Mr. Douglas and the Doctrine of Coercion.* Charleston, SC, 1860.

Smith, Goldwin. *A Letter to a Whig Member of the Southern Independence Association.* London: Macmillan, 1864.

Smith, William R., ed. *History and Debates of the Convention of the People of Alabama.* Montgomery, AL: White, Pfister, 1861.

Spence, James. *The American Union: Its Effect on National Character and Policy, with an Inquiry into Secession as a Constitutional Right, and the Causes of the Disruption.* Richmond, VA: West and Johnston, 1863.

———. *On the Recognition of the Southern Confederation.* London: Richard Bentley, 1862.

Spratt, L. W. *The Philosophy of Secession: A Southern View.* Charleston, SC, 1861.

Stephens, Alexander. *The Assertions of a Secessionist: From the Speech of A. H. Stephens, of Georgia, November 14th, 1860.* New York: Loyal Publication Society, 1864.

Story, William W. *The American Story.* London: George Manwaring, 1862.

Train, George Francis, ed. *Union Speeches Delivered in England during the Present American War.* Philadelphia: T. B. Peterson and Brothers, 1862.

Tuckerman, Henry T. *The Rebellion: Its Latent Causes and True Significance.* New York: James G. Gregory, 1861.

Wikoff, Henry. *Secession and Its Causes, in a Letter to Viscount Palmerston, K. G., Prime Minister of England.* New York: Ross and Tousey, 1861.

Online Databases

Chronicling America: Historic American Newspapers. National Digital Newspaper Project. National Endowment for the Humanities and Library of Congress. https://chroniclingamerica.loc.gov/.

Documenting the American South. University Library, University of North Carolina at Chapel Hill. docsouth.unc.edu.

Georgia Historic Newspapers. Digital Library of Georgia. https://gahistoricnewspapers.galileo.usg.edu/.

Google Books. books.google.com.

HathiTrust Digital Library. www.hathitrust.org.

Illustrated Civil War Newspapers and Magazines. Alexander Street, ProQuest. https://lincolnandthecivilwar.com.

Making of America. University of Michigan, Digital Library Production Service. https://quod.lib.umich.edu/m/moagrp/.

Newspaper Articles—1690–2016. Genealogy Bank, Newsbank, Inc. www.genealogybank.com.

Newspapers.com. Ancestry. newspapers.com.

North Carolina Newspapers. Digital NC. http://newspapers.digitalnc.org/.

Richmond Daily Dispatch. University of Richmond, Perseus Project, and Virginia Center for Digital History. http://dlxs.richmond.edu/d/ddr/.

Secondary Sources

Anderson, Benedict. *Imagined Communities: Reflections on the Origin and Spread of Nationalism.* London: Verso, 1983.

Armitage, David. *The Declaration of Independence: A Global History.* Cambridge, MA: Harvard University Press, 2007.

Ashworth, John. *The Republic in Crisis, 1848–1861.* Cambridge: Cambridge University Press, 2012.

Bailyn, Bernard. *Ideological Origins of the American Revolution.* 1967. Reprint, Cambridge, MA: Belknap Press of Harvard University Press, 1992.

Barnes, L. Diane, Brian Schoen, and Frank Towers, eds. *The Old South's Modern Worlds: Slavery, Region, and Nation in the Age of Progress.* Oxford: Oxford University Press, 2011.

Bender, Thomas. *A Nation among Nations: America's Place in World History.* New York: Hill and Wang, 2006.

Beringer, Richard E., et al. *Why the South Lost the Civil War.* Athens: University of Georgia Press, 1986.

Bernath, Michael T. *Confederate Minds: The Struggle for Intellectual Independence in the Civil War South.* Chapel Hill: University of North Carolina Press, 2010.

Binnington, Ian. *Confederate Visions: Nationalism, Symbolism, and the Imagined South in the Civil War.* Charlottesville: University of Virginia Press, 2013.

Blackburn, George M. *French Newspaper Opinion on the American Civil War.* Westport, CT: Greenwood Press, 1997.

Blackett, R. J. M. *Divided Hearts: Britain and the American Civil War.* Baton Rouge: Louisiana State University Press, 2001.

Bonner, Robert E. *Mastering America: Southern Slaveholders and the Crisis of American Nationhood.* Cambridge: Cambridge University Press, 2009.

Brewer, David. *The Greek War of Independence: The Struggle for Freedom from Ottoman Oppression.* New York: Overlook Press, 2001.

Brown, David. *Southern Outcast: Hinton Rowan Helper and "The Impending Crisis of the South."* Baton Rouge: Louisiana State University Press, 2006.

Bruce, Susannah Ural. *The Harp and the Eagle: Irish-American Volunteers and the Union Army, 1861–1865.* New York: New York University Press, 2006.

Campbell, Duncan Andrew. *English Public Opinion and the American Civil War.* Rochester, NY: Royal Historical Society and Boydell Press, 2003.

Cash, W. J. *The Mind of the South.* New York: Knopf, 1941.

Clavin, Matthew J. *Toussaint L'Ouverture and the American Civil War: The Promise and Peril of a Second Haitian Revolution.* Philadelphia: University of Pennsylvania Press, 2011.

Cobb, James C. *Away Down South: A History of Southern Identity.* Oxford: Oxford University Press, 2005.

Cooper, William J., Jr. *Liberty and Slavery: Southern Politics to 1860.* New York: Knopf, 1983.

Coulter, E. Merton. *William G. Brownlow: Fighting Parson of the Southern Highlands.* Knoxville: University of Tennessee Press, 1999.

Crofts, Daniel W. *Reluctant Confederates: Upper South Unionists in the Secession Crisis.* Chapel Hill: University of North Carolina Press, 1989.

Dal Lago, Enrico. *Agrarian Elites: American Slaveholders and Southern Italian Landowners, 1815–1861.* Baton Rouge: Louisiana State University Press, 2005.

———. *William Lloyd Garrison and Giuseppe Mazzini: Abolition, Democracy, and Radical Reform.* Baton Rouge: Louisiana State University Press, 2013.

Davis, David Brion. *The Slave Power Conspiracy and the Paranoid Style.* Baton Rouge: Louisiana State University Press, 1969.

Degler, Carl N. *The Other South: Southern Dissenters in the Nineteenth Century.* New York: Harper and Row, 1974.

———. *Place over Time: The Continuity of Southern Distinctiveness.* Athens: University of Georgia Press, 1997.

Dew, Charles B. *Apostles of Disunion: Southern Secession Commissioners and the Causes of the Civil War.* Charlottesville: University of Virginia Press, 2001.

Dowe, Dieter, et al., eds. *Europe in 1848: Revolution and Reform.* New York: Berghahn Books, 2001.

Doyle, Don H., ed. *American Civil Wars: The United States, Latin America, Europe, and the Crisis of the 1860s.* Chapel Hill: University of North Carolina Press, 2017.

———. *The Cause of All Nations: An International History of the American Civil War.* New York: Basic Books, 2015.

Doyle, Don H., and Marco Antonio Pamplona, eds. *Nationalism in the New World.* Athens: University of Georgia Press, 2006.

Dufour, Charles L. *Gentle Tiger: The Gallant Life of Roberdeau Wheat.* Baton Rouge: Louisiana State University Press, 1957.

Engle, Stephen D. "Yankee Dutchmen: Germans, the Union, and the Construction of Wartime Identity." In *Civil War Citizens: Race, Ethnicity, and Identity in America's Bloodiest Conflict,* edited by Susannah J. Ural, 11–56. New York: New York University Press, 2010.

Faust, Drew Gilpin. *The Creation of Confederate Nationalism: Ideology and Identity in the Civil War South.* Baton Rouge: Louisiana State University Press, 1989.

Fitz, Caitlin. *Our Sister Republics: The United States in an Age of American Revolutions.* New York: Norton, 2016.

Fleche, Andre M. *The Revolution of 1861: The American Civil War in the Age of Nationalist Conflict.* Chapel Hill: University of North Carolina Press, 2012.

Foner, Eric. *Politics and Ideology in the Age of the Civil War.* Oxford: Oxford University Press, 1981.

Ford, Lacy K. *Deliver Us from Evil: The Slavery Question in the Old South.* New York: Oxford University Press, 2011.

———. *Origins of Southern Radicalism: The South Carolina Upcountry, 1800–1860.* New York: Oxford University Press, 1988.

Fox-Genovese, Elizabeth, and Eugene D. Genovese. *The Mind of the Master Class: History and Faith in the Southern Slaveholders' Worldview.* Cambridge: Cambridge University Press, 2005.

Gallagher, Gary W. *The Confederate War.* Cambridge, MA: Harvard University Press, 1997.

Gay, H. Nelson. "Lincoln's Offer of Command to Garibaldi: Light on a Disputed Point of History." *Century Magazine,* November 1907, 63–74.

Gemme, Paola. *Domesticating Foreign Struggles: The Italian Risorgimento and Antebellum American Identity.* Athens: University of Georgia Press, 2005.

Genovese, Eugene D. *The Slaveholders' Dilemma: Freedom and Progress in Southern Conservative Thought, 1820–1860.* Columbia: University of South Carolina Press, 1994.

————. *The Southern Tradition: The Achievement and Limitations of American Conservatism.* Cambridge, MA: Harvard University Press, 1996.

Gleeson, David T. *The Green and the Gray: The Irish in the Confederate States of America.* Chapel Hill: University of North Carolina Press, 2013.

Gleeson, David T., and Simon Lewis, eds. *The Civil War as Global Conflict: Transnational Meanings of the American Civil War.* Columbia: University of South Carolina Press, 2014.

Grant, Alfred. *The American Civil War and the British Press.* Jefferson, NC: McFarland, 2000.

Greenberg, Kenneth S. *Masters and Statesmen: The Political Culture of American Slavery.* Baltimore: Johns Hopkins University Press, 1985.

Guterl, Matthew Pratt. *American Mediterranean: Southern Slaveholders in the Age of Emancipation.* Cambridge, MA: Harvard University Press, 2013.

Harris, Sheldon H. "John L. O'Sullivan Serves the Confederacy." *Civil War History* 10, no. 3 (September 1964): 275–90.

Hobsbawm, E. J. *The Age of Revolution, 1789–1848.* New York: Mentor, 1962.

————. *Nations and Nationalism since 1780: Programme, Myth, Reality.* Cambridge: Cambridge University Press, 1990.

Holt, Michael. *The Political Crisis of the 1850s.* New York: Wiley, 1978.

Hubbard, Charles M. *The Burden of Confederate Diplomacy.* Knoxville: University of Tennessee Press, 1998.

Israel, Jonathan. *A Revolution of the Mind: Radical Enlightenment and the Intellectual Origins of Modern Democracy.* Princeton, NJ: Princeton University Press, 2010.

Johnson, Walter. *River of Dark Dreams: Slavery and Empire in the Cotton Kingdom.* Cambridge, MA: Belknap Press of Harvard University Press, 2013.

Jones, Howard. *Blue and Gray Diplomacy: A History of Union and Confederate Foreign Relations.* Chapel Hill: University of North Carolina Press, 2010.

Karp, Matthew. *This Vast Southern Empire: Slaveholders at the Helm of American Foreign Policy.* Cambridge, MA: Harvard University Press, 2016.

Kolchin, Peter. *A Sphinx on the American Land: The Nineteenth Century South in Comparative Perspective.* Baton Rouge: Louisiana State University Press, 2003.

————. *Unfree Labor: American Slavery and Russian Serfdom.* Cambridge, MA: Harvard University Press, 1987.

Kramer, Lloyd. *Nationalism in Europe and America: Politics, Cultures, and Identities since 1775.* Chapel Hill: University of North Carolina Press, 2011.

Lawrence, Paul. *Nationalism: History and Theory*. New York: Routledge, 2004.

Leerssen, Joep. *National Thought in Europe: A Cultural History*. Amsterdam: Amsterdam University Press, 2014.

Levine, Bruce. *The Spirit of 1848: German Immigrants, Labor Conflict, and the Coming of the Civil War*. Urbana: University of Illinois Press, 1992.

Lonn, Ella. *Foreigners in the Union Army and Navy*. Baton Rouge: Louisiana State University Press, 1951.

Mack Smith, Denis. *The Making of Italy, 1796–1866*. London: Macmillan, 1988.

Mahin, Dean B. *The Blessed Place of Freedom: Europeans in Civil War America*. Washington, DC: Brassey, 2002.

Marraro, Howard R. "Lincoln's Offer of Command to Garibaldi: Further Light on a Disputed Point of History." *Journal of the Illinois State Historical Society* 36, no. 3 (September 1943): 237–70.

Mattson, Gregory Louis. "Pariah Diplomacy: The Slavery Issue in Confederate Foreign Relations." PhD diss., University of Southern Mississippi, 1999.

May, Robert E. *Manifest Destiny's Underworld: Filibustering in Antebellum America*. Chapel Hill: University of North Carolina Press, 2002.

———. *The Southern Dream of a Caribbean Empire*. Baton Rouge: Louisiana State University Press, 1973.

McCurry, Stephanie. *Confederate Reckoning: Power and Politics in the Civil War South*. Cambridge, MA: Harvard University Press, 2010.

McDaniel, W. Caleb. *The Problem of Democracy in the Age of Slavery: Garrisonian Abolitionists and Transatlantic Reform*. Baton Rouge: Louisiana State University Press, 2013.

McGovern, Bryan P. *John Mitchel: Irish Nationalist, Southern Secessionist*. Knoxville: University of Tennessee Press, 2009.

McPherson, James M. *For Cause and Comrade: Why Men Fought in the Civil War*. New York: Oxford University Press, 1997.

Neely, Mark E., Jr. *The Fate of Liberty: Abraham Lincoln and Civil Liberties*. Oxford: Oxford University Press, 1992.

O'Brien, Michael. *Conjectures of Order: Intellectual Life and the American South, 1810–1860*. 2 vols. Chapel Hill: University of North Carolina Press, 2004.

Öfele, Martin W. *True Sons of the Republic: European Immigrants in the Union Army*. Westport, CT: Praeger, 2008.

Onuf, Nicholas, and Peter Onuf. *Nations, Markets, and War: Modern History and the American Civil War*. Charlottesville: University of Virginia Press, 2006.

Osterweis, Rollin G. *Romanticism and Nationalism in the Old South*. Baton Rouge: Louisiana State University Press, 1949.

Owsley, Frank Lawrence. *King Cotton Diplomacy: Foreign Relations of the Confederate States of America*. 2nd edition. Tuscaloosa: University of Alabama Press, 2008.

Pappas, Paul. *The United States and the Greek War for Independence, 1821–1828.* New York: Columbia University Press, 1985.

Pessen, Edward. "How Different from Each Other Were the Antebellum North and South?" *American Historical Review* 85, no. 5 (1980): 1119–49.

Potter, David M. *The Impending Crisis, 1848–1861.* New York: Harper and Row, 1976.

Quigley, Paul. *Shifting Grounds: Nationalism and the American South, 1848–1865.* New York: Oxford University Press, 2011.

Rable, George C. *The Confederate Republic: A Revolution against Politics.* Chapel Hill: University of North Carolina Press, 1994.

Reinhart, Joseph R., ed. *August Willich's Gallant Dutchmen: Civil War Letters from the 32nd Indiana Infantry.* Kent, OH: Kent State University Press, 2006.

Reynolds, Donald E. *Editors Make War: Southern Newspapers in the Secession Crisis.* Carbondale: Southern Illinois University Press, 2006.

Riall, Lucy. *Garibaldi: Invention of a Hero.* New Haven, CT: Yale University Press, 2007.

———. *The Italian Risorgimento: State, Society, and National Unification.* New York: Routledge, 1994.

Roberts, Timothy Mason. *Distant Revolutions: 1848 and the Challenge to American Exceptionalism.* Charlottesville: University of Virginia Press, 2009.

Rubin, Anne Sarah. *A Shattered Nation: The Rise and Fall of the Confederacy, 1861–1868.* Chapel Hill: University of North Carolina Press, 2005.

Rugemer, Edward Bartlett. *The Problem of Emancipation: The Caribbean Roots of the American Civil War.* Baton Rouge: Louisiana State University Press, 2009.

Sexton, Jay. *The Monroe Doctrine: Empire and Nation in Nineteenth Century America.* New York: Hill and Wang, 2012.

Shalhope, Robert E. *The Roots of Democracy: American Thought and Culture, 1760–1800.* Boston: Twayne, 1990.

Sinha, Manisha. *The Counterrevolution of Slavery: Politics and Ideology in Antebellum South Carolina.* Chapel Hill: University of North Carolina Press, 2000.

Spencer, Donald S. *Louis Kossuth and Young America: A Study of Sectionalism and Foreign Policy, 1848–52.* Columbia: University of Missouri Press, 1977.

Sperber, Jonathan. *The European Revolutions, 1848–1851.* Cambridge: Cambridge University Press, 1994.

Stampp, Kenneth M. *The Imperiled Union: Essays on the Background of the Civil War.* New York: Oxford University Press, 1980.

Storey, Margaret M. *Loyalty and Loss: Alabama's Unionists in the Civil War and Reconstruction.* Baton Rouge: Louisiana State University Press, 2004.

Tate, Adam L. *Conservatism and Southern Intellectuals, 1789–1861: Liberty, Tradition, and the Good Society.* Columbia: University of Missouri Press, 2005.

Taylor, William R. *Cavalier and Yankee: The Old South and American National Character.* New York: Oxford University Press, 1993.

Thornton, J. Mills, III. *Politics and Power in a Slave Society: Alabama, 1800–1860.* Baton Rouge: Louisiana State University Press, 1978.

Ural, Susannah J., ed. *Civil War Citizens: Race, Ethnicity, and Identity in America's Bloodiest Conflict.* New York: New York University Press, 2010.

Walther, Eric H. *The Fire-Eaters.* Baton Rouge: Louisiana State University Press, 1992.

———. *The Shattering of the Union: America in the 1850s.* Wilmington, DE: Scholarly Resources, 2004.

Weber, Jennifer L. *Copperheads: The Rise and Fall of Lincoln's Opponents in the North.* Oxford: Oxford University Press, 2006.

Wiltse, Charles M. "A Critical Southerner: John C. Calhoun on the Revolutions of 1848." *Journal of Southern History* 15, no. 3 (August 1949): 299–310.

Winterer, Caroline. *The Culture of Classicism: Ancient Greece and Rome in American Intellectual Life, 1780–1910.* Baltimore: Johns Hopkins University Press, 2002.

Wood, Gordon S. *The Radicalism of the American Revolution.* New York: Vintage Books, 1993.

INDEX

abolitionism: and European revolutionaries in United States, 78–80; and free-soil movement, 42, 54, 76, 79; international movement, 47–48, 64, 116, 123–24, 125, 131–32, 163–64; rise of, 39, 42, 47–48; as tyrannical, claims of, 12, 42–43, 44–50, 64, 97–100, 109–11; white southern abolitionists, 134–37; white southern fears of, 218n54. *See also* slavery
Adler (Confederate colonel), 88
age of revolution, defined, 1–2, 4–5, 15. *See also individual nations by name*
American exceptionalism, 51–52, 141–45, 152–54, 209n17. *See also* American Revolution; conservatism, as international perspective
American Revolution: legacy of, 10, 18–19, 47; as model for nationalist movements, 21–23, 25–27, 31, 36, 51–52; South as true heir of, 73, 80, 122–24, 180. *See also* republicanism
Americanus (pseudonym), 51
anarchy, 28–30, 51, 120, 121, 124, 131, 141–44, 187
Anderson, Benedict, 207n6
Anglo-Californian (pseudonym), 110
aristocracy, 129–33, 150–51, 196
Aspromonte, 169–70
Austria, 24, 34, 48, 59, 86, 193. *See also* Hungary; Italy; tyranny

B., H. L., 192
Bailey, David J., 45, 97
Barnard, Frederick A. P., 51
Bassett, George W., 110
Beecher, Henry Ward, 148
Belgium, 20–23, 110, 238n11

Bell, James H., 141
Benthuysen, Alfred van, 88
Bertinatti, Chevalier Joseph, 147
blockades, 175
Bomba, king of Naples, Ferdinand of the Two Sicilies, 58
Boyd, Samuel S., 51
Brown, Albert G., 46, 49–50
Brown, Bedford, 139
Brown, Benjamin Gratz, 146
Brownlow, William, 143–44, 195–99. *See also* Unionists (southern), international perspective
Brownlow's Knoxville Whig, 195

Calhoun, John C., 28
Canisius, Heinrich Theodore, 170
Cantwell, Patrick, 21
Carlile, John, 144
Carroll, Anna Ella, 145
Catholics, 189–94. *See also* Pius IX
Central Southern Rights Association of Virginia, 46
Charles Albert, king of Piedmont-Sardinia, 27, 33, 84
Charleston Mercury, 119
Chat (pseudonym), 60, 70, 72, 76
Citizen newspaper, 67, 80. *See also* Mitchel, John
Clark, James S., 140
Clarke, H. C., 136, 166
Clay, C. C., 123
Clay, Clement, 98
Clayton, Alexander Mosby, 98
Clemens, Jeremiah, 71
Cline, A. J., 150
Clingman, Thomas Lanier, 45